AF408614

WHITE NOISE & LIGHTNING

The Continental Drifters Story

BY SEAN KELLY

White Noise & Lightning:
The Continental Drifters Story

by Sean Kelly

Forward by Brett Milano

Edited by Tim Lee

Published ℗ 2024 by Cool Dog Sound
P.O. Box 454 • Water Valley, Miss. 38965
www.cooldogsound.com

Continental Drifters lyrics used by permission.

ISBN: 979-8-218-49116-1

Book design by Susan Bauer Lee

Cover painting by Marti Jones Dixon

Dedicated to Carlo Nuccio

Contents

Author's Note

Being in a band is a strange phenomenon. It's difficult to describe to the layman the feeling of an innate musical chemistry within a group of people. When you really have it, though, you know it. You feel it. I've found that it's always there—even when there are years and miles between band members.

When something doesn't work, it's usually pretty obvious. This is often due to a combination of factors, but the role that personality plays in band chemistry can't be overstated. Every great band is a combination of personalities that work well together, even when those personalities clash or the relationships change, evolve, or deteriorate. So much of the time, chemistry and personality trump musical skill.

When personalities merge in such a way within a band, it tends to translate to a more emotionally-driven approach to art. Take Fleetwood Mac, for example. Here's a band where pretty much everyone in its "classic lineup" was either married to, or in a romantic relationship with, one another through their initial run. Everyone knows the story, so there's no need to elaborate. But imagine what *Rumours* would have been were it not for the tension, and at times volatility, that existed during that process.

For the Continental Drifters, the effect that emotion, personal connection, and tension had on their art was largely the same. When you talk to any of the people who were integral parts of the Drifters journey, you immediately get the sense that the experience was unlike any other.

Multi-instrumentalist and vocalist Peter Holsapple likens the band to a "locomotive going down a hill."

"It might run off the rails, but boy, it's exhilarating while it is," he says.

In following the thread of this band's story, I found myself rediscovering what I immediately loved about this group of people. On the surface, they were a supergroup; a band composed of musicians who'd previously been part of successful musical entities. I say "supergroup" only because of the fact that they'd all come from bands with varying levels of success, but we won't be using that terminology here because I find that it cheapens this band and the devotion everyone had to it.

That said, everyone did come from somewhere. Its longest-serving members all had notable careers before the band formed.

Peter was known as songwriter and frontman for The dB's, a cult band whose members grew up in North Carolina before joining together in New York at the jumpstart of new wave in the late 1970s. Original drummer, founder, and songwriter Carlo Nuccio was a session player and L.A. heavyweight who played on major records by the likes of Tori Amos and Emmylou Harris. Singer and guitarist Susan Cowsill was the child star of the bunch, having spent the majority of the 1960s as part of the popular family band The Cowsills. Vicki Peterson was the lead guitar player in The Bangles, the massive 1980s group that started off as a sixties-inspired garage band and went on to achieve major mainstream success with hits like "Walk Like An Egyptian." Bassist and founder Mark Walton was a Los Angeles staple, best known as the bassist in Steve Wynn's beloved group The Dream Syndicate.

Sure, their pedigree is impressive. When I first discovered them, however, I had very little of that context. I was an impressionable kid from New York who was an aspiring musician. I'd been immersing myself in R.E.M., by way of Hootie & the Blowfish, a band that I grew up listening to with my family. Hootie will always get the acknowledgement of being my introduction to music, and R.E.M. is my north star; always has been.

The connection between these bands was Peter Holsapple. Peter notably served as an auxiliary member on R.E.M.'s *Green* world tour in 1989, before contributing to 1991's monster hit *Out Of Time* and its single, "Losing My Religion." After leaving R.E.M., Peter joined the Continental Drifters and then accepted an offer to join Hootie in an auxiliary role, which he held for more than a quarter-century.

As a kid (we're talking anywhere from age 4 to 6), I was fixated on Peter because of his ability to both augment these bands on multiple instruments and remain relatively inconspicuous near the back of the stage. In my mind, it was the perfect job. I'd watch Peter intently and imagine myself one day doing the same thing with some popular band. I had a VHS of a Hootie concert that my parents bought me, and I'd watch closely as he switched between guitar, keyboards, mandolin, and accordion. I also distinctly remember Peter wearing a Continental Drifters t-shirt during the show.

Intrigued by the name on the shirt, I decided to investigate. I found the band and was delighted to see that Peter was a member. I also recognized the name Susan Cowsill, which I'd seen in the liner notes of Hootie's 1998 album *Musical Chairs*—an album that my mother bought from Best Buy when it was released. Thanks to a now-defunct music radio app, on which I'd find new music almost every single day, I started listening to the Drifters right away. I was immediately taken by the songs, the melodies, and the guitar parts. I also remember really noticing the bass lines, which I believe started to unlock the way I would listen to music.

I was a fan from the first song, and it was only then that I discovered the many other projects that the Drifters had been involved in. My first foray into their catalog was 1999's *Vermilion*—a beloved album that is a near flawless representation of this group of six people who were doing something special. It was the perfect encapsulation of a moment in time, but it also felt timeless.

As someone who now writes and records music regularly, I can attest to how difficult it is to truly capture chemistry on a recording. On stage you can see it, but the album is a different medium altogether. *Vermilion* is a rare example, in my opinion, of an album bursting with chemistry.

Having the smallest amount of context possible regarding the members' histories, the Continental Drifters really weren't a supergroup to me; they were a band. I connected with what they were doing on levels that made me start to think about music differently, and it was the first time I'd ever truly studied songwriting.

There was just something very special about their songs and the way they performed them. As a fan, it felt like a gravitational pull. It wasn't something I'd experienced with other bands. This is something that hasn't gone away, even after so many years. Even as someone who now considers these people friends (and many of them family), the pure fandom and love of this music remains.

This was, and is, a band that started out rather ragtag in its approach; forming in Los Angeles

Sean Kelly

and staging a weekly residency at a dive bar called Raji's, before migrating to New Orleans a few years later. The original version of the band that emerged from a transitional moment in rock and roll Los Angeles, compared to the one that splintered in New Orleans a decade later, was its own thing entirely. Formed by Carlo, Mark, guitarists Gary Eaton and Ray Ganucheau, and keyboardist Danny McGough, the earliest version of the Drifters was as much a Parsons-esque country rock band as it was a swampy blues band, as it was a pop band, as it was a New Orleans soul band.

It was everything you wouldn't expect a band from Los Angeles to sound like in 1991, rolled into one. And when Peter entered the fold, followed by Vicki and Susan, the pop songs were certainly more emphasized, but they didn't lose the soul. The music simply morphed into something new.

Songwriting was the name of the game for the Continental Drifters, and there was no shortage of great songs to go around. Among the ten members who circulated through the band in their decade together, nine contributed to the catalog.

This was a band that had a lot going for it, at a time when terms like "Americana" and "alt-country" were either on the come-up or hardly in the lexicon at all. They were following the same path as their peers; the Wilcos, Son Volts, and even Hooties of the world. So why didn't everybody know about them?

That's something we'll explore in this book, and it's a question that many people ask themselves today. Even now, as the Drifters continue to reunite on occasion, they remain something of a best-kept secret in pop music.

In 2024, as some of the members' other bands have had resurgences—The Dream Syndicate touring and recording full-time, The Bangles getting their due as the trailblazers they were, The Cowsills experiencing a lucrative career renaissance, and The dB's finally getting acknowledged for their influence on the new wave and college rock movements of the 1980s—the Continental Drifters remain safely under the radar.

I've got no delusions that this book will change that, but I do hope that there's a faction of passionate music lovers out there that discovers this band and appreciates the Drifters for what they are, and what they are capable of together. What you will discover is a master class-level repertoire of music; songs that surprise you, make you cry, make you laugh, and make you understand that what you are hearing is something rare and unique. What you are getting is an education.

I am a student of the Continental Drifters. That education continues to this day, even as they've become part of my life both personally and professionally.

And, to this day, the story of the Continental Drifters remains, to me, a fascinating and compelling one. They're a group of people who became forever linked to one another through marriage, relationships, divorce, and children. They're a group of people whose desire for musical exploration led them to one another at a dive bar in Los Angeles. They're a group of people who followed each other to New Orleans, where they began a short-lived yet prolific chapter that yielded some of the most emotionally potent music you'll hear.

There were some ugly moments in the band's history, for sure. I could hear very real sadness in each of the members' voices as they retold their perspective on the final days. This was a band where romantic relationships became entangled and the seriousness of a dissolving marriage weighed heavily on its day-to-day operations in the last couple of years. This was a band in which the beer flowed heavily; in which a drug addiction closed one complicated chapter and opened another. This was by no means a simple story to tell.

All of that will be examined here, but we're not here to dig into people's personal lives. What I want to explore is the why of it all. What makes a band carry on through such turmoil, especially when there is no money or fame involved?

Indeed, there was so much turmoil, and so much pain. It's what brought the Continental Drifters together, and what tore them apart.

With plenty of time and distance, though, the members of the Continental Drifters ultimately healed the wounds that were left from their breakup. When asked to sum up their experience, the answer is always about love. The love of the music, of the memories, of the beer, and the love they have for each other.

That love was abundant at two reunion shows in Los Angeles in September of 2015, where old friends, fans, and family gathered—as many of them had, decades earlier, on a weekly basis. The seeds of this book were planted during those shows, as I watched in awe of the people I grew up learning so much from.

I even learned something new that night—when you have that innate, explosive, palpable musical chemistry, it really never goes away.

— Sean Kelly

Foreword

"Are you heading to the Drifters tonight?"

It was late Tuesday afternoon in Los Angeles and life was good, since one friend or another would be making that call before I left work. Time to get changed, forget about whatever album the small label I worked for was putting out that week, and join the crowd at Raji's. Few things are more gratifying than having a world-class band to yourself, and those of us who discovered the Continental Drifters at that early stage had no doubt that they'd soon be recognized as one of the flagship American bands. Or barring that, maybe they'd still be playing 30 years later, their albums would be getting reissued and someone would be writing a book about them. Score one for the good guys.

I'd love to snap my fingers and transport you back to Raji's in 1993, or Carrollton Station in New Orleans five years later, but Sean Kelly's wonderful book does the job for me. It also explains why so many of us have sworn by a band that never quite got the success it seemed destined for. We can only wonder if history would have been different if the Drifters had played this or that big showcase, if they'd aligned with one or another trend, if they'd released an album at some exact moment. But nonetheless, for those of us who did come along, those shows are treasured memories and the songs have become the proverbial soundtrack of our lives. They simply had too much heart, too much meaning and too many killer hooks not to.

And I'm here to tell you what a joy it was to be in that room on a random Tuesday—especially in the wee hours when the acoustic guitars came out and they launched into "Dedicated To the One I Love" because there was nothing else left to play.

I can't claim to be one of the very original Drifters fans: I came in mainly as a fan of Peter Holsapple's work with the dB's and Mark Walton's with the Dream Syndicate, so I missed the very first lineup with Danny McGough on keys (though I did see his other band, the wonderful 7 Deadly 5). I was a recent East Coast transplant who'd come to Los Angeles with music-biz ambitions. The city was hardly a musical wasteland at that time, but tastes were changing: Sunset Strip metal and punk were the happening things, and while great bands like the Muffs and L7 were in that mix, I was still looking for the Hollywood of my childhood dreams—the spot where the spirits of Gram Parsons, Danny Whitten, and the Mamas & the Papas came out to play. I found that at Raji's.

I also found a roomful of people who were united in music fandom. During one of my first visits a woman—who happened to play bass in a band I loved—told me I looked like Zal Yanovsky, possibly my favorite compliment I've ever received. Cover tunes would get played once and never heard again; one night before closing the Drifters struck into an epic "Dear Mr. Fantasy"—because well, why not? This prompted a predictable batch of Traffic requests, including mine for "Shoot Out at the Fantasy Factory." "We'd need to get our fuzzbox for that one," Holsapple shot back.

At that point you were never sure who'd be onstage on any given night; there seemed to be as many auxiliary Drifters as full-fledged ones (When guitar hero Robert Maché became a member, it was a surprise that he wasn't one already). These people had a lot of friends, and they dared to write songs that were a bit mythic. Carlo Nuccio was the towering, Dionysian presence—but man, what a voice, and what sly wordplay was in his songs. I recall the room going dead quiet when Ray Ganucheau—a band member who wasn't there every time—did their most lovelorn song, "I Didn't Want to Lie." Most of all, I remember the song "Dallas" and the sound of the five-part chorus harmonies bouncing off the walls. The arrival of Susan Cowsill and Vicki Peterson added that beautiful element of classic California pop vocalizing; few other bands under the Americana banner had that. And for us fans, it closed a circle with our own musical history: Most of what you'd loved at various points in your life—whether it was sunshine pop or open-road Americana—was now under one roof. This was a band to fall in love with. And in one or two cases, to be a bit crushed on as well.

Yes, the alcohol flowed a little more freely in those days, and the good spirits did as well, and quite a few friendships sprung up around Drifters gigs. David Jenkins, who most often made those Tuesday-afternoon calls remains a good friend—of mine and of theirs—to this day. I never again saw the woman who kindly gave me a cassette she'd recorded at a random Raji's night, but I wore that tape out over the next year while waiting for a real album to appear.

The band itself were the friendliest of cult heroes, and even if you didn't get to visit the legendary "bachelor pad," you probably had a few good connective moments. Toward the end of his tenure Gary Eaton wrote "Vatican Blues," a road song about a very specific incident: A marathon drive home from New Orleans during which Carlo, known as the Pope to his bandmates, refused to surrender the wheel. But to these ears the song went a little deeper, talking about that long road of life ("This old state keeps getting bigger and bigger") and the little things that make it worth traveling ("We're rolling … we're sleeping … we're drinking … and we're singing"). I waited for the song to come up the night I said my own good bye to Los Angeles, Vicki leaned forward and said "This is for you" when it did. Meant a lot.

Turns out the band left Los Angeles soon after I did, taking to New Orleans which had always been their spiritual home. Part of the mystique always was that they were a piece of New Orleans that somehow landed in Hollywood; there was even a Mardi Gras show where everyone was in drag (I've had people compliment me on my outfit for this night, even though I wasn't actually there). Louisiana also provided the perfect drummer to step in after Carlo's departure—Russ Broussard, who can be easy to overlook because he's so in the pocket all the time. The preferred stomping ground moved to a couple Crescent City clubs, and now the shows could truly stretch close to dawn. My favorite of those spots, Carrollton Station, wasn't especially close to anything, but that made the shows seem more special—even if getting home at four in the morning could be a bit of an adventure.

The albums don't tell the whole story, but they do tell a lot. During a time of personal turmoil the band made its last (to date) studio album *Better Day*, which evinces heartbreak and optimism of the most dogged kind. It's an album that's served me well in later years. Likewise, those Raji's-era tracks (now on the double *Drifted* compilation) still convey that sense of the world stretching out ahead, which still makes sense on a good day. But mostly it's the *Vermilion* album that I've carried along all this time. Musically and spiritually it sums up what the band was about: There's some shimmering pop, epic balladry, and deep roots. Like most great albums, its songs have taken on new resonance over time. When I hear the opening line of "Way of the World":

> *There's a mean wind blowing this way*

Sean Kelly

...I'm amazed it wasn't written last year. And there's "Drifters," a warm embrace of a song that Susan and Peter wrote for the band and its audience, but could apply to any family you find yourself in.

Lest this turn into a "good old days"-type of screed, I'll say that two of my sweetest Drifters memories are the more recent ones. I was there in New Orleans during 2015 when they got all ten people who'd ever been official band members together for one epic show. Even on the sacred ground of Tipitina's, this was something special: At four-and-a-half hours it was the longest show I'd ever seen by anybody (and I saw Bruce Springsteen's second-longest concert, a mere four hours, two minutes). And yeah, it could have gone on even longer, since nobody onstage or in the crowd seemed fully out of energy yet. The lineup by then included two former couples, one going-strong couple, a pair of stepsisters, a bunch of close friends and even a couple of folks who hadn't met. Every song got a fresh twist from the expanded lineup, and as usual they made all that genre-jumping look perfectly natural. In terms of pure musicality it made a damn fine crowning statement.

But that of course wasn't the end either. My most recent show, just three months ago at this writing, landed on the more emotional side. It was during the 2023 New Orleans Jazz Fest when they managed four shows in a week, including their first on the fairgrounds for more than a decade. It was still a celebration, but one of a different kind: They'd always had songs about loss and the passage of time; but you tend to notice those more distinctly as the years go on. These were the first shows since the passing of Carlo Nuccio, who was very much present: Susan joked once or twice about how pissed he'd be if they messed up. The occasional teary moments were not hidden; such things happen when extended families come together. Yet the upbeat moments still rang true as well, with "Drifters" calling everyone together and an unchanged (and unplanned, and unrehearsed) "Dedicated To the One I Love" taking things out on the usual high. All that love and all those experiences are still there in the songs. And while we're here, we might as well just sing along.

— Brett Milano

Chapter One:
L.A. to LA

"What matters in the end is the love, and the connection; the camaraderie. The whole foundation of the original reason for the Continental Drifters was the journey. Not the destination."

— Susan Cowsill

There's a line in "Drifters," the de facto theme song of the Continental Drifters, that precedes keyboardist Peter Holsapple's heartbreaking organ solo and serves as a bridge between the song's second and third choruses. It's a simple statement of assertion; one that's repeated and alternated by Peter and co-vocalists Susan Cowsill and Vicki Peterson, amid a crescendo of melodic ascension and a wide stereo flange with increasing intensity.

"You don't understand."

In the telling of this band's unique and complex history, the phrase "you don't understand" is one that can most assuredly be used to sum up its twelve-year existence. To witness them on stage was to watch something unfold that you knew was special; a rare and palpable artistic connection between humans.

No matter how captivating and unique it was to the audience, though, nobody except the people on that stage would ever really understand it.

Russ Broussard, the second of two drummers in the band's run, recalls many of his gigs with the Continental Drifters as being "out of body" experiences.

"It was like the six of us together had an invisible director. A conductor with a presence greater than any of us," he said. "There was definitely a power that was greater than our members. And a sound, too."

The line in question can actually be traced back to early band rehearsals in Los Angeles, when bassist and co-founder Mark Walton would argue with drummer/co-founder Carlo Nuccio. The arguments often escalated to a point where both men would shout over each other.

"You don't understand!"

"No, YOU don't understand!"

This oft-repeated phrase became an inside joke among the other band members, poking fun at their bandmates. The line was a nod to that joke, as well as to the arguments that would break out at band meetings and rehearsals—which often resembled those of a dysfunctional family debating over Thanksgiving dinner.

"In retrospect, people talk over each other," Peter said. "They do that in a band, they do that in a family. And somebody prevails. So, somebody always prevailed. And sometimes it was the loudest talker."

In pulling back the layers of the Continental Drifters, and investigating their complicated story, it's impossible not to come back to that simple phrase that started as a joke but ultimately serves as the perfect disclaimer for listeners.

"There's a familiarity that is so comforting that, you know, others don't understand it," Susan said. "You don't get us, and you never will, and I don't even want you to."

There's also a familial level to this band that makes their story, and this inexplicable chemistry, all the more compelling. Complex interpersonal relationships between band members would tear the band apart, but in the end unite all of these individuals forever; they were part of each other's lives for better or worse, Drifter or no.

In that way, they were something of a working class Fleetwood Mac. The romances, the breakups, the clashing of personalities, the excess of alcohol; all of that existed in the Continental Drifters. As did the pure creative magic that happened when their energies combined.

The Continental Drifters essentially lived two existences; one in Los Angeles and one in New Orleans. Both were planted primarily under the umbrella of Americana, but the Los Angeles band was a bit more on the rock and roll and country rock side. The New Orleans band started as an extension of that, but quickly began veering into a more folk rock and roots rock territory; almost a New Orleans-infused Fairport Convention.

Both versions of the band were often fueled by alcohol, neglected the usual band routines, and operated under the idea that it would be the antithesis of a mainstream venture. No industry pressure to succumb to, no "hit single" mentality driving the creative process, and no desire to become the biggest band in the world.

That's not to say they weren't a band full of star power and enormous commercial potential. In fact, nearly every member had come into the Drifters to get away from that very thing.

The band's founder, Carlo Nuccio, was a session and touring drummer who cut his teeth in Los Angeles and made a name for himself with a John Bonham-meets-New Orleans swagger and impeccable feel. The "classic" Drifters lineup, which was cemented in New Orleans in the mid-1990s and recorded two studio albums, featured a frontline *and* backline of impressive stature.

Susan was best known as the little girl in the hugely successful 1960s pop group The Cowsills, and Vicki rose to fame as the guitarist and founder of The Bangles. Mark had a lengthy turn as bassist for The Dream Syndicate, and guitarist Robert Maché cut his teeth in the 1970s New York CBGB's punk scene. Peter was part of cult new wave band The dB's before going on to tour and record as an auxiliary member of both R.E.M. and Hootie & the Blowfish, and Russ was a workhorse New Orleans drummer best known for his stint with Terrance Simien.

There was a wealth of notable talent in this group, which made them a buzz band for many years and garnered them critical acclaim worldwide (and even some commercial success in Europe). They were never concerned with image, marketability, or commercial appeal, though. These people, who'd all spent time in the music industry pressure cooker, wanted connection, creativity, and joy.

For a long time, they had all of that. It didn't matter what was happening at home or behind the scenes; as soon as they stepped on stage, all of the baggage stayed behind. What came from all of that was an appetite for indulgence that followed them from lineup to lineup, from L.A. to LA.

"You can't do a history of the Continental Drifters without putting the alcohol in perspective," Peter said. "Because a lot of it was consumed by many of us. Constantly. Repeatedly."

Whether it was alcohol, cocaine, or mushrooms, most of the band took a strong liking to substances. Mostly it was alcohol and pot; but as we'll learn, the Drifters almost never said no to a party. In the early days, especially, it was all beer all the time. Lots and lots of beer. "Cases and cases and cases of beer," as Vicki Peterson—the only Drifter who wasn't much of a partier—said.

Vicki recalls often being tasked with retrieving "suitcases" of beer, which was a term she hadn't heard before. And in those days, there was one brand that ruled them all.

In 1986, the Miller Brewing Company rolled out an innovative new product called Miller Genuine Draft—a bottled beer that was cold filtered and pasteurized, so as to mimic the taste and mouthfeel of draft beer.

At just 4.7% ABV, the tagline for MGD was famously, "Twist the cap, beer on draft." It quickly became a best-seller, accounting for three percent of the U.S. beer market by 1988.

Unbeknownst to the brass at Miller, the caps were being twisted regularly at the Batch (shorthand for 'bachelor') Pad, a house in Studio City occupied by three disparate musicians—Mark Walton, Carlo Nuccio, and Gary Eaton—who kept the brew in stock on a consistent basis. Genuine Draft was the fuel that kept the Continental Drifters going during marathon rehearsals.

Those rehearsals would often become sleepovers, which would then become barbecues, which would last for days at a time. Surrounded by guitars, the Batch Pad became the incubator for some of the band's most inspired early material.

Miller Genuine Draft, as Peter Holsapple recalls, was the "beer of necessity" in those early days; their penchant for indulgence was something they remember fondly about the band's thrilling period of musical infancy.

Just over the hill from that beer-soaked musical incubator, a competing brew reigned supreme. During its heyday, Raji's—a dive bar in Hollywood originally owned by the late Danny "Dobbs" Wilson—was famous for only serving Budweiser in a bottle.

Paula Thurber, a former Raji's employee who witnessed many of the legendary performances that graced the club's stage, takes care to note that they'd serve Bud in a can "when punk rock bands were playing."

It was a dive in the truest sense of the word. Dobbs himself remarked in a 1990 interview with the Los Angeles *Times* that Raji's—located in the basement of the Hastings Hotel on Hollywood Boulevard, in a space that used to be a Greek restaurant called The King's Palace—was "the McDonald's of nightclubs."

"I don't know if I would say it was the McDonald's of nightclubs, but sure, man, sure," Dave Catching, guitarist and studio owner who was a frequent substitute Drifter in the Raji's days, said with a laugh. Catching played there with many different groups, including Devil Squares, The Ringling Sisters, and Tex & the Horseheads.

"[Raji's] was kind of like my home because all of my bands played there all the time, all of my best friends worked there, my roommate was the chef—it was just like my home away from home," Catching added. "If I wasn't working delivering pizzas or playing a gig, that's where I was hanging out."

Raji's wasn't just where the Drifters played, it was also where they'd stage pre-show rehearsals that involved standing around with instruments in the club's near-defunct kitchen.

"The kitchen, of course, was kind of a gross no man's land," Peter recalled. "There wasn't a lot of food being prepared there anymore, as far as I know. On the occasion where food was being prepared, I wasn't eating it."

Given the club's limited drink menu and its already storied history as a punk-centric venue that hosted bands like Nirvana, Redd Kross, and even Guns N' Roses, it's a wonder the Continental Drifters ended up there every Tuesday night playing what was basically Americana roots music.

Los Angeles spearheaded and nurtured a pay-to-play culture in the 1980s, which meant that artists who wanted to play at a certain venue were required to pay a fee up front to use the facility. Pay-to-play was commonplace at the time the Drifters were up and running, but the practice had started to become stale and artists were looking for another option. For Mark Walton, pay-to-play felt like bullying.

"I didn't want to play any of those places," he said.

According to original Drifters keyboardist Danny McGough: "Most of them were just like, 'Okay, here you go. Here's a beer coupon.' Which wasn't any way to pay the rent or anything. The Whisky, I think, you would owe them money if you played there."

Raji's provided an alternative for bands; a place to play where they could actually get a percentage of the door (in this case, 100% of the door plus as much beer as they could drink) rather than have to pay anything to the venue up front. In fact, it was Carlo Nuccio who pushed for the venue to adopt a system that was fair to bands and artists.

For Carlo, making a living as a drummer in Los Angeles was a difficult endeavor in the mid-1980s, as he navigated the frustrating pay-to-play climate.

"It was tough," Carlo said. "Fortunately, I was really arrogant and I had a few other tools in my skill set."

With enough knowledge to work as a front-of-house engineer, studio engineer, producer, session and touring drummer, and drum tech, Carlo was ultimately able to cast a wide net and develop a big enough network to become a viable player in the L.A. scene. It didn't happen overnight, though.

Before he landed in L.A. on a long-term basis, the New Orleans native spent a bit of time living there with his friend Ben Delgadillo. They both returned to New Orleans, where they were in a band together called The Radical Shiite God Squad, along with NOLA bassist and WTUL (Tulane University's radio station) deejay Ivan "Funkboy" Bodley.

Bodley, who would go on to be a bass player to the stars in New York City, says that the band was "on fire." But that would all change after only a couple of months and two gigs.

"The songs were great; the audience loved us," Bodley said. "There was no question in our minds at all that we had definitely captured lightning in a bottle and were on our way to do great things.

"Then only a month or two into the life of the band, Ben got into an argument with his brother at their house. The brother shot Ben to death. And that was it. It was all over."

Devastated by the loss of his close friend, Carlo was compelled to get out of New Orleans. A call from producer Jim Hill in L.A. opened the door for him to make a move.

Hill, a producer known for his work with The Plimsouls and The Rain Parade, mentioned to Carlo that The Rain Parade wanted to hire him as their front-of-house engineer. He said he'd accept on one condition—if the band, who was also scouting for a drummer, hired Carlo as well. The band, according to the Rain Parade's Matt Piucci, had just been overseas on tour and returned home to search for a drummer. They settled on someone, until the call came in from Hill.

"After we came back to the States we were gonna tour, and we didn't have a drummer," Piucci recalled. " We were rehearsing people, and we picked some guy—and I get this call from Jim. He goes, 'Did you find a drummer?' I go, 'Yeah.' He goes, 'Fire him. I have your drummer.'"

The band linked with Carlo and hit it off, and Carlo relocated once again to Los Angeles to hit the road with the Rain Parade.

"I took my cocky ass out to L.A. again," he said.

Working with the Rain Parade guys and returning to L.A. was heavy for Carlo, who had his world turned upside down when Ben was murdered—costing him a best friend and a musical partner.

"He didn't talk about it in that way, but I know it fucked him up. Ben was his good buddy," Piucci said.

Carlo's first Rain Parade gig was at The Palace in Hollywood, where he met Steve Berlin of Los Lobos fame, who at the time was climbing the ladder as a producer. Berlin told Carlo that he was going to make him "a star."

Hearing Carlo's recollection of their first meeting. Berlin himself laughs off the notion that he would have had "the power to make anybody anything."

"I certainly hope that was [said] with a twinkle in my eye," Berlin said with a laugh.

The comment may have been in jest, but Berlin says he'd never met a drummer like Carlo before and sensed he had the chops and unique characteristics to make his way in Los Angeles.

"It was sort of a joke and sort of wasn't, really," he said. "I thought, 'This guy's going to come to town and play with everybody.' He was funnier and cooler and groovier than anybody I knew."

True to his word, Berlin started hiring Carlo for as many sessions as he could. Soon enough, the work became constant.

"[Berlin] was just getting his feet really wet, and he kept me along for the ride in the beginning," Carlo recalled. "I said, 'Man, let me move out here and see what the hell happens.'"

It's also true that Carlo played with everybody. He could play anything, and perhaps that is best emphasized by his friendship and musical relationship with hardcore punk icon Keith Morris, founder of seminal bands Black Flag and Circle Jerks.

"The first time I met Carlo he was doing sound," Morris recalled of their first encounter at a Circle Jerks gig in the 1980s. "This was in New Orleans, and he was set up and ready to go for a soundcheck. That was the afternoon after I'd discovered [the famous New Orleans cocktail] the Hurricane. I got up early, skipped breakfast, and went straight to Preservation Hall. And I just started to get plastered. Over the course of the day I consumed, I'd say, a minimum half a dozen Hurricanes."

Drunk by soundcheck, Morris took it upon himself to start pulling cables from the snake where all of the microphone XLR cables were connected.

"I get a tap on my shoulder," Morris said. "And I should have been punched in the face and knocked out; that probably would have been the best thing for me. But it's Carlo, and he's turning red. He's got steam coming out of his ears and he's, like, breathing fire.

"I didn't make it through soundcheck because I got pissed off and stormed out of the club."

Their first meeting may have been tense, but the pair became friends after Carlo moved to Los Angeles. When they linked up in L.A., Morris' favorite local band quickly became Laughing Sam's Dice—a band that featured Carlo and Mark Walton—and Morris would hang out with them while they were recording or go and see as many gigs as he could. He estimates seeing them at least six or seven times in the band's short run.

Carlo was introduced to Mark in 1985, when The Dream Syndicate was working on the *Out of the Grey* album. They were introduced by Jim Hill, hit it off, and their friendship led to Carlo—while back in New Orleans—getting regional work as a drum tech and front-of-house engineer for The Dream Syndicate.

By that point, Mark had already established himself in the L.A. scene thanks to Uncle Studios, the rehearsal studio he founded in 1979 that became home base for countless bands in the city. Uncle was Mark's foot in the door as a young, ambitious musician.

"Music was always my life—I wanted to live that life," Mark said. "I didn't care to go off to college. I started the studio, and I wanted to play music and do what I have to do."

When he joined The Dream Syndicate in 1984, the band was coming off the success of their 1982 cult classic *The Days Of Wine And Roses*—a seminal album from the Paisley Underground period. The Dream Syndicate was riding a wave of critical success and buzz at the time, but lackluster performance from the follow-up album prompted a brief breakup before they ultimately reunited a short time later in the mid-eighties.

As a tech, Carlo would tune and play drummer Dennis Duck's kit to get the sounds right.

"Once he tuned the drums and started playing them, I was enamored," Mark said. "I thought this guy was the best drummer I'd ever heard."

When Carlo moved to L.A. for the second time, he ran into Mark and the two began playing together. They even moved in together, at the infamous Batch Pad, and little by little the seeds were being planted for collaboration.

Some of the most important songs in the early history of the Continental Drifters were penned by Carlo during the earliest days at the Batch Pad. He had started writing songs after a falling out with a former band leader.

"Most of the songs I'd been working on, I worked on up in the Batch Pad," Carlo said. "To be quite honest, I was just kind of getting frustrated because, you know, I left another band where the guy—it was clear and evident that it was his band and he was going to fuck everybody.

"I gotta put my fate in my own hands; I've got to start writing some songs. I can, so why not?"

Mark was immediately drawn in by Carlo as a singer and songwriter, just as he was with his drumming during the Dream Syndicate session. He recalls stealthily signing Carlo up for an open mic as a way to encourage him to play his own compositions.

"He's like, 'What the fuck are you doing?'" Mark said. "I'm like, 'Just go sing!' That's kind of, I think, the moment the band idea started."

Soon enough, Ray Ganucheau, another New Orleans transplant and friend of Carlo's who moved to Los Angeles to work for Microsoft, started hanging around the house with the guys. Ray had bounced around a bit by that point, originally moving to Los Angeles in 1985 before going back to New Orleans, and also spending time in Dallas. He recalls meeting up with Carlo in Dallas when he was in town working as front-of-house engineer for the Circle Jerks.

"He said, 'You know, you ought to come back out to L.A.,' and I said, 'Yeah, I dunno, maybe we could work our way out there," Ray said. "So I ended up back in L.A. around '91 or so."

Ray and Carlo's connection went back to bands in the early 1980s, including a group called Apt. B, which also featured musicians Vance DeGeneres and Scott Goudeau. The two also played together in both RZA and Pop Combo; both of which also included New Orleans rock linchpin Lenny Zenith.

"RZA was initially a punk band inspired by [NOLA punks] The Normals and UK punk bands," Zenith said. RZA played "dingy, poorly attended shows," he adds, but was propelled by critical attention as well as opening slots for bands like U2, Iggy Pop, and Mott the Hoople's Ian Hunter.

RZA essentially "transitioned" to the band that became Pop Combo, which leaned in more of a new wave direction.

Ray was also collaborating, including in an iteration of Apt. B, with Barbara Menendez, singer and keyboardist of hugely popular NOLA new wave band The Cold. That band also featured DeGeneres, and made a solid impact across the southeast in the early 1980s despite not finding national success. Ray ultimately married Menendez, and the two started a family in the time between their two Los Angeles moves.

Lenny Zenith recalls hearing some of Ray's earlier songwriting efforts and being significantly impressed by what he was doing.

"I remember when RZA was transitioning to Pop Combo, and he played a couple of songs from a demo deal that he had been shopping, and together with his voice and guitar skills, I was a little embarrassed and confused why he wanted to play with me," he said. "He is an exceptional guitarist, singer and songwriter, and there have been few people I've worked with who were so musically 'in tune' for whatever genre, or who I enjoyed singing with more."

When Ray returned to Los Angeles for the second time and he began collaborating more with Carlo, a two-day writing binge resulted in songs like "The Mississippi" and "New York"—which would become classics in the early Drifters catalog.

"Fucking four or five songs came out of the two days, that are still arguably the most requested Drifters songs of that time," Carlo said. "We all kind of sat down, opened a beer, and said, 'Well, this is fucking good!'"

While there's debate on what exactly was *the* first song worked up as a band, "The Mississippi" is almost always cited as one of the earliest as well as the song that clicked most immediately at the initial gatherings. That Ganucheau/Nuccio co-write, with Ray on lead vocals, would unquestionably become the centerpiece of the band in the earliest days.

"I had kind of the bones of it together, when we got together in L.A., and then [Carlo] refined it," Ray said. "He wrote a large portion of the lyrics, and I had that chorus and some other key lines in it."

The song, with its references to the South and the quasi Delta Blues musicality, was the perfect platform for each member's individuality.

"I got to play guitar the way I wanted to hear the guitar on it," Gary Eaton said. "I was allowed to do what I wanted to do on [the song]. The fucking pocket is so damn deep."

Those initial writing sessions turned into demo sessions, after Ray and Carlo set up a studio in Ray's basement.

"I had a place in Dixie Canyon that had a basement in it. He had some recording gear and he said, 'We ought to do some tunes.' I had some recording gear; I had a console and some other stuff," Ray said. "So we combined our gear, and we just started making demos. We set up a little studio in the basement of our house."

Meanwhile, Gary Eaton was playing in multiple bands and befriended Carlo after he left his newborn son's mother, with whom he was playing in an L.A. buzz band called The Ringling Sisters. Gary found refuge at Raji's and the two became friends.

One day, Gary called Carlo to mention that he needed a drummer and a bass player.

"I happened to be at his house at the moment, and he goes, 'Well maybe Mark will do it.' I said, 'Well, sure,'" Mark recalled.

When Gary's relationship ended, he got the chance to move into an apartment rented by the then-girlfriend of his Ringling Sisters bandmate and future auxiliary Drifter, Dave Catching. Solo living lasted just a short time, though, before he got a fateful call from Carlo.

"Carlo and Mark, who had been living together, asked me to move in because [Rockpile and Pat McLaughlin guitarist] Billy Bremner had just moved out," Gary said. "So they needed another roomie there to help with the rent. And so I thought, 'Well, that beats living alone. There's furniture there!'"

And so, the Batch Pad was born.

Carlo, Mark, and Ray invited Gary shortly after they began playing together, and things started gelling. There was no one line of direction in terms of what the band was going to be; all of the individual Drifters had different musical backgrounds and weren't very much concerned with genre or fitting inside of a certain box.

"I'm not really a country guy, because I didn't grow up in the hills," Gary said. "I'm not an OG punk guy really. And I grew up listening to all kinds of music, so I just wanted the people that I like to appreciate what I was trying to do."

That wasn't to say that there wasn't somewhat of a shared sense of where the music could go and how they wanted to play it.

"We all liked Crazy Horse. We all loved that sort of 'teetering on the edge of disaster,'" Ray said. "It was really pretty honest, the way that stuff came together. We all brought something to the table and just would turn up and play."

However haphazardly it was happening, an actual band *was* starting to form. They recruited Danny McGough on keyboards, who Carlo was working with through his 7 Deadly 5 bandmate, Ilene Markell.

"Carlo called me up one day and he was like, 'Hey man, I'm starting a band with my friend Ray Ganucheau, and Mark Walton and Gary Eaton and you. How do you feel about this?' And I was like, 'Yeah, well, okay sure. I can do that,'" McGough laughed. "I was almost abducted."

When he joined the Drifters, Danny was already a working keyboardist with a full plate of projects rotating regularly—something he'd worked up to for years. He'd been playing since he was a teenager, finding an interest in music in part through his brother's record collection.

"My big brother, he's like twelve years older than me," Danny said. "He would buy records and basically treated them like they were magazines. So he would give me all of his records after a week. He was never moved by the records in the way I was.

"I got the first couple of Band records through him, and *Disraeli Gears* by Cream, and Jethro Tull records and whatnot."

Inspired by players like Garth Hudson of The Band, Danny took an interest in keyboards and asked his mother for a piano. She had other ideas.

"Eventually she bought me a guitar and I was like, 'Oh, great,'" he said.

Danny's first gig was as a guitar player with an early punk rock band that featured former Adolescents guitarist Rikk Agnew, who persuaded him to join a band of his despite Danny being just 14 and not having played guitar for very long.

"I'm 14 years old and they're like, 'Dude, you're in our band,'" Danny recalled. " And I'm like, 'What? I don't know how to play guitar!' They go, 'No, it's gonna be punk rock. It doesn't matter if you can play or not."

He lasted just a month in that role, eventually starting bands of his own in his late teens and buying himself a Vox Continental combo organ. He began doing gigs on both keyboards and guitar, which proved successful enough.

"I would get actual jobs doing that," Danny said. "I think probably because I played keyboards like I played guitar—I understand support, and a lot of shreddy keyboard players don't get that."

He formed a band called The Swing Set, which featured Ilene Markell on bass and sometimes Carlo on drums. At the time, Markell was dating Peter Holsapple and the couple was playing together with Peter's dB's bandmate Chris Stamey. From that collaboration came a tour in 1990 as the Peter Holsapple Band with McGough, Markell, and Carlo.

"That was sort of the real beginnings of the Continental Drifters," said Danny, who'd become a regular around Los Angeles when he was abducted into the band by Carlo. Everyone had other projects, but the Drifters quickly became a focus.

Gary, especially, saw the band as his songwriting vehicle after the demise of the Ringling Sisters just a couple of years earlier. His early contributions to the band included songs like "Dallas" and "Let It Ride," aided by Danny's tasteful work on piano and organ.

"It just started falling together. One by one, we were finding each other," Mark said.

While some songs emerged from the co-writes happening between Ray and Carlo before the band got together, and some of Carlo's songs were born of necessity and survival, Gary's songs had been around for a few years and were even being tried out in other bands. "Dallas" dated back to the Ringling Sisters before getting the Drifters treatment.

That song, with its anthemic chorus and vivid imagery portraying memories of his military childhood in Wichita Falls, Texas, happened almost instantaneously.

"I was working part time as a dispatcher for my buddy," Gary recalled. "He knew I needed a job and he gave me this job as a dispatcher at his little messenger service. He let me bring my guitar, he let me bring my son. I wrote it in about ten minutes sitting in this office. I was sitting there with my guitar, and I picked it up and I just started playing it and then I started writing the words."

> *Wichita Falls is trailers and dust*
> *Blowin' tornadoes and hail as big as golf balls*
> *Dirt roads in dark town*
> *And blues on a Hammond organ*
> *It was a cool November mornin'*
> *Mahalia Jackson sang*
>
> *Not old enough to know any better*
> *But all roads led to Dallas*
> *I remember it in black and white*
> *All roads led to Dallas*

The Ringling Sisters version of "Dallas" was worked up for what was supposed to become that band's second album for A&M Records after their debut—the Lou Adler-produced *60 Watt Reality*.

There was a bit of social crossover between the Drifters and the Ringling Sisters, as it turns out. Gary's bandmate, Dave Catching, was also a friend of Carlo's. Carlo's girlfriend at the time, Martha Gehman, had a half-sister named Pleasant Gehman (high school classmate of Mark Walton's) who was one of the singers in The Ringling Sisters. Another singer in the band was Annette Zilinskas, whose career started as an original member and bass player of The Bangs, Vicki Peterson's band that went on to become The Bangles.

Going to Raji's to see the Drifters became a regular thing for Zilinskas after The Ringling Sisters broke up, and it was a chance for her not only to see Gary but also in time to catch up with Vicki. They didn't see a lot of each other at that point, as they each had their own things going on. Raji's was their hangout, as it was for so many people and so many bands.

"It was such a meeting place for all types of bands," Zilinskas said. "Alternative country to punk rock to rockabilly. All the different sectors of music. And that's where people would go to hang, you know? I could go there alone and I would know somebody."

The first time Zilinskas encountered the Drifters, she walked into Raji's and heard them playing "Dallas"—impressed by how different it was from the version she sang alongside Gary in the Ringling Sisters.

"It was always a kick for me to sing that song because I could really just stretch, you know? Just really belt it," she said, "It was so fun to see it done with his new creative endeavor."

One of the things that Zilinskas emphasizes about the brilliance of "Dallas" is the lyrics. Robert Lloyd, keyboardist in the Steve Wynn Band and Gary Eaton's post-Drifters band Kingsizemaybe, agrees.

"Every line in 'Dallas' is a thing," Lloyd said. "You don't necessarily know what the story is. There's a secret to it; it's behind the narrative. But they're all completely real. It just was exciting to play. 'Dallas' is just a fucking amazing song."

Lloyd's relationship with the Drifters started with the Steve Wynn Band, where he played alongside Mark, Robert Maché, and drummer Kevin Jarvis. But he'd seen the others around Los Angeles and had connections with some of them through his day job as a writer for the *L.A. Weekly*. He even saw Gary play in his pre-Drifters days.

"I can remember seeing [Gary] play with a band called the Ringling Sisters at the Roxy and just thinking, 'That guy looks like a rock star.' He was wearing, as I recall, kind of like a tuxedo shirt with frills on it. Looking very commanding. He just had a lot of presence; stage presence," Lloyd said.

The first lineup of the Continental Drifters was born from the Batch Pad at the end of 1991, and the first rehearsal at Ray's house, where they worked up a handful of songs, signaled that something special was happening.

"We played the songs and they sounded freaking amazing, you know?" Gary recalled.

"We just hit it off. We played, and we all brought in a few tunes, and next thing you know we had a gig," Ray adds.

The band made their debut at Club Lingerie not long after, and the Continental Drifters were off and running. Around this time, Raji's was suffering from a bit of an attendance slump, leading to Carlo being asked to organize a weekly residency with his new group.

The Tuesday residency at Raji's launched in January of 1992, starting as a fairly structured showcase of the newly-formed Drifters and their increasing repertoire of songs. Some of the nights were pretty ramshackle, as the standing concern among Carlo, Mark, Gary, Ray, and Danny was to play music and have a good time.

"The first couple of times, it wasn't that big of a thing. But people caught wind of it pretty quickly, and then it was pretty steady," Ray said. "There was a pretty steady line of people who wanted to get up and play."

Raji's, Mark recalls, was the perfect location for the band because of how close it was to the legendary Frolic Room.

"We would go, run across the street to the Frolic Room, have a few drinks, come back to the club, drink beer, hang out on stage, and just stay there all night long," he said.

The looseness of Raji's was the ideal setting for the Drifters' residency, especially as more musicians showed up to sit in. It was a welcoming environment; one where nobody was too precious about anything.

"I had a little garage studio with a bunch of old tube gear and stuff, and I sold an old Ampex four-track tube machine to this guy Tom Newman, who produced *Tubular Bells*," Danny said. "I invited him down to one of the shows, and he was like, 'Wait, you guys all let other people touch your equipment?'

"I was like, 'Yeah, they're all our buddies!' He goes, 'That would never fly in my hometown.'"

As word started to spread about the Drifters and their weekly gig, friends and acquaintances (musical or otherwise) started showing up with greater frequency. One of those friends was Peter Holsapple, who at the time had just left a gig with R.E.M.

Peter's stint with R.E.M. began when The dB's ended in 1988 and he moved to Los Angeles. He was invited by the band, with whom he'd become friends in the early 1980s, to play guitar and keyboards on the *Green* World Tour in 1989. That nine-month world tour was their first foray into arenas and planted the seeds for 1991's *Out Of Time*.

Peter stayed on through 1991, augmenting the band during recording and promo for *Out Of Time*. He contributed bass, guitar, and keyboards to the album (including the acoustic guitar on the massive hit "Losing My Religion"), and participated in subsequent promotional efforts.

By late 1991, songwriting disputes prompted him to leave the band, and he returned to Los Angeles, burned out by frustrating industry experiences. He decided to pursue work as a producer and session player, rather than joining another band.

Around that time, Peter had begun producing an album for Barry Cowsill, who was two decades removed from his time as a child star with the 1960s pop group The Cowsills. His introduction to Barry was made by way of Paul du Gré, owner of Paul and Mike's Recording in Los Angeles, who played Peter some of Barry's songs one day without telling him who it was. Peter was blown away; his response to what he heard being, "What the fuck is this?"

"Paul finally turns it off and he says, 'That is Barry Cowsill,'" Peter said. "And I'm like, 'You've got to be kidding me. You've *got* to be kidding me!'"

Peter's marriage to musician Ilene Markell was coming apart by this point, and he started going to see the Drifters play at Raji's, and was even in the audience at their first show. He was fascinated by the band and what they were doing, and wanted to be involved—as a producer.

"[There was] Carlo, and Mark with these loopy, Chris Hillman-like dive bombs on the bass," Peter said. "Ray with his beautiful voice. Gary with his songs. Danny made everything sound better. It was very alluring."

Eventually, Peter was asked to fill in on guitar one night (alongside Dave Catching) for an absent Ray Ganucheau—cementing his infatuation with the band.

"I got off that stage and just couldn't get the experience out of my mind," he recalled.

In August of 1991, a "surprisingly acquiescent" Barry Cowsill agreed to go with Peter and see his siblings—who'd been recording and gigging together again without his involvement—play at Club Lingerie.

At The Cowsills' gig, Peter was introduced to Barry's sister, Susan. He was enamored immediately.

"I could not focus on anything except Susan, and listening to her sing," he recalled.

Susan, at the time, was back with her childhood band after a period of what she refers to as "the dormant years."

Those years are integral to the Continental Drifters story because of a song that would start with the Drifters and ultimately have a life of its own—"The Rain Song."

Consider this: Susan Cowsill, whose life in music started when she joined The Cowsills at the age of 8, wrote her very first song in her 30s. It was "The Rain Song." Not only did she bring it to the Continental Drifters when she joined the band in 1992, but it was later recorded by Hootie & the Blowfish *and* The Bangles. Not many songwriters have that kind of luck with their first song.

That song was born of those aforesaid dormant years, which began in 1978. Prior to that, Susan had spent a few years pursuing a solo career after The Cowsills initially broke up in 1972, releasing a pair of singles for Warner Bros. Records in 1976. When she met singer/songwriter Dwight Twilley in '78, all of that ended. She and Twilley—best known for his 1975 hit "I'm On Fire"—started dating, and she was ultimately cut off from anything relating to music outside of his.

"Effectively, by my own choice, as I've owned my 50 percent of my part in any relationship—when I fell in love with Dwight and became his gal, I left The Cowsills and I became his muse and his singer chick," Susan said.

Once she joined Twilley's band and started a relationship with him, Susan's time in The Cowsills came to an end. Aside from the rare special occasion, her involvement in music was limited to the Dwight Twilley Band; she was not allowed to pursue or even listen to anything else.

"I had also turned down two record deals behind their backs that people were trying to make with me," she recalled. "Whatever Dwight wanted, I was going to do."

The same year she met Twilley, Susan was playing with her brothers at a club when she was introduced to aspiring teenage musicians Vicki and Debbi Peterson—two lifelong Cowsills fans who were just starting a band of their own. They introduced themselves to Susan and her brothers, including bandleader Bob Cowsill.

"I met them that night, made no real connection with anyone other than Bob, but I kind of stayed in touch with him," Vicki recalled.

Susan remembers them being eager to learn about harmony from their childhood idols.

"I don't know how I even remember them, but they were so annoyingly pure-looking," Susan laughed.

Through those years, Vicki and Bob Cowsill stayed in touch—she'd send him Christmas cards and he'd give her advice as her career was starting to take off. By the mid 1980s, Vicki's garage band The Bangles became one of the biggest in the world.

"[Bob] was kind of like my mentor, in certain ways," Vicki said. "He reminded me to stay in the moment and to take a deep breath and go, 'Oh my god, you have a number two hit record right now. Can you please just enjoy that for four seconds before you start thinking about all of the things that are wrong in your world?'

"I didn't have anyone else in my world who'd been a pop star before, so it was really helpful to me, actually."

One day, in 1988, Susan was watching MTV and recognized two familiar faces—Vicki and Debbi Peterson. She realized that the two Cowsills fans who were enamored with her group just a decade earlier had become superstars.

"She was like, 'They're on fucking MTV?! What?'" Vicki said.

On a random night the following year, Susan ventured down to a pub where her brother Bob was playing, despite Dwight not allowing her to. That's where she ran into Vicki once again, only this time The Bangles were breaking up.

"There she was looking like Riz from *Grease*," Susan recalled with a laugh. "I guess there was a silent truce made that evening, because we exchanged numbers and spoke every day from that point on."

Susan and Vicki's friendship quickly blossomed into a full-on songwriting partnership, and it also became the catalyst for her to leave her relationship with Twilley.

Though she'd discovered that Twilley had an affair with her best friend, Susan stayed in the relationship for two more years before finally leaving for good. It was then that she started writing songs, and started linking up with Vicki to work on music together.

Very late one night, after she started getting back into music, Susan frantically called Vicki.

"She literally called me at four in the morning, in a panic, and said, 'I think I have a song. I don't know what to do. I'm sorry to wake you up,'" Vicki recalled. "[I said], 'Do you have a tape recorder in the house, anywhere?'"

That late night epiphany became "The Rain Song," a triumphant pop masterpiece that was essentially Susan's "fuck you" to her former boyfriend.

> *I don't think about us much anymore*
> *And frankly the topic has become a bore*
> *You don't come up much in my conversations*
> *And I don't think about you on vacation*
> *But when it rains*
> *That's when I remember*
> *I remember you*

Susan and Vicki, who by then were calling themselves The Psycho Sisters, started thinking more seriously about recording and quickly found a kindred creative spirit in Peter Holsapple, who came to the aforementioned Cowsills gig at Club Lingerie.

Peter and Vicki, as it turns out, first met on December 7, 1984, when both The Bangles and The dB's were playing in Kansas City, Missouri. The Bangles, who were touring with Cyndi Lauper, had just finished a show at Kemper Arena and went to see The dB's play at Parody Hall.

They missed the dB's set, but ended up hanging out together at the motel where The dB's were staying. Peter and Vicki stayed in touch rather infrequently, mostly by postcard, until meeting again through The Cowsills. By then, Peter was sitting in with the Drifters at Raji's, and Vicki and Susan were aware of the Tuesday night action through Mark Walton, who told them about it when The Cowsills were rehearsing with Vicki at Uncle Studios.

"Mark just started saying, 'You've just gotta see this band I'm playing with. It's the craziest thing. It's these two guys from New Orleans, and Peter's coming,'" Vicki said. She and Susan eventually made their way down to Raji's to see the band, and were immediately hooked.

"They were just so incredible," Vicki said.

One of Susan's first major Drifters interactions occurred when Peter approached her about recording a duet of Gram Parsons' "A Song for You" for a tribute album, with most of the Drifters as the backing band. That song would become a staple at Raji's.

"The next thing you frickin' know, we're going to Raji's every Tuesday," Susan said. An undeniable connection between Susan and Peter was happening, as they began to play together and worked up a demo of "The Rain Song" together.

The allure of the Continental Drifters at that time was the freewheeling vibe—the feeling that what they were doing was much more about the emotion of the moment than any level of musical precision.

"On the nights that we did have it going, it was amazing. On the good nights, good lord," Gary said.

The wealth of songwriters and singers might have easily made for an uneven experience in other bands, but in the Drifters there was something about the blend that added to just how captivating and unique they were.

"None of them was like dead weight," said Kevin Jarvis, a drummer who filled in for Carlo frequently at Raji's. "Every one of those guys, you just would love to hear them sing all night."

"The songwriting is really the bottom line of what makes them so great," legendary rockabilly guitarist and songwriter Rosie Flores says of the band. "How they handle each song with so much intent and heart and soul. It's a feel-good band. You feel good when you go see them."

What the Drifters clearly had, particularly in the earliest days of the band, was the kind of chemistry and balance of personalities that is not always easy to find.

"Coming off a band like The dB's, which in a lot of ways was a more intellectual exercise—don't get me wrong, there was plenty of emotion in the dB's. Especially in the latter day band, I think," Peter said. "But the Drifters were a whole different kettle of fish for me. I was suddenly part of a family."

With Peter in the producer's chair and Susan and Vicki guesting on background vocals (none of the three were full-on members just yet), the Continental Drifters recorded a six-song demo at Doug Messenger's Studio in North Hollywood, owned by engineer Doug Messenger. Those sessions wouldn't see the light of day until late 1992, when the Messenger version of "The Mississippi" was released as a single for Bob Mould and Nicholas Hill's S.O.L. label.

Those sessions were a solid template for the upstart Drifters, but they'd soon find themselves shuffling things up for the first time.

Chapter Two:
"The Vatican"

"A few of us thought that the Continental Drifters was, in some form, a prize for having survived our other bands. That we could lapse into this beautiful family mode."

— Peter Holsapple

Part I

The year 1992 was a pivotal one for the Continental Drifters, with Tuesday night gigs at Raji's in Hollywood, recording sessions, and a bunch of non-Drifters activity that often took band members away from their weekly gig and put a substitute in their place. The original five members—Mark Walton, Gary Eaton, Ray Ganucheau, Carlo Nuccio, and Danny McGough—were all busy enough with other endeavors that the weekly night gigs sometimes overlapped with other commitments. Mark toured with Carlene Carter, Danny was in several other bands, and Carlo was jet setting all around the country working as a drummer, engineer, or producer.

That fluidity within the band would remain pretty consistent throughout the tenure of the L.A. Drifters. But the Raji's gigs became enough of a nucleus for the band's musical activity that word quickly got around, and there was already some buzz happening not long after they started the Tuesday night shows in early 1992.

"Drifting" was *always* the name of the game in this band. After all, the entire existence of the Continental Drifters was the result of Carlo's initial landing in Los Angeles just a few years prior, his brief move back to New Orleans, and then ultimately his return in the short time preceding the beginning of the band. And if calling your revolving door of a band the Continental Drifters wasn't fitting enough already, the origins of the name might just cement it.

It goes all the way back to the mid-1980s, when New Orleans musician Tommy Malone was coming off of a stint with Li'l Queenie and the Percolators, a band he played in with the late NOLA legend Leigh "Li'l Queenie" Harris.

The early 1980s yielded some success for the Percolators, with their song "My Dawlin' New Orleans" becoming a local hit and ultimately a New Orleans standard. Harris, who died in 2019, became an icon of New Orleans music and remains beloved in NOLA.

Malone and his Percolators bandmate John Magnie ultimately decided that they wanted to do their own thing. They hooked up with musicians Johnnie Ray Allen and Steve Amedee, and the group started writing together.

"We started jamming together and writing songs together and all that, and started gigging a little bit," Malone said. "And somewhere in there, we were looking for a name." They found one courtesy of the late Clark Vreeland, a New Orleans funk pioneer known for his work with the pre-Radiators band The Rhapsodizers.

According to Malone, "Clark actually coined the name Continental Drifters, and we said 'Oh, that's great! We like that. Can we use it?' He said, 'Yeah, yeah. Sure! Go ahead.' So we got it from Clark."

By 1986, the first iteration of the Continental Drifters were playing regularly around New Orleans and had gone through a few personnel changes. Things gelled for the band, though, and they felt they had something interesting happening.

"It was like this crazy music club for writing and performing weird shit," Malone recalled. "And everybody was juiced. Just jacked up to play and write."

During their run, the original Continental Drifters actually did a gig in New Orleans opening for local legends Dash Rip Rock, NYC toy instrument band Pianosaurus, and The dB's.

Around this time, Malone's Continental Drifters went to a recording studio in Metarie, Louisiana, to work on some music, hiring Carlo Nuccio as producer. When the band's drummer didn't show up for the session, Carlo decided to break a longstanding rule to not play drums on anything he produced.

"Somehow, over the next year, I ended up being their drummer," Carlo said.

Despite having gigs lined up in New Orleans with the Continental Drifters, Carlo was also getting calls from Steve Berlin in Los Angeles, being flown out several times a month for recording sessions.

"Steve was calling and going, 'Tuesday. I'll overnight you a ticket.' I go, 'Oh, shit. I've got two gigs this week with the Continental Drifters," Carlo said. "I've gotta make my call. So it became understood that if I had to leave, I was going to leave."

One of those West Coast trips happened to occur synchronously with Malone and his bandmates deciding that they wanted to try something different for an upcoming gig without their usual drummer.

"We were always being dogged for being too fucking loud," Malone said with a laugh. "[And] Steve's a pretty musical cat. What if we got some of these songs down to a place where we could just focus on the material, you know? And actually hear it. So I thought we'd do a gig where we'd only bring in what we could carry."

With Steve Amedee on tambourine, the band reconfigured themselves into a more acoustic format with two guitars and accordion. Amedee played the tambourine in a way that would almost simulate a drum kit, accenting both kick and snare hits in different positions. The combination proved to be a revelation for the band; Malone remembers a gig in the summer of 1987 where they tried out the new format and got a tremendous audience response.

"We did another set and went back to somebody's apartment, put on the board tapes, and we're like, 'Fuck, this is pretty interesting, This is really different. Well, fuck the old band!" he said.

Carlo, meanwhile, had come back early from an L.A. trip and decided to go watch his Continental Drifters bandmates play.

"I saw them at Carrollton Station and just sat there with my mouth open," he said. "And when Tommy came off he went to the bar. He goes, 'Hey Carlo!' I said, 'Dude, that was fucking amazing. *This* is the band. He goes, 'You think so?' He was kind of trying to avoid me, because he was feeling the same way."

That enthusiasm led to the newly reconfigured band changing their name to the subdudes, and by November they'd moved themselves and their families to Colorado. They had a record deal within a year, with a little nudge from their pal Carlo Nuccio.

After Carlo had gone back to L.A. to stay, he was working on a record with Pat McLaughlin, produced by Mitchell Froom. Froom, as it turned out, was a judge for *Musician* magazine's annual Best Unsigned Band competition. One of the bands entered in the competition that year was none other than the subdudes.

"So I said, 'Hey Mitchell, check out the demo you got for the subdudes,'" Carlo recalled. The band won the contest, were signed to Atlantic Records, and soon flew to Los Angeles to work on their debut album with R.E.M./John Mellencamp producer Don Gehman. Carlo ultimately connected with Malone and the band when they arrived.

"I went homeless," Carlo said. "I left the place I was staying because I didn't have much money, and I moved in with them for the two months they were there, and cooked for them every day."

He also called Clark Vreeland, the man who coined the Drifters name, to ask if he could use the now freestanding name for a new project he'd begun working on with Ray Ganucheau, Mark Walton, and Gary Eaton.

"When I called Clark Vreeland to ask if I can have the name, he goes, 'Well fuck yeah you can have the name. That ain't my fuckin' name!'" Carlo said.

In those days, the hustle-or-die of Los Angeles meant that Carlo Nuccio found himself everywhere all at once. Playing drums for countless artists in studios and at clubs, working as the front of house engineer at Raji's, producing when opportunities arose, and drum tech-ing for bands like the Dream Syndicate. It's why he started writing songs in the first place, and ultimately found a platform for those songs in the Drifters.

"I couldn't understand how I was getting work, because I'm like, 'What? They ain't got no fuckin' drummers here?' And boy, when I started going out I said, 'Goddamnit, they got no drummers here.' It was weird," Carlo said of his workload during that period. "It was like spandex drummer wannabes with their drumsticks in their back pocket. Who are you? Who are you under all of that makeup?"

By the time the Drifters got going, Carlo was a well-connected guy. It's no wonder, then, that many worlds would collide at Raji's. People would show up who knew Carlo, Mark, Ray, Danny, or Gary, and often those people would invite other people who'd turn out to also be connected to Carlo, Mark, Ray, Danny, or Gary from some other band or some other life.

That is what turned the Drifters into something amorphous; a seemingly limitless canvas on which any number of people could paint.

And paint, they did. When word started to spread around L.A. about the residency, not only did an audience start to build, but so did a roster of guests that included everyone from Rosie Flores to Jackson Browne, Victoria Williams to The Cowsills, and Thelonious Monster's Bob Forrest to Martin Phillipps of The Chills.

"You didn't feel like there was a sideman," Flores recalled of the Drifters. "Each person was an entity all to their own. Each one of them had a light that was shining off of them. And of course Raji's would be packed because *everybody* loved the Continental Drifters."

There was a veritable who's who of artists that would either open any given Tuesday night, or the Drifters themselves would back up for a short set. More often than not, both things would occur, and it was Carlo, Peter, and Mark calling friends, inviting them down, and making arrangements.

"Playing with Rosie Flores was really fun," Gary recalled. "I've always loved Rosie Flores. She was a queen, to me, of doing it the right way."

With the freewheeling vibe and relative unpredictability of Tuesday nights at Raji's, it's no wonder that so many musicians were attracted to the Drifters' residency each week.

"This was the scene you would dream of having in L.A., where you could go to a place and you're guaranteed to have a fun time, hear great music, and shoot the shit with all of your good friends," Steve Wynn, singer and principal songwriter of The Dream Syndicate, said.

The Dream Syndicate had a history at Raji's that preceded the Continental Drifters, recording their 1989 live album *Live At Raji's* there. By the time the Drifters residency started, Mark, Carlo (who was the front of house engineer the night of the *Live At Raji's* show), and Steve Wynn knew the venue well.

"It was the kind of place where you could do things spontaneously," Wynn said. "You could take chances; you could just do things for no reason besides just to have some fun. It just had that feeling that you'd want to have in a local scene that didn't exist."

Of course, spontaneity lent itself well to the guest performances during the Drifters' run of shows at Raji's, but it wasn't necessarily just a bunch of people winging it every week. Peter, according to Carlo, would be in charge of making "quick charts" for a guest set, and rehearsal did occur—albeit rather loosely.

"We'd get to the club and before they came, long before they came, we'd try to run them down. We'd always get there early," Carlo said. "We'd run them down a little bit with somebody singing or humming the melody line and we'd go, 'Yeah, that's cool. That works.' And then they'd come to the gig that night and we'd try to show off how badass we were."

Jackson Browne, a close friend of Susan's going back to the 1970s, was a particular highlight for Carlo.

"I know we did 'Doctor My Eyes.' I remember being shocked at how quiet he [sang]. He's like, 'If I sang like you, I'd have to only do one gig a week,'" he said. "I was like, 'Yeah, I'm kind of a bullhorn.'"

As with any weekly gig, it wasn't always possible for every Drifter to show up every single Tuesday. To keep the momentum, many of the Drifters employed substitutes—affectionately dubbed the "auxiliary Drifters"—to take their place when other commitments took precedence.

In their place, they'd call in friends like Dave Catching, who would go on to run Rancho de la Luna, a recording studio in Joshua Tree, and play guitar with Eagles of Death Metal. Catching would sub for Ray, while Bangles bassist Michael Steele subbed for Mark on a few occasions.

Carlo recalls Steele, whose playing he describes as "so fucking amazing," dropping her low E string to D—which Mark did for "Invisible Boyfriend"—and assuming it was what Mark did for the entire set.

"So she got on stage and she had learned all the songs with the E string dropped to D. It had the coolest sound," Carlo said. "She crushed the gig. I just remember that night I was like, 'Mark who?' I had him fired in my head. Actually, I had him fired and I was married to her."

Calexico drummer John Convertino filled in on occasion, although Kevin Jarvis was a more frequent sub.

"It was actually a daunting task to fill those shoes, just because he is such an amazing drummer. One of my favorites for sure," Jarvis said of jumping in for Carlo.

Convertino shares similar feelings on Carlo as a drummer, and counts him as an important early influence going back to Carlo's days in Laughing Sam's Dice.

"I saw him play once with them, and I was like, 'That's the first time I've seen a drummer come close to John Bonham.' He has that thing that, like, nobody else has that John Bonham has," Convertino said. "He has this way of, like, driving the bus that very few drummers have."

As a young upstart drummer, who was then in his earliest days of playing with Giant Sand (years before he and singer/guitarist Joey Burns left that band and formed Calexico), Convertino admired Carlo's singular playing style. He even learned a valuable lesson about drums, courtesy of another singular Carlo trait: his large personality.

"I saw him backstage with Mark, and they had a bass drum and he was trying to get this certain tone out of the bass drum and couldn't get it," Convertino recalled. "And he was like, 'I'm not going to be able to play because I can't get this bass drum right.' And I was just standing there with my jaw agape. I just thought it was so cool.

"Here he is, so into his bass drum tone that it's going to make or break the show. And ever since I saw that I was like, 'I'm paying more attention to the bass drum.' And then I started understanding why. I learned that from him, in just that five or ten minutes that I saw him backstage."

Robert Maché also started his Drifter life as an auxiliary player, as well as a guest. He was invited by Mark, with whom he played in the Steve Wynn Band, alongside Kevin Jarvis, Wynn, and Robert Lloyd on keyboards. Maché, along with Robert Lloyd, would sit in on "Dallas" and "The Mississippi" on mandolin and accordion, respectively.

"The feeling of getting up and playing those couple of songs at the end of the night was really exhilarating," Lloyd said.

Robert Maché started getting calls to fill in, subbing for Ray when the guitarist would have work commitments keeping him away.

"Nobody can sub for Ray, he's just, like, perfection on earth," Maché said.

In Drifter world, it wasn't uncommon for friends and auxiliary players to be "adopted" by the band, as Robert Maché ultimately was.

"We were like these adjunct little pets," he said. "It's kind of like we were all cats showing up on somebody's porch. And every once in a while somebody says, 'Oh that's a cute one, we should feed it.' And then all of the sudden it's your cat."

"It just became kind of a medicine almost," Lloyd said. "Whatever else was happening in your week, going there was just really kind of a relief."

Like cats to a porch, musicians flocked to Raji's, and some showed up week after week. The same can be said for attendees, many of whom were regulars.

"Raji's couldn't have been more opposite of show business, yet music business people certainly went there," Raji's regular and former Dave Davies bassist David Jenkins said.

At the time, Jenkins was working as a scout for a music publisher and would rave about the Drifters any chance he got. Jenkins was among a core group of regulars that also included Brian Kehew, keyboardist and longtime tech for The Who, actor and musician Robbie Rist, and Gary Stewart—a music industry executive best known for his work at Rhino Records and as Chief Music Officer at Apple Music.

"If Gary was there, it was cool," Steve Wynn said. "If Gary was there, it became an instant scene. Gary was a scene in himself. So Gary being at all those Drifters shows, it was like, 'Wow, this is the place to be!'"

Added Kevin Jarvis: "[Stewart] was always at everything I ever went to. And even non-music stuff. He was in the know of these interesting cultural benchmarks."

Stewart, who took his own life in 2019, had a presence that seemed to make an impact on the Drifters and those who were alongside him in the audience every week, and his influence is felt to this day by Wynn and his contemporaries.

"I always felt like Gary was one of my best friends, and vice versa. What I realized after he died was, there were hundreds of people who felt that way," said Wynn, who Stewart signed to Rhino as both a new and reissue artist. "And it wasn't because he was fake or phony, because he wasn't in any way. I think he just really made so many people feel that connection. He would help people with advice, he would help people with money, he would help people with ideas. He was a filter, a curator, a person who would say, 'Oh, if you like this music you've gotta hear this.'"

Undoubtedly, the Drifters and its members often ended up in Stewart's orbit—one of the most notable connections being Peter's landmark 1990 album *Mavericks*, a duo album with his dB's bandmate Chris Stamey, which was released on the RNA (Rhino New Artists) label under Stewart's leadership.

Gary Stewart and other like-minded music fans and musicians ultimately made Raji's a home base of sorts, relishing in the rare and unusual thing that was happening there; something they couldn't find elsewhere in Los Angeles.

Among those regulars was photographer Greg Allen, who took early (including the very first) photos of the band and would go on to co-own the Omnivore Recordings label.

"That was the Tuesday thing; heading down to Raji's," Allen said. "I'd get there a couple hours early so I could get on the Rudy's FunHouse pinball machine and hog it for myself.

"To me, it sort of felt like there was no real scene in L.A. It's not like it was the power pop era or the new wave era or what have you. It was just a lot of whatever. The kind of void that the Drifters filled, especially with the shows happening every week—that was its own scene. But it didn't seem to expand more broadly into the zeitgeist of the moment or anything like that."

Another Tuesday regular, record label executive and industry veteran Cheryl Pawelski, was just as interested in hogging the FunHouse machine as Allen was. In fact, the two—who didn't know each other at all—unknowingly competed for time on the machine by stacking the machine with quarters.

"I would try to get there before this jerk would come and put a stack of quarters on it so I couldn't play," Pawelski recalled. Amazingly, more than a decade later, Allen and Pawelski met and worked together at the Rhino Handmade label, before going on to launch Omnivore together. They eventually discovered their pinball feud from the Drifter days.

"Years later I was like, 'That was you? You're an asshole!'" Pawelski laughed.

While there was buzz around what the Drifters were doing at Raji's, it tended to fly under the radar in mainstream press, save for an article in the *L.A. Weekly* written by journalist Karen Schoemer.

Schoemer was friends with Mark at the time, who he met through Robert Lloyd. Lloyd had been assigning Schoemer, then a freelance journalist who'd done a lot of work for the *New York Times*, stories for the publication and she was spending a lot of time in Los Angeles on assignment.

"I was kind of getting flown around a bit at that point," Schoemer said.

Her first introduction to the Drifters happened when she was sent to L.A. for a story.

"Somebody flew me to L.A. for something, and my recollection is that I had rented, on an expense account, a convertible," she said, adding that she stayed a few days past the completion of her assignment to hang out with Mark. "[We] came up with this idea to drive out to the desert, where Howe Gelb was living, near Pioneertown."

When she picked up Mark in her rented convertible for their trip to the desert, Schoemer said he started telling her about what he was doing with the Drifters. It was enough for her to want to visit the Batch Pad and see it for herself. What she witnessed there was like nothing she'd seen before.

"I, and other people of my generation as well, had kind of grown up a few or more years after the sixties," Schoemer said. "So we kind of missed the sixties, but the mainstream rock press was still totally stuck in [that decade]. *Rolling Stone* was putting Bob Dylan and Jerry Garcia on the cover until Jerry Garcia died. The mainstream press was so stuck in the sixties, and having kind of missed it I was sort of resentful of constantly being told how the best moment in rock history was something that had preceded me.

"But at the same time, there was this longing to have some of those experiences, but among ourselves. And I feel like the Drifters were tapping into that kind of seventies Fleetwood Mac vibe. Flying Burrito Brothers, Gram Parsons—that kind of really free-spirited Valley / L.A. vibe. And I think as soon as I met them that day, it felt like stepping into a little commune."

It certainly was unique at the Batch Pad, which spilled over to and expanded at Raji's. Peter remembers a singularly Batch Pad occurrence from a long night of music: "One night, we thought we should work up the Mamas & Papas' version of 'Dedicated to the One I Love' but nobody had a copy of it. So Susan gets on the phone and calls Jim Ladd, famous FM deejay in LA, and requests it.

"Ladd plays it but not without a little 'side-eye' introduction about how he'd never play this if it wasn't that an old friend had requested it. And so we listened and caught all the chords and worked it up."

There was a lot of this happening at the house, and Schoemer's visit made such an impression that she decided to profile the band in what became the *L.A. Weekly* piece.

"They were more than a band. They were a bunch of people living ideals that were familiar to me from what I'd heard about the sixties but had never experienced myself," she said. "They were living a life where the band and the life were this totally intermixed, blurred-line situation."

The songs hooked her, too, after she was given a cassette that included "The Mississippi," "Karen A," and "Green."

"I just loved them all," Schoemer recalled. "I loved Carlo's voice—all those guys had voices that were kind of soulful and had a lot of longing. Those songs, right away, I loved."

Like many others, Susan also made a huge impression on Schoemer during that initial hang at the Batch Pad.

"The minute I laid eyes on Susan, I was just in love with [her]," Schoemer said. "She was this incredibly charming and mischievous, and smart and hilarious person. I just thought that Susan could sing the alphabet and I could fall madly at her feet. I just loved her voice."

What Schoemer loved about the band was what most everyone who loved them was attracted to: their ability to create something cohesive out of so many different personalities and inclinations.

"When you're able to harness all of that and put it in service of a band, that is really kind of miraculous," she said. "So I do think they were harnessing a lot of unique styles and unique energy into a band. They were able to channel that into a band rather than themselves as individuals."

Many of the Raji's regulars, like Cheryl Pawelski, recall feeling a deep connection with the band because of how much they felt as if they were cut from the same musical cloth.

She explains: "We wanted to play music like that. Because we had crappy little bands, right? We were destined to become producers and record business people and not artists. I wanted to sound like the Continental Drifters. I wanted to have that level of talent where you could just show up and blast through anything and have a ball doing it.

"It was rock but it had all of the right folk and roots underpinnings that we really loved. In our bands we had rules like 'no guitar solos' because they were boring. Play that solo but do it on accordion or do it on mandolin. So they were a little bit in that vein that we were interested in."

Pawelski, for her part, says she taped several radio appearances that the band did throughout 1992 on KCRW, where they'd play songs like Gary's "Match Made in Heaven" and the Psycho Sisters' "Who We Are, Where We Live." To her, those performances felt like the album that they hadn't yet made; so much so that she listened to them constantly.

Three decades later, the Drifters and the people they surrounded themselves with tend to look back at what was happening in the Raji's bubble and realize that it was something extremely unique; not just what the band was doing musically, but the whole overarching experience of being there with them week after week.

"They weren't always really well attended, which doesn't make it any less important, for sure," Kevin Jarvis said. "But it's just interesting because when you look at those things 30 years later, you're going, 'God, it was such a beautiful, unique time.' You just don't have that perspective when you're in the middle of it."

Though the Drifter buzz didn't always expand beyond the confines of Raji's, what was happening inside the building became something of a club; a world in itself. It was a world that Vicki Peterson became quickly infatuated with, but her infatuation with the Drifters went far beyond just connecting with a band. For Vicki, the Raji's residency became a source of healing after the loss of her fiancé, Bobby Donati, the previous year.

Vicki and Bobby's relationship went back to late 1988, when Bobby was hired as a tech by Steve Botting, Vicki's now-brother-in-law who worked for The Bangles and had previously worked with Bobby touring with Air Supply. Botting, Vicki says, thought the world of him.

"He called him the 'International What-a-guy.' Everyone loves this guy! He's got a great personality, he's incredibly capable. A blisteringly brilliant guitar player and singer," Vicki said. "He came on literally just as a guitar tech. You know, a vastly overqualified guitar tech."

The two didn't start dating until the end of the recording of the third Bangles album, *Everything*, after Bobby had broken up with his girlfriend.

"And then all of the sudden it was like, 'Oh! Well, in that case…you're kind of cute!'" Vicki recalled.

Their relationship blossomed, and they were engaged by the following year.

Said Susan: "Vicki and I were inseparable, and now she wants to bring a boy into the scene. I was happy, because she really loved him a lot. And he was really a normal guy. He was not a rock star. He was just a fucking guitar player in L.A. who fell in love with her, and she fell in love with him."

In late June of 1990, Bobby started experiencing strange and serious symptoms.

"It took us about six weeks to get him diagnosed, because nothing was really presenting clearly," Vicki said. "He went to an infectious disease doctor; we thought maybe he had some kind of a blood infection, like strep in the blood. He was having bone pain, which was very disconcerting."

A trip to the emergency room prompted the doctor to refer them to a hematologist.

"I called the doctor, but she was on holiday for four weeks. And like idiots, we waited for her," Vicki recalled. Around July 4, 1990, they finally were able to meet with the hematologist and get Bobby examined.

"She had to do a spinal puncture on him because his blood was coming up kind of funny but they weren't really seeing anything definitive. And that's where she saw the white cells that were lymphoblast, and so she diagnosed him with Acute Lymphoblastic Leukemia. Which, in kids, you do chemo and you have a good eighty percent chance of beating. In adults, it's more like a 50/50 shot with treatment," she said. "We got the diagnosis that day, I'll never forget, and we literally—the next day or two days later—got on a plane for Philadelphia."

Philly was where Bobby's family was, and where Vicki spent the next year of her life. She lived between hotel rooms and a room at the University of Pennsylvania hospital, a teaching hospital where Bobby got treatment.

"They were brilliant. They were great," Vicki said of the hospital's staff. "They got him admitted immediately and started him on chemo and radiation to get him to a level of remission so that they could harvest his bone marrow."

A typical bone marrow transplant, Vicki says, wasn't possible because none of Bobby's four siblings were a match. Doctors ended up doing an experimental treatment that involved harvesting his bone marrow, treating it, and then re-infusing it. The treatment was one of the first of its kind.

"The bone marrow transplant itself was brutal because they basically bring you to the brink of death," she explained. "They kill your immune system completely, and then they re-infuse you with your own stem cells, basically, which magically find their way into the marrow and regenerate blood cells."

Bobby got out of the hospital by April of 1991, and following the procedure and chemotherapy treatment, he went into remission. Although extremely weak, Vicki says Bobby was "happy to be alive."

Being in Philadelphia allowed Vicki to become close with the Donatis, who she calls a "wonderful, wonderful Italian family." His father was a physician, but Vicki says that didn't make the situation any easier to bear.

"Having a sick child, I just can't imagine," she said.

Things took a turn in June of 1991, when Bobby suddenly started feeling unwell.

"There was one night where Bobby was feeling kind of weak and I said, 'I just need to take your temperature.' Because they said, 'If he spikes a fever, you've got to come back here right away.' So I took his temperature and it was 101.1, which is the lowest that they call a real fever. But it's a fever," Vicki recalled.

She took Bobby to the hospital, where he was readmitted.

"His disease had returned, but we didn't quite know that yet," she said.

Bobby was in the ICU just a few days later, where he spent ten days before his death in the summer of 1991.

"She was beyond devastated," Susan said of Vicki. "She was not prepared for that at all."

"He was such a force of nature, this guy," Vicki said of her late fiancé.

Navigating her grief after the unimaginable loss of Bobby was possible in large part, she says, because of the fact that she woke up every morning to take care of his dog.

"I had his dog, Buddy. I had a very large Samoyed ElkHound mix. This beautiful dog watched me every morning," Vicki said. "If you have a dog that gets you up in the morning, it's like having kids. It gets you out of bed. Thank god. Thank god I had it."

Bobby's passing, to paraphrase a lyric from Vicki, "blew a hole" in her life. But by that point she'd become extremely close with Susan, who was also in a dark place.

"We were kind of each other's safety nets, in a way," Vicki said. "She was a constant in my life. She was a very important landing place for me."

Susan herself had developed a "sibling-like" relationship with Bobby after he and Vicki started dating.

"He teased her to death, and adored her, but just gave her shit all the time," Vicki recalled.

"He was a pain in the neck, but he was cute as a bug's ear," Susan added. "He loved Vicki to pieces. But he definitely saw the target on my forehead as a sibling."

That relationship ultimately led to Susan recruiting Bobby for a band she was putting together.

"It's another one of those funny Venn diagram intersections in my life: he played bass in a band backing up Susan," Vicki said. "She'd first left Dwight [Twilley] and was trying to resuscitate something in the way of a performing career. She put together a band and she needed a bass player, and Bobby said, 'I'll play bass.'

"And the drummer was John Cowsill!"

Something to note: not only was Vicki a massive Cowsills fan as a kid, but John Cowsill, specifically, was her childhood celebrity crush. As you can imagine, the *Twilight Zone*-esque circumstance of these two specific people being Susan's rhythm section was not lost on Vicki.

"'This is hilarious! My boyfriend and the love of my childhood,'" she remembers thinking. "It was very funny. And those two just got along like brothers."

Bobby's passing brought Vicki closer to music than she had been in some time, and when she and Susan began writing and playing music together, she brought a song about Bobby to the table. That song, "Who We Are, Where We Live," would become not only a Continental Drifters staple, but one of two songs that would cement her and Susan's place in the band.

"That was the anthem of people who've lost very close loved ones," Vicki said. "It felt like a club. Susan and I were in that club; she'd lost family members and her first love to cancer, when she was very young. It's not a club you want to be in, but it's kind of nice to know that there are others who share your experience."

Grief, Vicki says, was something that presented itself much differently than she envisioned, but it's what ultimately led her to the healing place that Raji's became, just months later.

"I was, I think very fortunate, because I was being very Capricorn about how I was dealing with my grief," she explained. "I was like, 'Okay, I'm going to grieve very efficiently. I'm going to feel bad for six months and then I'm going to feel great.' And it's like, 'Yeah, no. It doesn't work like that.'

"But within a very short period of time, I was hanging around the Batch pad and singing Fairport Convention songs and Emmylou songs with Gary Eaton. And that's why I felt like the Drifters saved my life, in a lot of ways. They put the love of music back, because I'd been grieving *that* loss before I even lost Bobby. It felt completely restorative."

In the earliest days of the Drifters, Vicki was grieving, and the band lifted her up and helped her through.

"She needed the power of music, I think," Peter said. "And she found that in what she heard at Raji's, and she found the camaraderie."

Peter was so moved by Vicki and what she'd been through that he, who himself had never met Bobby but learned his story mostly through Susan, wrote a song called "Invisible Boyfriend."

"The entire creation of that song was a product of the shows at Raji's, and the attendance thereof by Vicki Peterson, in her mourning phase," he said. "She was our wonderful, happy, cheerful Vicki. But there was a definite palpable vibe about it."

> *There in the back of the dimly lit room*
> *Stands a woman alone, or so you'd assume*
> *But there to her right, all through the night*
> *Stands her invisible boyfriend*

"I just remember thinking that it was the most loving, beautiful gesture," Vicki said of the song. "And, also, obviously somehow he intuited my reality—it was very empathic. It was like, he really did get what I was doing those nights at Raji's. I think he had a moment where he actually did think he saw him one night."

By the middle of 1992, the Raji's residency was in full force. Those who found solace in what was happening at Raji's found that in each other, and Tuesday nights in Los Angeles became a place of refuge from the pain of loss, whether that was the loss of a loved one or the loss of a relationship. For others in the Drifters, it was simply a refreshing and often thrilling musical exercise.

"It worked like a machine," Danny said. "It kind of functioned like a reggae band or something like that, where there's all these interlocking pieces. I always liked that."

As the months progressed, Peter became more of a fixture at Raji's and his infatuation with the band grew stronger. The same can be said for Susan and Vicki, who would show up frequently, doing background vocals as well as guest sets as the Psycho Sisters. It was during a Psycho Sisters guest appearance that the Drifters first played "Who We Are" and "The Rain Song," which would both become key songs in the band's catalog.

While initial attempts to get Peter to join the band had failed because of Peter's disinterest in joining a band, at some point the allure of the Drifters was so much that he wanted in.

"One night, I got home from the gig and it was late at night," Carlo recalled. "It was, like, two in the morning. I'm smoking a joint, snorting a line of cocaine or something. The phone rings and it's Peter. He goes, 'I wanna be a Continental Drifter.' I went, 'Well, that's a problem. We've got a keyboard player.'"

Throughout his time in the Drifters, Danny McGough was, by his estimation, playing with four other bands, which was not unusual for an in-demand keyboard player around Los Angeles. He acknowledges, though, that the Continental Drifters was a unique experience.

"I did love all those guys, and loved playing with them. I knew that they were special, and high quality. The real deal," Danny said. "Everybody was pretty knowledgeable about all sorts of music. All the different genres and stuff like that. And I think everyone loved sitting in with us because Carlo was so… the way he plays is so unique and comfortable. He makes you play [well]. He's way behind the beat. It's like sitting in a giant catcher's mitt."

It was ultimately decided that the band didn't need two keyboard players, despite it being something they had done before. The decision was made that Danny would be asked to leave, which he says he ultimately had no hard feelings about given the amount of work he was doing.

"I was just busy doing stuff," he said. "I was probably in five bands at any given time."

Gary recalls hearing about the decision to replace Danny from Carlo directly, although in a rather curious way.

"All of the sudden Carlo comes up to me [and says], 'Hey man, Ray really wants to replace Danny with Peter.' And I'm like, 'Really? Why?' It was just like, 'What the fuck are you talking about?'" Next thing I know, Peter's in the band and Danny's out," he said. "Maybe a year later or so, I was talking to Ray, and Ray told me that Carlo told him that *I wanted* to replace Danny with Peter Holsapple."

Regardless of how sketchily the situation was handled with the remaining members, Danny McGough left the Drifters just a few months after the start of the Raji's residency, and Peter cemented his place as the band's keyboard player.

It was something that he hadn't come in looking for or wanting, instead hoping to produce them. And when he became a member, Peter was initially adamant about not writing any songs or playing guitar; he simply wanted to be behind some keyboards. That didn't last very long.

"The longer I was around the Continental Drifters, the more I wanted to be a part of it. I was pretty much ready to run off and join the circus," Peter said.

The circus, by April of 1992, was off and running like a high speed train. Often exhilarating, sometimes jarring, and always loud as fuck.

Part II

"I just had never been around anybody like her, and it was like a blast of oxygen."

That's how Peter describes his earliest days with Susan, who he'd met through her brother Barry and was now spending time with at Raji's, as his marriage was falling apart at home. Singing with Susan and playing with the Drifters was as much an escape as it was a gig.

"I felt that I was having issues of depression myself, again. I'd suffered from that before at various times in my life that were variously dealt with or not dealt with," he said. "I just wanted to sing with her."

In some ways, Peter saw Susan as his great singing partner; the kind of combination of voices that stand the test of time, like Gram Parsons and Emmylou Harris.

"I found that in Susan. She was Emmylou, she was Linda [Thompson]. She was Linda

McCartney: Great loves of music, great loves of sound. Singers that sang together and sounded like they were loving every minute of it," Peter said.

Sealing the deal on his duo dreams, Gary Stewart approached Peter in mid-1992 to contribute to the aforementioned Gram Parsons tribute album, titled *Conmemorativo: A Tribute to Gram Parsons*, at the same time that he was working on an album for New Zealand cult band The Chills.

That album, *Soft Bomb*, was produced by Gavin MacKillop, who at the time was known for his success producing Toad the Wet Sprocket.

Peter was able to secure time at Master Control Studios in Burbank, where The Chills were recording, found a day off in the Chills' tracking schedule, and assembled a group of musicians to play on the song.

He chose "A Song for You," one of the definitive songs in the Parsons catalog, and arguably one of Parsons and Harris' most beautiful and enduring duets.

The recording featured some of the Continental Drifters—Mark on bass, Carlo on drums, and Gary on lead guitar—plus the Psycho Sisters, Vicki and Susan. They also asked The Chills' Martin Phillipps to play acoustic guitar, and enlisted MacKillop to engineer.

It was, in Peter's words, "an afternoon of hijinx, and cocaine, and a lot of beer."

"We got a bunch of people in here, we're all drunk, we're all high. Smoking pot, sneaking around, making a Gram Parsons record," he said.

This makeshift band was billed for the tribute as Peter Holsapple & Susan Cowsill with the Walkin' Tacos, a play on Parsons' seminal post-Byrds band The Flying Burrito Brothers. And as an homage to Parsons, Peter had the idea to overdub the band (and everyone in the studio at the time) applauding as if it was a live recording with an audience present.

It was something Parsons had done on "Medley Live from Northern Quebec," a recording that included canned applause, which ended up on his posthumously-released *Grievous Angel* album from 1974.

Capturing the "hinjix" of that afternoon in Burbank wasn't hard for Peter and his Walkin' Tacos, who set up some microphones at the end of the session and listened back to what they'd just recorded.

"We were all drunk and stupid by that point, and we just put some mics in the room and pretended like we were watching the show," Mark recalled. "If you listen closely you can hear somebody yelling, 'Whipping Post!' or something."

That session not only yielded a memorable contribution for the *Conmeorativo* compilation, but it also cemented "A Song for You" as a staple in the Drifters' cover song catalog. The band started playing it at Raji's after those sessions, and it was, in large part, the launching pad for Peter and Susan's harmonious future.

Back at Raji's, the residency continued in full blast. Some three decades later, much of it is a blur for the Drifters themselves, but the guest sets remain highlights.

"A lot of them were memorable," Carlo said. "That, I think, was the good thing about having guests. Because that kind of marked that night as being 'that night.'"

One particularly raucous night featured a dizzying slew of guests and cameos; Victoria Williams, Annette Zilinskas, Robert Maché, Rosie Flores, Dave Catching, and Michael Steele all crammed on the stage at different times (or all at once) throughout the night.

With Kevin Jarvis subbing for Carlo on drums, the band blazed through a version of "Dallas" flanked by Zilinskas, Susan, Vicki, Robert, and Williams. They also brought up Flores for "Wild

Thing," tapped Steele for bass on Crazy Horse's "Look At All the Things," and offered up a harmony-rich rendition of The Fifth Dimension's "Stoned Soul Picnic."

It was a remarkably covers-heavy night, which also included a rarity: Susan and Vicki swapping lead vocals on the 1970 Five Stairsteps hit "O-o-h Child."

Williams was a constant on this night in particular, joining the band on covers and Drifters songs as a backup singer. The Drifters also backed her up on several of her own songs including "Crazy Mary," perhaps her most well-known composition.

"Victoria was just, like, so self-effacing," Robert said. "And we'd nail that shit. And then we'd finish and she'd just kind of look around and go, 'Well, that wasn't very good, now was it?'"

On and off stage, the Continental Drifters, with their Psycho Sisters compatriots, were forming something of an exclusive club all to themselves. Or, perhaps, it was more like a gang.

Even Dave Catching remarked to Gary on one occasion that the Drifters seemed to be getting especially "clique-ish."

"Man, I don't want to do *that*," Gary remembers thinking. "I felt bad, because I felt like I was deserting him."

The clique-ish atmosphere cultivating within the Drifters camp unquestionably nurtured two relationships in the early version of the band: Peter and Susan, and Gary and Vicki.

That foursome, along with John Convertino on drums, contributed recordings of two Raji's cover staples—the Brian Wilson/Mike Love-penned "Farmer's Daughter," and a version of "Stoned Soul Picnic"—to a single released by White Flag founder Bill Bartell on his Gasatanka Records label. That was released under the moniker Double Date, and recorded in a session engineered by Vicki's brother, Dave Peterson.

The relationship between Vicki and Gary was born of the earliest days at the Batch Pad, where this rag-tag group of music business refugees gathered to pick up the pieces of their lives and find some meaning in it all.

"I guess, on one level, it was looking for healing. It was my version of a one-night stand, but of course it lasted eighteen months," Vicki said of that relationship. "He was just a sweet man with a beautiful voice, and that's where it started."

As a romantic relationship formed between Gary and Vicki, and another between Susan and Peter was bubbling just beneath the surface, the band was looking for opportunities to make a record.

Their first chance at record label financing came at the hands of Jimmy Ford and Frank Quintini, two New Orleans characters who started a local label called Monkey Hill Records. Jimmy Ford was the connector between Monkey Hill and the Continental Drifters, as his relationship with Peter dated back to the early 1980s when he tour-managed The dB's, and then became their manager while the band was working with Bearsville Records.

Bearsville was a label and recording studio based in Woodstock, New York, and was founded by legendary artist manager Albert Grossman, who was most notable for managing the likes of Janis Joplin, Bob Dylan, and The Band.

"He really was a tyrant," Ford recalled of Grossman.

The dB's signed with Bearsville for what became their 1983 album *Like This*, and were facing pushback from Todd Rundgren, who was in and out of the picture, doing A&R for Bearsville. Peter recalls Rundgren disapproving of the initial mixes, saying that the songs "sounded like shit."

While Ford was smoothing things over for The dB's, he started managing bands via Bob Singerman's Singermanagement company, where The dB's had been at the time.

"I ended up with The dB's and Richard Hell and The Gun Club and all these bands," Ford said. "I did management for a while, which was not my favorite thing to do. There's more gratification being a dogcatcher."

Ford ultimately got The dB's off of Bearsville (after at least a year of negotiating) and ultimately on I.R.S. Records, the label that had been home to R.E.M. prior to that band signing with Warner Brothers in the late eighties. They remained there through the rest of their tenure.

Before The dB's dissolved in 1988, Ford brought the band to New Orleans to record some demos at a friend's house and recording studio that he had access to.

"My buddy wasn't living there anymore, and that house was there with the studio in it," Ford said. "And he just gave me the keys and said, 'Hey, man, make some music,' basically."

Plans to put an album together were abandoned, however, and The dB's disbanded. Those demos later came out on Monkey Hill as an album called *Paris Avenue*, named after the street on which the house was located.

"The dB's, in a better world, would have had ten percent of the success that R.E.M. had, and they'd be millionaires right now," Ford said. "They were phenomenal, but it just wasn't meant to be."

Peter's relationship with Jimmy Ford continued past the dissolution of The dB's, through his touring and recording work for R.E.M., and into his start with the Drifters. Ford also had a history and friendship with Carlo from their days in New Orleans.

Because of these relationships, Ford was intimately aware of the Drifters and what they were doing out in Los Angeles, and quickly became interested in helping them shop demos to labels. When nothing came of those efforts, he started entertaining the idea of starting a rock label. Frank Quintini, one-time manager of Li'l Queenie and the Percolators and later the subdudes, was brought on board and the two launched Monkey Hill Records, named after a cement mound in the Audubon Zoo which is the highest point in New Orleans.

It was decided that Quintini would manage the band, and Ford would work more on the label side. And with investors soon on board, Monkey Hill was off and running.

Now that management was in place and Monkey Hill was ready to front enough money to make an album with the Holsapple, Walton, Nuccio, Ganucheau, and Eaton lineup, the band decided to rent an RV and make the trek from Los Angeles to New Orleans to make it official.

Bringing Vicki, Susan, and their pal Dave Catching along, the Drifters booked two weekends of gigs during Jazz Fest in April of 1992 and headed off on I-10 for Louisiana. Bringing the Psycho Sisters was a no-brainer, and it wasn't just because of ongoing or percolating romantic relationships.

"We did feel at that point that we had a deep bond, and we felt like we should have them belong with us. They just belonged," Mark said. "Even though we didn't ask them to be in the band and they didn't ask to be in the band. They just wanted to come out and play with us, and hang out with us."

Because there were so many strong personalities in the band, the Drifters developed protocols for keeping people in check and maintaining order, so to speak. In the studio, it was a Pirates baseball cap with a "P" logo that was dubbed the "producer hat." Anyone wearing the hat would effectively become the producer in that particular moment.

In the RV, it was the person in the driver's seat who took charge. They dubbed the RV "The Vatican" and created a system of governance, in a sense, by which the non-drivers would abide.

"It was its own city-state, and it contained rules and regulations. And whoever was the driver was the Pope," Vicki said. "Carlo, when he was the Pope, he was denying us stops; truck stops, pee stops. Because he wanted to freaking get to New Orleans before the bars closed."

Dave Catching recalls the drive to New Orleans being largely musical.

"The whole way there, we just sang songs and played songs. There was nothing that Peter didn't know how to play," he said.

They arrived in New Orleans at the Monkey Hill offices in the early morning hours, greeted by Ford, Quintini, and their girlfriends.

"I knocked on the door at Monkey Hill, and Jimmy Ford opened the door. And I remember seeing all of these empty tequila bottles, and I said, 'Oh, margaritas?'" Catching recalled.

Indeed they were. Ford presented them with the margaritas, which Vicki says were "his own special recipe"—mushroom margaritas.

"Do you know the movie *Trouble With Angels*? All of us Catholic school girls loved it," Susan said. "So we're coming into town, and now this little dude is offering. And Vicki was like, 'Yeah, no, but do you have one of those *without* mushrooms? Because I would love one of those.' It was like Fantasy Island a little bit."

While being in New Orleans certainly didn't faze Carlo or Ray, for the Psycho Sisters from California it was much more foreign. Jimmy and Frank's girlfriends at the time, Daisy and Shelley, made a particular impression on them.

"They were New Orleans girls. And I think Vicki and I found them to be unbelievably intriguing," Susan recalled. "One of the girls had a N'awlins accent and she talked like this: 'Cahlo and I went tah grade school tugethah.' That kind of thing.

"And we're just like, 'Oh my god, what movie are we in?!' We're staring at each other just talking with our faces going, 'What. The. Fuck.' Because it was so far from Los Angeles, California, and anything either one of us knew, collectively or individually."

The two-week stay in New Orleans consisted of a few gigs at the Howlin' Wolf, and one backing up their friend Pat McLaughlin at the Warehouse Cafe.

"Everywhere we went to eat was fucking amazing, the gigs were fun, we actually made money," Gary recalled.

Carlo told the story of the NOLA trip on an episode of the *Troubled Men Podcast*, hosted by New Orleanians Rene Coman and Manny Chevrolet—emphasizing, as Gary did, the fact that they made good money playing in New Orleans, as opposed to what they were used to at Raji's in Los Angeles.

"We were all just dumbfounded, like, 'What are we doing in L.A.?'" he said.

Everybody was enamored with New Orleans—even Dave Catching, who Carlo brought to the Saturn Bar while they were in town and it was love at first round.

As Catching recalled: "The first place that Carlo took us after going to Monkey Hill—he took us to the Saturn Bar, which became my favorite bar on Earth. Since I was the tagalong I was like, 'I'm buying the first round. Everybody order up!' I remember ordering a drink for everybody, and the bartender kind of looked around and he was like, '$18.50.'

"And it was for, like, eight drinks or something. I was like, 'Oh my god! What the fuck?' So I bought another round for everybody but a couple of people didn't want a second drink. And he kind of looked and he was like, '$18.50.' And then the third round, maybe some other people were in there and it was $18.50. Every time."

The trip proved successful for the Drifters, and Ford describes it as a "big love fest." Individually, though, members of the band were struggling; some more outwardly than others. For Peter, the deterioration of his marriage back in L.A., coupled with the intensifying magnetism of the Drifters, was starting to bring him to a breaking point.

"I was torn in a lot of places; I remember going to the liquor store and buying a bottle of tequila and dropping it on the ground," Peter said. "And weeping profusely, and then going back to the liquor store and getting another bottle of tequila to replace it.

"A lot of wandering off; a lot of thousand-yard stares from me, because I felt like I wasn't really inhabiting myself at that point. I was trying to chemically induce some kind of spiritual levitation to get me away from the mess that I had made of my life."

Gary was also in a difficult position, navigating single fatherhood while also trying to pursue his work with the Drifters.

"I was split," Gary said. "Because I felt really bad, but it was like, I can't waste this time and just be in the doldrums this whole time. I have to enjoy this, because this is a blessing. It's amazing that I get to be here with this amazing band and we're going to fucking play in these places.

"So I was kind of split. I was totally schizophrenic at that time, between being really happy and feeling like a failure as a father."

Needless to say, some Drifters were ready to get home to Los Angeles. Following their back-to-back Jazz Fest weekends, they packed up the RV and did just that. With Peter opting to fly home, the remaining crew piled into "The Vatican" and decided to make two stops—Holt Cemetery, a potter's field cemetery on City Park Avenue, and Gram Parsons' grave at Garden of Memories Cemetery on Airline Drive.

It was at Holt Cemetery where Dave Catching made what some Drifters believe was an ill-fated mistake.

"I had my camera and I'm like, 'I'm going to go across the street and take some pictures of the graveyard.' And Carlo's like, 'Cool. Don't take anything, though,'" Catching said.

"We pulled up the RV at the graveyard, and Dave Catching walked up to me with some chunks that came off of some of the concrete headstones," Carlo recalled on the *Troubled Men Podcast*. "He's like, 'Look!' And I'm like, 'Dave, go put that stuff right back where you found it.'"

Catching did return the chunks of headstone to the graveyard, though not all of them.

"I went over and I was taking photos, and there was a broken headstone. And one of the pieces had a 'D.' And I was like, 'Oh, D for David. I'm gonna grab that.' And I put it in my pocket and didn't think anything about it until we're driving across the country," he said.

After taking a photo with a gravedigger working at the cemetery, the group was on their way to Garden of Memories to visit Parsons' grave. Mark, in particular, was interested in Parsons' burial spot because he wanted to lift a copy of the plaque on his grave with wax paper. He did, while the band sat around the grave with guitars singing Parsons songs.

"It was just a round little disc on the ground. Embedded in the ground. And we just sat around and drank, and poured whiskey on his grave. We sang his songs. That was fun," Mark said. At the time, the disc displayed the phrase "God's Own Singer," a reference of Bernie Leadon's tribute song to Parsons. It was later replaced by a more traditional marker.

Following their cemetery detour, the band officially hit the road back to Los Angeles. Carlo, by this point, had become concerned about the RV being able to make it back to California without breaking down. When he took a break from driving to catch some sleep, he instructed the band not to fill the RV with Shell gas in particular.

"At that time, Shell was having a real issue with their gas. There was some kind of muck in it. My car, back in L.A., I had to, twice, change fuel filters," he recalled.

Adds Mark: "From day one of the trip, Carlo's like, 'Yeah, we've got to put good gas in here.' He kept saying it before we even left, basically."

Sure enough, not long after the band passed through Katy, Texas, Carlo was awakened by Gary and Mark telling him that the RV was stalled and something was wrong.

"Who the fuck put Shell gas in the RV?" he immediately asked the group, before deciding to check the fuel filter first since that was an issue with which he had some experience. His bandmates weren't nearly as sure as he was that the fuel filter was indeed the problem.

"We'd be like, 'Well, come on! It can't just be the fuel filter.' But of course as soon as he did that, it started up right away. So it was indeed the fuel filter," Mark said. "None of us were trying to piss Carlo off. More power to him that he was right."

Carlo found the fuel filter, and decided to take it out to clean it before putting it back in.

"I put a wrench on the front of the fuel filter, and a wrench on the back, and I turn one time and this hideous noise happens. And gas just sprays everywhere. Covers me head to toe," he said. It was then that he resorted to more drastic measures.

"I take the fuel filter out, I put it in my mouth, and I'm blowing through it. Because at this point, who cares, you know?" he recalled.

Though not especially sanitary, the method worked and the RV started up again. Carlo decided to go back to sleep, but told his bandmates to stop at the next gas station and buy a new filter. The next thing he knew, he was rattled from his sleep by Susan and Gary standing over him, while the RV sat idle on the side of the road.

The band did, in fact, stop at a mechanic just prior to the second breakdown as per Carlo's instructions, only to be told that it wasn't actually the fuel filter. Furious, Carlo once again took out the fuel filter, cleaned it, put it back in, and started the RV again.

"I said, 'Now, motherfuckers. Stop at the first Pep Boys. Get that fuel filter,'" he recalled.

Carlo went back to sleep for a spell before being roused again, this time by Dave Catching. At this point, they'd made it to Blythe, California, and were stopped at a closed gas station with only one light on outside.

"It was very ill lit. It was like a horror film," Vicki recalled.

This time, they had a new problem: cockroaches.

"These are not your cute little California cockroaches," Vicki said. The roaches, which Carlo described as "thick-ass cockroaches," were all over the place because they were attracted to the single source of light at the station. With virtually no other choice, Carlo decided to brave the circumstances and try to fix the fuel filter anyway.

While the rest of the band stayed behind in the RV, Carlo—with Catching volunteering as bug destroyer—laid down under the RV to retrieve the fuel filter and within seconds was completely covered in bugs.

Carlo, who said he was "screaming like a little girl" the entire time, worked as fast as possible to undo the fuel filter and clean it to get back on the road. All the while, Dave Catching stood over him and swatted at cockroaches.

Finally, the fuel filter was fixed and a traumatized Carlo got back in the RV. His horrified bandmates said nothing, and the next hour of the trip was completely silent.

The RV made it the remaining 223 miles to Los Angeles, where it was returned by an angry Carlo who demanded a refund from the rental company. All told, the entire two-week rental only cost the band around two hundred bucks.

That would be a happy-enough ending to the story, had the band not returned to L.A. on April 29, 1992—the day of the verdict in the police brutality case of Rodney King, and the subsequent riots that consumed the city for days. No one could avoid the intensity and destruction that had overtaken Los Angeles.

"It was very scary because there was actual riot damage near where I had been living with Ilene. So it got very close to where she lived," Peter recalled.

After returning home to his city on fire following the cockroach-infested horror movie of trip home, Carlo met up with Dave Catching to smoke a joint.

"He looks at me and says, 'Carlo, man.' I said, 'What?'" Carlo recalled. "He stands up, sticks his hand in his pocket, and he pulls out all those stones from the graveyard. I said, 'You motherfucker! You caused all of this!'"

Catching did ultimately return the bits of headstone on his next trip out to New Orleans.

"I flew back, I went straight to that cemetery, and put that thing back," he said. "Everything on the way there was perfect, and everything on the way back was a pain in the ass. So who knows? Maybe I did break some voodoo laws and put everybody in harm's way."

Whether the band actually was cursed by headstones or not is debatable. But the chaos in L.A., while unnerving, didn't shake the Drifters too much. With the exception of Carlo, that is.

'I said, 'Man, fuck this,'" he said. "'Look, guys. I've decided that with all that just happened in L.A., and the hustle and bustle, I'm pretty sure I know what I want to do. And what I'm going to do is move back to New Orleans, but I'll still fly here. I'll fly here once a week for gigs, if I have to.'"

Carlo's mind was made up; he was going to find his way back to New Orleans and leave L.A. behind.

"That was his turning point," Vicki said. "He was just like, 'This is not okay. The city's on fire. There's just hate everywhere.' And I totally get that.

"[It] wasn't enough for me to feel like 'I need to leave this town.' Because I wasn't ready to do that. You have to remember, I was still kind of a grieving widow. So everything in my life was kind of overshadowed by losing my fiancé. So I didn't know what I was doing, or where I was supposed to be."

It would take Carlo roughly another year to follow through on his decision, but the Jazz Fest trip was the catalyst for a lot of change to come. Energized by the experience, the band returned from New Orleans ready to capitalize on the momentum of the trip, get into a studio, and make a Continental Drifters record.

Continental Drifters Mach 2 (L-R: Peter, Ray, Gary, Carlo, Mark) on their home stage at the Los Angeles dive bar Raji's in 1992. From the collection of Peter Holsapple

Continental Drifters and friends, Raji's, 1992 (L-R: Paul Cowsill, Gary, Lyn Bertles, John Convertino, Vicki, Joey Burns, Victoria Williams, Susan, Peter, Rob Stennett, Michael Steele, Mark, Robert Maché, Dave Catching). From the collection of Peter Holsapple

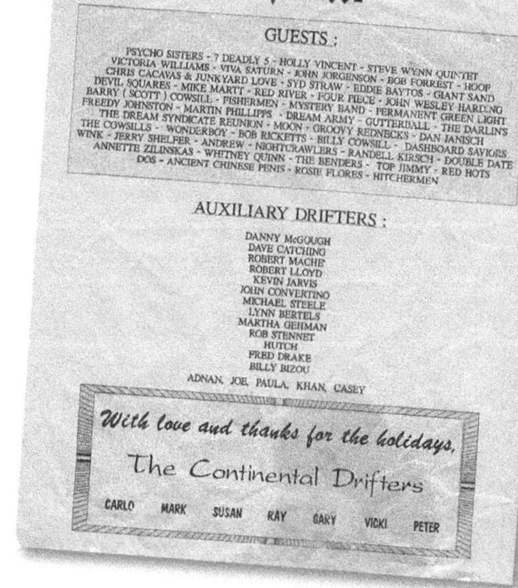

Continental Drifters
TUESDAY NIGHTS
Raji's 1992

GUESTS :

PSYCHO SISTERS - 7 DEADLY 5 - HOLLY VINCENT - STEVE WYNN QUINTET
VICTORIA WILLIAMS - VIVA SATURN - JOHN JORGENSON - BOB FORREST - HOOF
CHRIS CACAVAS & JUNKYARD LOVE - SYD STRAW - EDDIE BAYTOS - GIANT SAND
DEVIL SQUARES - MIKE MARTT - RED RIVER - FOUR PIECE - JOHN WESLEY HARDING
BARRY (SCOTT) COWSILL - FISHERMEN - MYSTERY BAND - PERMANENT GREEN LIGHT
FREEDY JOHNSTON - MARTIN PHILLIPPS - DREAM ARMY - GUTTERBALL - THE DARLIN'S
THE DREAM SYNDICATE REUNION - MOON - GROOVY REDNECKS - DAN JANISCH
THE COWSILLS - WONDERBOY - BOB RICKETTS - BILLY COWSILL - DASHBOARD SAVIORS
WINK - JERRY SHELFER - ANDREW - NIGHTCRAWLERS - RANDELL KIRSCH - DOUBLE DATE
ANNETTE ZILINSKAS - WHITNEY QUINN - THE BENDERS - TOP JIMMY - RED HOTS
DOS - ANCIENT CHINESE PENIS - ROSIE FLORES - HITCHERMEN

AUXILIARY DRIFTERS :

DANNY McGOUGH
DAVE CATCHING
ROBERT MACHE'
ROBERT LLOYD
KEVIN JARVIS
JOHN CONVERTINO
MICHAEL STEELE
LYNN BERTELS
MARTHA GEHMAN
ROB STENNET
HUTCH
FRED DRAKE
BILLY BIZOU

ADNAN, JOE, PAULA, KHAN, CASEY

With love and thanks for the holidays,
The Continental Drifters

CARLO   MARK   SUSAN   RAY   GARY   VICKI   PETER

Holiday flyer for the Continental Drifters' Tuesday night residency at Raji's, 1992. From the collection of Peter Holsapple

Sean Kelly

Group shot taken during the 1992 Walking Tacos session that yielded a version of Gram Parsons' "A Song for You" (L-R: Martin Phillipps, Vicki, Mark, Peter, Susan, Carlo, Gary). From the collection of Vicki Peterson

David Catching films while Mark makes repairs to the Drifters' rented RV and Peter gets out of the way during the bands' April 1992 trip to New Orleans. Photo by Vicki Peterson

(right) Auxiliary Drifter David Catching dons the "Pope Hat" and takes the wheel during the April 1992 RV trek to New Orleans. Photo by Vicki Peterson

(above) Drifters, friends, and Psycho Sisters (minus Peter) at Holt Cemetery, New Orleans, 1992 (L-R: Mark, David Catching, Gary, Susan, Carlo, Vicki) From the collection of Vicki Peterson

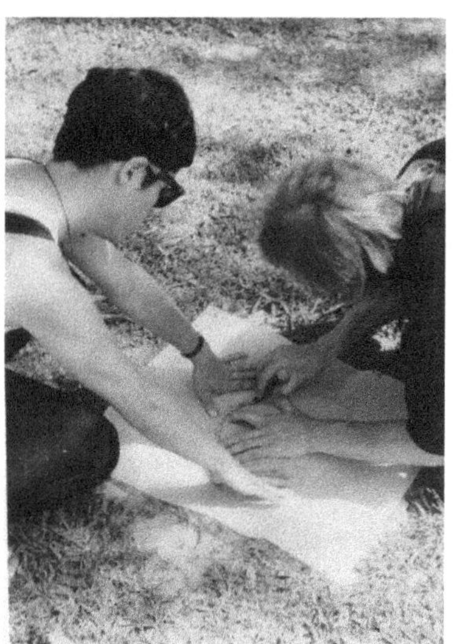

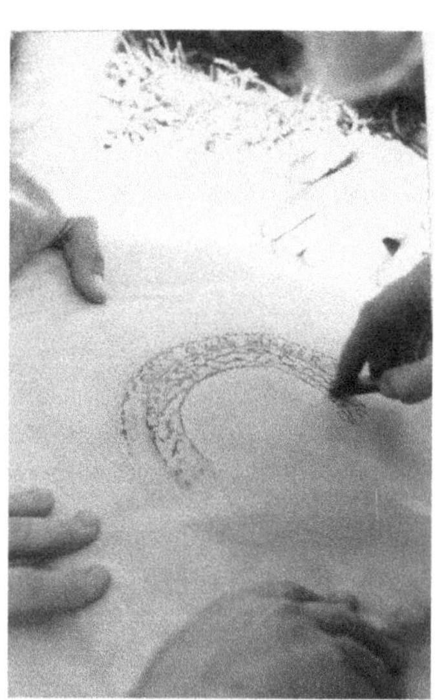

Mark makes an etching from the "God's Own Singer" engraving on Gram Parsons' grave with assistance from Vicki, Susan, and David Catching, New Orleans 1992. From the collection of Vicki Peterson.

Gary with the RV that carried the Drifters to New Orleans in April of 1992. Photo by Vicki Peterson

Sean Kelly

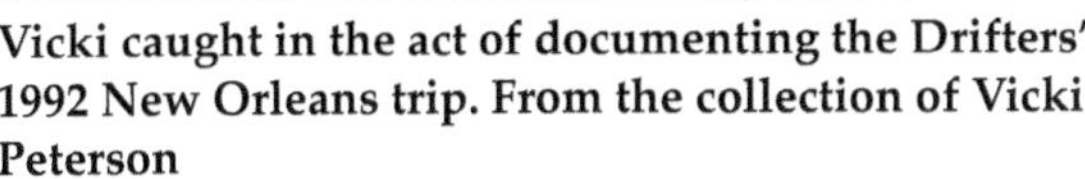

Vicki caught in the act of documenting the Drifters'
1992 New Orleans trip. From the collection of Vicki
Peterson

(right) Carlo's legs sticking out from under the
rented RV was a common sight during the April
1992 NOLA trek. Photo by Vicki Peterson

Vicki Peterson prepares to add an acoustic guitar track during sessions for the proposed first Continental Drifters album at Milagro Studios in 1992. Photo by Greg Allen

Original Drifters guitarist Gary Eaton during an early session at Milagro Studios in Glendale, California, 1992. Photo by Greg Allen

Peter Holsapple lays down a Hammond organ take at Milagro Studios, 1992. Photo by Greg Allen

Mark gets in tune for recording at Milagro Studios, 1992. Photo by Greg Allen

(right) Ray Ganucheau records guitars for a proposed first Continental Drifters album at Milagro Studios in 1992. Photo by Greg Allen

Sean Kelly

Continental Drifters Mach 2 with the Psycho Sisters, 1992 (L-R: Peter, Susan, Mark, Ray, Carlo, Gary, Vicki). Photo by Greg Allen

Carlo Nuccio between takes at Milagro Studios, 1992. Photo by Greg Allen

Susan Cowsill during a Drifters session at Milagro Studios in Glendale, California, in 1992. Photo by Greg Allen

Chapter Three:
Nineteen Ninety-Three

"It felt like I could do this for the rest of my life."

— Mark Walton

Returning to Los Angeles from a monumental trip to New Orleans, the Continental Drifters jumped back into their Raji's residency in May of 1992, invigorated by the allure of Carlo and Ray's home city and ready to deliver a proper Drifters record for Monkey Hill.

Those sessions would be a ways away, however, as opportunity knocked early that month when the band was given the chance to open for Bob Dylan at one of his ten residency shows at the Pantages Theater. The Pantages, a storied L.A. theater that was notably the venue for Talking Heads' landmark 1984 concert film *Stop Making Sense*, was just a short walk from the band's usual haunt, and adjacent to The Frolic Room.

Peter's friend Bill Thomson, guitar tech for Dylan who also worked with him on the *Green* tour with R.E.M. (as Bill Berry's drum tech), helped facilitate two nights for Peter; a solo spot on May 12, the first night of the residency, and a Drifters set the second night. Those nights were followed by a slew of artists for the remaining eight shows that included Counting Crows, Marc Cohn, and the Fabulous Thunderbirds.

Not content on doing the show simply as a five-piece, the band invited the Psycho Sisters to sit in and also welcomed Robert Lloyd and Robert Maché to round out a nine-piece Drifters extravaganza.

It was a much different gig than the Drifters were used to, particularly because of union rules that prevented band members from touching gear, moving monitors, and generally being able to adjust things as needed.

"I don't even remember much about playing the show except that it sounded like crap on stage because we couldn't really touch anything," Gary said. "So we were just left guessing, and it was like, 'Well, what did The Beatles do? What did everybody else do back in olden times?' Just fucking suck it up and play."

Play they did, offering up a spirited, albeit truncated set of songs with auxiliary Drifters in tow.

"To me, it was a blur. The place was beautiful. I just remember walking out on stage just in awe of the whole situation," Ray recalled. "And then we got a really good response. Which was surprising, because you know how openers go."

The band did, indeed, get a great response from the audience, and word even got around that the elusive Dylan was watching from the side of the stage. It was a memorable night for all, with the possible exception of the headliner.

"I remember when I was walking back towards the stage, I could see Bob Dylan had a big dressing room right off the stage," Gary said. "He had a big dressing room, and [in] it was a coffee table with a big bottle of Jack [Daniels] on it. We walk by and it's full, right? We're downstairs and stuff, and come back up and it's a little less full.

"We play our set, and I come back up. I wanted to see the set from the side of the stage so I'm standing by the monitor guy, and I look in the dressing room and that fucking bottle is three quarters gone. You could see it through the fucking door!

"And they start playing. Bob walks out, he's got his acoustic, plugs in and starts playing, and he's not fucking playing [the right] song. They solo him up at the desk there, and he's not even close to playing that song!"

That night at the Pantages, while a far cry from their regular dive just across the street, was a successful showcase for the Drifters and a chance to show off the depth of the material they'd had at the time. For Peter, it was also an audition of sorts for Bob Dylan.

"We may have gotten those gigs because Dylan kind of wanted to see what I was about," he said.

A month after the Pantages show, Peter was in New York doing a show with songwriter Peter Blegvad when he got a call that Dylan was interested in auditioning him.

"I found out about it and I was like, 'Oh shit.' I ran to the first record store I could find," he recalled, adding that he came away from that errand with Dylan's 1985 career-spanning box set *Biograph*. He listened to the LP when he arrived home to his recently-rented bungalow on Blix Street in North Hollywood. It was the house where some of Peter's fondest L.A. memories took place, and the house where Susan lived when the two ultimately got together.

"We had a pair of trees that Paul Cowsill was able to string one of those string hammocks from. It was lovely. And on Friday nights and Saturday nights; our back wall backed up against a Mexican restaurant with a live band, so that was a big part of our music, and that was beautiful," he recalled. "It was a cool place, and I had my Tascam 388, a seven-inch reel-to-reel deck with a built-in mixing board. It was the size of a fuckin' foosball table. So I would wake up and [go] in the next room and it was like, 'Oh! Gotta record.'"

That bungalow was also where Bob Dylan himself showed up for Peter's audition, which didn't pan out but did free Peter up to keep the party going with the Continental Drifters.

"We're just having a ball," Peter said of the Drifters. "And we're drinking a lot, and you know, that's fun. Smoking a lot of pot, and playing in this band together."

Back at Raji's, the Tuesday night residency continued with reliably lively (and long) Drifters sets. By this point, the shows were well attended—even the cast of *Beverly Hills 90210* was known to drop by. One Tuesday night audience even included iconic British singer/songwriter Kirsty MacColl, her then-husband and producer of note Steve Lillywhite, and the 1990s hitmaker Seal.

Employing auxiliary Drifters was the band's way of keeping that momentum going during this time, particularly during the summer of 1992 when Mark and Carlo toured alongside Robert Lloyd as the band for Carlene Carter. Mark was a longtime friend of Carter's, and she was, herself, a Drifters fan.

A key song in the Drifters catalog came out of this particular tour with Carter, thanks to a book loan to Carlo from Robert Lloyd.

"When we were on the bus, I lent Carlo a novel by a guy named Nicholson Baker," Lloyd recalled. "He wrote a book called *The Mezzanine*, which all takes place on an escalator ride going from a ground floor to a mezzanine."

That book spawned "Mezzanine," an essential Carlo tune with a distinctively country rock twang and guitars chugging along percussively in a style unique to the song's drummer composer.

> *Ain't it funny how you whistle a tune*
> *It passes on from room to room*
> *Still I'd take time and note the sun shinin' through a grid*
> *Oh I'm caught in a daydream*
> *Between ground floor and the mezzanine*

A key relationship during this time was Carlo's romantic partnership with Martha Gehman, who was pursuing an acting career in L.A. at the time. Gehman recalls meeting Carlo at tennis great John McEnroe's birthday party, where Carlo was playing drums with the band McEnroe's wife hired to play the party—The Ringling Sisters.

She remembers Carlo arriving at the McEnroe residence and not being able to find the entrance to the house, "peeking over the fence" and asking her where he needed to go to get in. They sat next to each other at the party and by the end he'd offered her a ride to an audition the next day.

"It was warm, it was broad daylight, and he had on a t-shirt and a black leather jacket and a wallet on a chain in his back pocket," Gehman said. "At the time, I was engaged with someone in New York. I came to L.A. to work and decided to stay to get more acting jobs. My sister Pleasant was the booking person for Raji's, she knew everyone and she had said to me, 'You're going to love Carlo.' And so he just gave me a lot of rides because I didn't have a car and we got to know each other. And then I ended up going with him to all of his gigs."

The relationship between Carlo and Martha Gehman would have perhaps seemed unlikely to some given their backgrounds. Carlo, a boxer's kid from a well-connected New Orleans Italian clan, and Gehman, the daughter of actress Estelle Parsons and journalist Richard Gehman.

"There was something odd and special about our relationship," she said. "There was this feeling that two roads from two opposite directions met and rerouted the landscape. We joined in creativity in music, the unspoken universal language. We had a shared sensibility."

Things were complicated at first, mostly due to Gehman's engagement.

"We knew we couldn't be together because of my engagement," she said. "And we would just kind of be like, 'We shouldn't be together, we shouldn't be doing this.' Also, I was worried about how much he drank, but it really didn't matter that much at all, quite frankly."

Their relationship inspired a few songs, one of the most notable in the Drifters catalog being "Here I Am." Few other songs among Carlo's Drifter contributions were as vulnerable.

> *Oh, it might be toxic, but the thing I'm doing is right*
> *Put away your microscope, no need to magnify your side*
> *'Cause here I am*

They would ultimately start a relationship formally when Gehman ended her engagement, and she met Ray and Barbara Ganucheau soon after—quickly becoming a fixture at Drifters shows and joining them in the studio. Naturally, she became part of the crew that had formed among the band but also had the chance to witness what they were building at Raji's.

"I mean, these were really, really incredible musicians," she said. "Watching that come to fruition was really powerful."

In the entire run of the Raji's residency, the band—in some form or another—played every Tuesday except for one. And even on that one occasion when schedules got in the way of the gig, Mark showed up and handed out demos to people who came to the door.

Though there was certainly a desire to make a record and grow their audience, other gigs and job opportunities were still pulling focus from the Drifters for several band members—something that didn't sit well with Gary. He maintains that he always felt the band should've been more of a priority than it was among some of the others.

"That was a big problem for me as time went on, because it didn't seem like everybody else felt that way," he said. "I felt like it was *the* band and it could be a great fucking band. It was like, 'Are you kidding me? Let's do this! We've got all the weapons, let's go.'"

As countless musicians in L.A. had done before him, Gary Eaton spent years cutting his teeth in local bands; playing gigs and writing songs in pursuit of success. When he joined the Drifters, he had just come from the Ringling Sisters—a band that experienced a taste of the upper echelon of the industry when they were discovered by famed producer Lou Adler and ultimately signed to A&M Records in the late 1980s.

Gary's musical path was forged as a teenager when he started playing in bands, but music was a part of his life from very early on.

While his paternal grandfather was a professional sax player who played with artists like the Dorsey Brothers, and his father played harmonica, Gary credits his mother with really shaping his own interests and taste in music.

"In England she was kind of a hipster," Gary explained. "She liked Latin music and jazz, mostly. African American musicians. So me, growing up, I can remember from being a baby just listening to a lot of soul music and a lot of Latin and Latin Jazz music."

He says that he always knew he had an interest in music, but can't really identify a defining moment that made him want to pursue it as a career. It was something that happened organically. He began as a drummer when he was young, before getting into flute thanks to early Jethro Tull and renowned jazz flutist Herbie Mann.

When Gary was 14 he started playing bass, which quickly laid the groundwork for what was to come. He joined a band in high school called Spike, which primarily focused on heavier rock music.

"It was a bunch of guys from Hermosa Beach that were surfers but we played covers of Blue Öyster Cult, Aerosmith, old Peter Green's Fleetwood Mac," he recalled. "I became kind of an early music snob because of those guys."

Disillusioned by what mainstream radio was playing at that time, Gary gravitated towards what KROQ was playing—music that at the time would have been considered underground such as Patti Smith, Lou Reed, and the Ramones.

He started a new wave band called The View soon after Spike dissolved and met guitarist Severo Jornacion at a wedding. Jornacion's band, which included a former bandmate of Gary's, was playing at the event.

"L.A. back then was a really great place to be if you were a musician, because punk was happening, and the new wave stuff was happening," Jornacion said.

Jornacion, who today is the bassist for The Smithereens and The Romantics, was much more musically aligned with what Gary was interested in doing than his previous band.

"He and I hit it off and I asked him to come out and play with us, and it worked out great," Gary said. Jornacion quickly joined the band, and they started playing and writing songs together.

The View fizzled out but they kept working together, writing songs and trying to make their way in the L.A. scene.

"We started out playing covers a lot, and then we started writing songs and did the usual struggle to stay afloat in the L.A. area," Jornacion said.

Gary eventually parted ways with Jornacion and formed, with his then-girlfriend Debbie Dexter, a band called the Devil Squares. It was then that he became friends with Carlo, who he asked to fill in at a Devil Squares gig. But it was when he met, through Dexter, artists Pleasant Gehman and Iris Berry that everything really changed. Gehman and Berry had started a poetry collective called The Ringling Sisters with Dexter and Annette Zilinskas, and Gary and Dave Catching started hanging out with them. A band formed organically.

"[Dave] and I would be over there drinking or smoking weed or whatever, and we'd have our guitars," Gary said. "And we started writing music to their poems. We started doing shows like that—Dave and I would go up there and just play acoustic guitar while they sang these songs that we came up with."

Zilinskas recalled: "I had a piece called 'Velvet Crush,' which was sort of an homage to when I was a teenager and I was really into Elvis—like *Sun Sessions*; early Elvis. And he turned that into a song. Gary would transform these spoken word pieces into music."

The band started getting some attention around L.A., and soon enough people such as producer Lou Adler (The Mamas & the Papas, Carole King) started noticing.

"Somebody had come to a show we did; there were, like, five people at this place," Gary recalled. "And I guess somebody from Lou's office was at the show and saw us. They confirmed to Lou that we were okay, and he called us up. We auditioned for him at the Roxy. It was just us and Lou, standing in the middle of the fucking floor in front of the stage."

Adler signed the band and produced *60 Watt Reality*, which received good press in and outside of Los Angeles. When they started doing demos for their second album, things went south.

"We finished them and handed them off to Lou, and Lou listened to it and threw the tape out the window," Gary said. "He wanted us to be more esoteric, and everybody's predilection was towards rock. He didn't dig it. Then all of the sudden, A&M dropped us."

After being dropped by their label, The Ringling Sisters went their separate ways.

While certainly a hard hand to be dealt, the end of The Ringling Sisters opened the door to Gary linking with Carlo and ultimately joining the Drifters. By the fall of 1992, he and his new bandmates were months into a weekly residency and armed with a growing catalog of songs that were in good shape for an album.

And so, with Monkey Hill on board in New Orleans, the Continental Drifters assembled at Milagro Studios in Glendale to record a proper full-length debut. Peter, who was asked to reprise his producer role for the album, brought in engineer Mark McKenna to record the band after the two had worked together on The dB's *Like This* (when McKenna worked at Bearsville as studio manager), as well as the *Mavericks* album with Chris Stamey.

At the time that the Drifters sessions came about, McKenna was doing freelance engineering following a stint as the engineer and studio manager at A&M Studios. McKenna says he was instantly a fan of the band, and saw parallels between what the Drifters were doing and the configuration, sound, and style of The Band.

"They had multiple lead singers and they were versatile," McKenna said. "And they were very much an 'Americana' band. Even though there wasn't any so-called idiom that was called Americana back then.

"It came from the South, it came from story songs, that kind of thing. The strong male lead vocals. It's indicative of what people think of as Americana music. They had an abundance of good songs. They all had a point of view to put across, and they all had a distinctive vocal style and a distinctive lyrical style. But yet they were cohesive."

The goal for the record was simple from Peter's perspective as both keyboardist and producer—capture the energy and spirit of the band as it had been on stage, and ultimately bring some order to the proceedings.

"It's not so much producing the record as it is wading through a lot of really valid ideas that all get said really loudly at once over each other, and nobody can figure it out," Peter explained. "I just wanted to catch it. I wanted to catch it. I wanted to catch what I heard. I wanted to catch what everybody was hearing."

The band spent about a week doing basic tracking at Milagro, before moving to a smaller room in Venice called Mad Dog Studios for overdubs and prepping the album for mixing. The Milagro sessions were largely successful in achieving what the band set out to achieve, though they were somewhat marred by a difference in opinion on the way the album should sound.

Carlo had a very distinct idea for the sonics of the album, particularly that there should be very little use of reverb. He wanted a much more dry and organic sound, which certainly would compliment Peter's almost minimalist, live-on-the-floor production approach. Gary, however, saw things much differently.

"It wasn't very comfortable," Gary explained. "Pete and Carlo had definite ideas of how things should be done. I was not really along with it, and I felt very outvoted on a lot of things. So it felt really tense to me most of the time.

"Everybody had a fucking opinion, man. Carlo had to have his drums a certain way, Mark had to hear his bass a certain way. And everybody was just fucking pushing and pulling."

There's something to be said for an album with a healthy dose of tension and strife, and the right amount of intensity can make for great art. But, as McKenna notes, it can also suck the vibe out of the room pretty quickly.

"Friction is not necessarily a bad thing, but you have to have some unity of thought," he said. "Or somebody has to be the guy who is sort of corralling everybody else.

"[The Drifters] were all kinds of big personalities in their own right. And successful bands aren't really democracies. There's usually somebody who kind of drags it along by the throat. Usually against the wishes of some others."

The album was finished at Mad Dog and then brought to Bearsville Studio where it was mixed by engineer George Cowan. Once finished, everyone was pleased with the results—mostly. Songs like "Invisible Boyfriend," which Gary took lead vocals on, translated well. But there was a feeling that "The Mississippi" didn't really get where it needed to go in the end, though ulti-mately there was a strong desire for it to be included on the record.

So, in January of 1993, the band assembled at Grinder Studios to record with the legendary Jim Scott, engineer and producer of note who already had an expansive resume (including Sting's 1985 album *The Dream of the Blue Turtles*, which earned him a Grammy® nomination for Best Engineered Album).

Scott, who later produced albums for the Red Hot Chili Peppers and engineer landmark works by Tom Petty and Wilco, was a friend of Ray's who had previously worked with him on demos that included soon-to-be Drifters songs like "I Didn't Want to Lie."

The Jim Scott sessions resulted in a much more agreeable version of "The Mississippi," and the band also took the opportunity to record a few more songs—including a couple with Vicki Peterson and Susan Cowsill.

By this point, if you've forgotten that Susan and Vicki aren't official members of the Continental Drifters yet, you're forgiven. The lines are so blurred that there's no clear timeline from anyone as to when exactly "the girls," as they were affectionately known, were asked to join.

Since we're already breaking the fourth wall, let's talk about "the girls." That doesn't quite feel like the right way to address our dynamic duo. How about we call them the Psychos?

Much better.

There were certainly members of the band who had a vested interest in the Psychos' continued involvement. They were, after all, *the* girlfriends in the band. And why not make it official? There was a bond between the collective that just seemed to grow stronger as time went on, and especially as the romantic relationships evolved between Susan and Peter and Vicki and Gary. It only made sense.

Music and booze were *the* going concerns by now for the ragtag group of musicians.

"We'd pull up to a venue and the Continental Drifter van would open up, and where Cheech and Chong had smoke coming out, we had 'clink, clank, clink.' We sounded like a bottling company every time somebody would get out of that van; it was hilarious," Susan recalled. "We used to say, every time somebody would pop some champagne, the words, 'Ahh, the sound of authority.' That was the line."

One could safely assume that alcohol is at least partly responsible for the lines being so blurred in regard to the Psychos being asked to join the circus. After all, there was a lot of it; not always consumed responsibly.

"I found that being with the Drifters made my drinking accelerate a lot," Peter said. "And even then, I would have to say, to a harmful degree. And I didn't have anybody coming after me and saying, 'Hey, you're too drunk to drive home.

"That's drinking on the road, that's drinking at gigs. And we'd have parties! There was no reason not to have a party."

Yes, the party switch was always turned to the "on" position. But this was also a group of human beings who all had strong personalities and strong opinions, so naturally there was plenty of tension as well.

"We had meetings with the band and rehearsals with the band, where [there were] seven of us in there with Vicki and Susan," Peter said. "And it was like, there was so much shouting going on over each other. And talking over each other. And I'd never been around that. Certainly not in my previous band, where we would rather not talk than break up.

"We were in each other's faces all the time, and then Susan and I would bring it home at night. And there was some shouting going on there, too. Because alcohol does that, and especially tequila."

Speaking of alcohol (and parties), there was another New Orleans trip with the Psychos still in auxiliary roles, in late February of 1993. There were a few other gigs along the way on this run, including their first-ever show in Austin, Texas on February 25.

Susan and Vicki had just been in Europe, where they (as the Psycho Sisters) spent several weeks on tour as backup singers for Giant Sand. They flew home with a few days to spare and then hopped in an RV to join the Drifters on another New Orleans adventure.

This time was different, though. Vicki recalled feeling that the band was starting to move ahead as a five-piece, and she and Susan had become concerned about getting in the way of that; so much so that they'd thought it might be their last trip with the gang.

"I remember being in New Orleans, and I remember sitting at the Rock N' Bowl, and being near tears thinking that this was going to be our last show with the Drifters," Vicki said. "And just being quite devastated by that thought."

Little did she know that Carlo's mind was already made up. Sometime after that trip, in the lobby at Uncle Studios, he proclaimed—rather nonchalantly—that Vicki and Susan were in the band.

"I guess they were talking either about a session or a gig coming up, and Carlo went, 'Oh, I don't know. I mean, the girls are in the band, so that's that.' I'll never forget it," Susan said.

Vicki has a slightly different memory of Carlo's invitation.

"Fuck yeah you're in the band!"

There was no big ask, no official discussion; just a gut feeling and an assumption that it made sense for everyone. And, of course, it did.

It wasn't a big stretch to make things official with Vicki and Susan, but it was not in the original plan for either Psycho.

"As far as I was concerned, we were fine with what was happening, which was: We were kind of the auxiliary club," Vicki said. "We were the women's auxiliary club to the Continental Drifters. And that was cool."

The selling point, ultimately, was that not only were good songs being written by good musicians, this was also a group of people whose intentions were purely musical at heart.

"I wasn't going back into the hurricane cesspool of the pop music industry again," Vicki insisted. "I wasn't going out trying to have a hit single. The pendulum swung as far as possible in the other direction here. Really, I went from wearing mini skirts and boots and fishnets to wearing baggy jeans and flannel shirts, and chopping my hair off. It really could not be more the other side of the coin, aesthetically, musically, and intentionally."

The addition of Vicki and Susan as official Drifters made sense, especially in light of the news that Susan and Peter were expecting a baby. This was exciting stuff for the burgeoning power couple, and they celebrated by getting married.

On April 18, 1993, at Vicki's house in Calabasas, Peter and Susan got married in an afternoon ceremony attended by their bandmates, a couple of Bangles, some Cowsills, and members of Giant Sand and Redd Kross.

Carlo, the best man, had the idea (of course) to throw Peter a bachelor party before the big day, despite Peter making a moral stand to Susan against such events.

"I think I had made some proclamation to Susan and Vicki that I would not be participating, and it was going to be some kind of moral, upright thing," Peter said. "I didn't walk the walk that night."

It was a simple and understated wedding, with Paul and Bob Cowsill providing six-foot Subway sandwiches for the guests, and a recording of the Holsapples' favorite song, "Moon River," played as part of the ceremony.

"I played that song as the last song, every night, of my New Orleans solo shows on Sunday nights," Peter said. "Sometimes Susan would sing it with me, sometimes I would just sing it to her. It's such a brilliantly simple song."

The song's lyrics referencing a pair of "drifters" on their way to see the world were certainly appropriate.

It wasn't long after the wedding that the band started to splinter, ever so slightly. Carlo was ready to make good on his pledge to leave Los Angeles and get back to New Orleans, and Ray followed suit.

"That whole year was kind of intense," Ray said. "There were riots, there was an earthquake; not a big one, but a fairly significant earthquake. And the hill behind my house where I was living caught on fire. And my wife was six or eight months pregnant at the time.

"I think all three of those events kind of led to rethinking the whole concept of living in L.A."

Ray, with his soulful tenor, understated stage presence, and colorful guitar work, was often a part-time presence in the band, but it was a presence that was no less important to the formula than the other Drifters.

With Ray—a working man with a wife and kids, and Carlo, restless and fed up with L.A.— ready to return to New Orleans, the rest of the band were faced with the obvious: move, keep the band going from opposite sides of the country, or pack it in.

Carlo was intent on returning home; something his girlfriend Martha Gehman wasn't especially sold on but wanted to give it a try for the sake of their relationship.

"I couldn't believe that I was going to move to New Orleans," Gehman said. "I mean, what was I going to do in New Orleans?

"And then the week we were all going to move—I don't remember if it was Ray or Barbara— one of them told me that he had been doing heroin. I just was like, 'I'm not going if you're doing heroin. I'm not going.' That was really, really heavy."

They technically broke up, but "didn't really break up," as Gehman puts it. She'd subsequently travel to NOLA to spend time with Carlo, and they would get together when he'd come back to Los Angeles.

Carlo made the move alone, but as it happened, some other Drifters were ready for a move, too. Particularly Peter and Susan, married and expecting a daughter, were ready for a change.

"For me, because I was pregnant, I was like, 'I am not raising a child here," Susan said. They decided on Rhode Island, where Susan grew up and where The Cowsills began some three decades earlier. "I want my baby to run in the grass and on the rocks and at the beach. And get what I got. The good part of my life."

While Peter agreed to give Rhode Island a shot, there was still the matter of the drifting Drifters to attend to. And so, conversations shifted towards a New Orleans move.

"I was cajoled by Jimmy Ford. They were going, and Peter came to me and was like, 'What do you think?'" Susan recalled. "I don't know what it's like there, so I agreed with Peter for a two-year stay."

There was also a financial incentive for the parents-to-be to make the New Orleans move, as living in Los Angeles was proving to be far too expensive for them.

Peter recalled: "We really just saw New Orleans as the potential of, 'Could we afford to live there?' I'd done exploratory trips down there and, you know, it isn't all Mardi Gras all the time. It seemed like, 'Wow, okay. So, this is a place to live, but it doesn't cost five dollars every time I want to walk out the door. We were entranced by the combination of laissez faire, which we loved. It'll happen when it happens. And also, the idea of 'lagniappe.' A little something extra."

With Vicki and Jimmy Ford's help, Susan and Peter made the trek to New Orleans with their belongings packed mainly in Peter's old Ford F150 (a border patrol vehicle in a previous life). Vicki and Susan trailed behind in Vicki's Ford Explorer, affectionately dubbed the Ford Exploder.

"We fuckin' looked like the Beverly Hillbillies," Peter recalled. "We looked like the goddamn Joad family."

They'd arranged to move into the house on Paris Avenue where Peter had recorded the *Paris Avenue* record for The dB's—a house that had just been occupied by Barry Cowsill, his then-wife, and their kids.

The plan was for Peter to move in and take over the recording setup that was living there and run it as a proper studio.

"It was going to be ready for us when we got there. Carlo was going to have it painted and stuff like that, and it was going to be in great shape," he said. On the trip down, however, they learned that none of the work had actually been done to prep the house.

Immediately upon arrival, Peter and Vicki started getting to work getting the house in order—cleaning, plastering walls, and tearing shit up.

"There was this nasty ass shag [carpet] in the back," Peter said. "And we pulled it up, and there was this terrazzo marble floor that was beautiful, except for wear they fuckin' dug holes in it to put carpeting nails in. But it was polished up beautifully, and it was bright and snappy. It was unbelievable, some of the shit that was in there."

The studio portion of the house ended up being a mess, but with a little work the Paris Avenue house became the home of the Holsapples. While Vicki, their devoted Psycho Sister, made multiple trips from Los Angeles to visit and play gigs, she wasn't sold on moving yet, though.

"I would stay with Susan and Peter, and then I would drive home," Vicki said. "And then I'd fly back and I'd rent a place somewhere. One August, I flew back to New Orleans and rented, you know, half of a double shotgun to see if I could handle a New Orleans summer."

Getting to New Orleans on the day that Peter and Susan moved in on Paris Avenue, Vicki recalls, was an exciting moment.

"It was a blast. We first got to Paris Avenue, and they had one of those beautiful New Orleans thunderstorms," she said. "And Susan and I, California girls, were out on the lawn jumping up and down, screaming, so excited that we were in the middle of a New Orleans thunderstorm."

Peter and Susan were the first of the non-expatriate Drifters to make the move, but Mark followed quickly behind.

Tired of living in L.A., he was at a crossroads and ready for a change. Initially torn between moving to Norway or Austin, he ultimately decided on (where else but?) New Orleans. His friends were moving there, after all.

"I hit a wall in Los Angeles, and I liked these people," Mark said. "I thought, 'I'd rather be around them than most people I know right now.' So even if we're not playing, I'd still like to be there with my friends and meet some more people."

And so, on August 10, 1993, the day after his 34th birthday, Mark arrived in New Orleans and found a house to rent right behind Frank Quintini's place. Like Peter and Susan's place, Mark's house also wasn't tenant-ready when he got to town. He had a bit of a different situation on his hands, though, given that the previous tenant not only died in the house, but in a chair that was ultimately left in the house when Mark arrived.

"So I ended up sleeping on couches for a few days until that finally got resolved,' he said. "And they said, 'Well, we cleaned the chair if you want to keep it.' So I did. I kept this dead man's chair. It was a really funny old chair, too." Susan and Peter later inherited the chair.

One by one, the Continental Drifters migrated to New Orleans. Enchanted by what the city offered musicians, they found a home and a new identity in the Crescent City. And, yes, there was the booze, too.

"I remember walking somewhere with Carlo," Peter said. "We were walking down a road in Metairie and he said something to me to the effect of, 'Peter, how has living in a place where you can purchase alcohol 24 hours a day affected your life?'"

Substances impacted the band in various ways, going back to their earliest days, but New Orleans took things to new levels. And that very first Jazz Fest trip in 1992 was certainly the catalyst for this seismic change of scenery.

"I think the New Orleans trip made the place look doable," Peter said. "And it looked like you could have a good time doing it. And I think that without a doubt we succeeded on all fronts. We did it from there, and we had a great time doing it until we didn't."

While the band wasn't especially active while moves were being made, there was still the issue of the Drifters album to attend to during this transition period. Vicki and Gary were still in L.A., too, "commuting" back and forth when needed for gigs.

Theirs was a romance that started in the wake of Vicki losing Bobby, as well as the end of Gary's relationship with his son's mother. Truly, the increasing closeness of the Drifters drew them together.

But Gary was feeling the strain of balancing his personal and musical lives, to the point where his behavior began impacting both his relationships within the band and with Vicki.

"He was not on his best behavior; I'll just put it like that," Vicki said. "There were definitely moments where, on tour, I'm sitting there thinking, 'Is someone going to come in and save me right now?'"

Gary admits as much. "I was acting like a complete asshole back then because I just hated everything," he said. "I was full of a lot of anger."

When the band started moving one by one to New Orleans, that anger reached a breaking point. Not willing to leave his son Sam to relocate to New Orleans, Gary became torn between a life going on in California and a band moving forward in Louisiana.

"I admire him for having always put Sam first in situations," Peter said. "He was really trying to take good care of Sam, in spite of being a member of the Continental Drifters and living at the Bachelor Pad, which had its own oversized problems."

Things came to a head, his relationship with Vicki ended, and the rest of the band decided that they couldn't continue on with Gary in the fold.

According to Gary, he was fired from the band via fax, while he was at Mad Dog working on the Steve Wynn record *Fluorescent*. It wasn't a surprising end to his tenure, but one he had conflicted feelings about.

"I fucking deserved it. I wasn't shocked; I deserved it," he said. "But I also didn't deserve it, you know what I mean? I was split on it. I felt like it was my band."

Vicki herself was conflicted about the idea of Gary being let go from the band because of the sheer weight of his contribution to the band, and despite knowing that their relationship couldn't continue. The situation, she says, was "untenable."

Initially, Vicki thought it best to step away from the band herself, but the other Drifters disagreed.

"For whatever reason, god bless them, the collective decided that they didn't like how he was behaving, and chose to let him go rather than let me go," she said. "I was very torn about that for a long time, because I saw Gary's input and his contributions to the band… for me, they were integral. For me, some of his songs were basic, important Continental Drifters songs."

Even though he was partly hurt by the band's decision, the band was already moving on and Gary was not willing to follow.

"I couldn't blame anybody, but there was no way I could go [to New Orleans]," he said. "My son was here in Los Angeles. It was like, 'Well, fuck. What am I going to fucking do?'

"My 'sinking into despair, sadness and anger' was getting even deeper. It was an easy choice at a very hard time."

Gary's departure from the Drifters took some of the band's most key compositions off the table and left a Dallas-sized hole in their identity. But, as bands tend to go, sometimes there's just no other way around it.

"He was really angry," Peter said. "He had a lot of anger. Some of it was directed at me. I was Carlo's famous showbiz friend, quote unquote. Fuck that. I was just trying to be part of a band and produce a record. I wasn't trying to make him uncomfortable, and I can't help where I came from.

"I hate that, because I think Gary is a supremely talented guitarist, singer and songwriter. Some of those songs are some of the best songs I've ever gotten to play."

The end of that era was a turning point for not just the band, but also Gary, who started going to therapy soon after and ended up meeting his wife of 30 years in the waiting room.

Now, with hindsight and decades of distance, Gary views the band as one with huge potential that seemed to always hit a roadblock.

"It was the best of times, it was the worst of times. It really was fucking crazy," he said. "We had a lot of great things at our disposal; we had people who wanted to help us all the time. But there was always something that stopped us. I don't know what it was."

If there was anything getting in the way of the band during those first couple of years that *could* be easily pinpointed, it was lineup shifts. First Danny left, then the Psychos joined. Then Gary left. It was as if the band was constantly morphing into something else.

Things were also changing on the label side, as Jimmy Ford had begun to take a step back from Monkey Hill after his son was born.

The Drifters' album, funded by Monkey Hill, hung in the balance now as one of the band's primary songwriters was out and two new songwriters were in.

And then came another major blow.

Ray, because of work and household commitments, was the most infrequent member of the band despite co-writing or writing some of the most essential songs in their catalog. In Los Angeles, they'd bring in auxiliary Drifters to fill the void. In New Orleans, though, they'd end up scaling down by one and just doing the shows without him, leaving lead guitar duties to Vicki.

The collective move to New Orleans was, initially, a curveball from Ray's perspective.

"I was surprised that there was all of the sudden this consensus that the band wanted to move to New Orleans," he said. "I was kind of shocked. That was sort of the last thing I expected.

"It seemed like an L.A.-based thing, you know? Everybody was from the area or had been there for a while, and that seemed like a good place to be doing what we were trying to do."

Nevertheless, the Drifters landed in New Orleans ready to keep things moving. In late 1993, they were booked at Café Brasil when Mark got a phone call from Ray's wife, Barbara. He was in the hospital after suffering an aneurysm in an artery near his shoulder, and wouldn't be able to play that night.

"I was doing a lot of sailing," Ray recalled. "I was doing a lot of overhead; pulling and tugging, a lot of that kind of activity. And then I started developing some weird pains in my upper body, like the left hand side in my shoulder. I didn't really make much of it. I was [experiencing] numbness in my arms and stuff like that.

"I just kind of shook it off. At that age you don't really think about—or, at least, I didn't think about—serious health problems, you know? Turns out I had an aneurysm in an artery. One day I was looking in the mirror and I saw this thing popping up out of my chest, like an egg in a tire."

It turns out that the bulge from his chest had been there a while, causing the aneurysm and almost destroying the artery.

"It was producing blood clots," he said. "My left arm was full of blood clots."

Ray spent roughly three weeks in the hospital recovering from this nightmare-ish scenario, and it was during that stay that he decided it was time to pull back from the band. With three young kids, a wife, a day job, and newfound health problems, the demands of the band no longer made sense for his life.

Of course, there was an invitation to return to the fold after he recovered, but by that point Ray had been gradually growing apart from the Drifters for some time.

"I probably could have continued with the band, but I guess at that point I'd kind of lost interest in the band, you know? Because the band kind of morphed into something else," he said. "That, combined with having the aneurysm and the surgery and not really being, sort of, road ready; I just decided to back off."

With Ray's departure, the band was down two songwriters who contributed nearly half of the material on the album they'd just recorded. On top of that, they'd added new members who were bringing material to the table. Losing Ray was a particular blow, though, one that Susan calls "devastating."

It was, in her words, "like losing the original reality."

Not only was the original vision of the band in question, the record they'd just made, after years of writing, demoing, gigging, and making a name for themselves in L.A., was completely obsolete.

And so…what now?

Chapter Four:
Eponymous

"The Drifters is my school—my high school, my grammar school, my everything."

— Susan Cowsill

"New Orleans was, and really still is, a very fertile place for musical discovery, and the creation of music. The music scene here has always been very welcoming and open, unlike a lot of other places."

So said Keith Spera, veteran music writer who has spent decades with *The Times-Picayune*, the city's longtime daily newspaper. Spera tackled the immense task of covering the cultural touchstone that is New Orleans music.

"Here, if you can play and you want to play, there's always a place for you," Spera says of the inviting spirit of the New Orleans music community. "New Orleans, then as now, was very conducive to musical cross pollination. You had guys that could play a little bit of everything, and did. You had R&B guys mixing with rock and roll guys, and jazz guys doing R&B gigs. You have all that intermingling, which partly defines what New Orleans is all about. It's no 'one thing,' musically."

You'd be hard pressed to find another active band of career musicians who would make such a drastic leap from a city like Los Angeles, where "the business" was, to a place such as New Orleans, where what one might consider "business" looked almost entirely different.

But New Orleans' open-armed approach to its culture, and that cross pollination that Spera refers to, might just be the thing that explains why the Continental Drifters ended up there.

That also might be why some Drifters were hesitant, or at the very least a bit reticent, to go all in on the idea initially. When Carlo announced his intention to move back home after the Rodney King riots in April of 1992, he recalls Peter being pretty unconvinced.

"Peter looked at me with the 'venom Peter,' and he goes, 'Isn't New Orleans the place where great musicians go to die?'" Carlo said. "I said, 'No, it's kind of like a music mecca. We got more great musicians in two square miles than we have in all of Los Angeles.' He always loved New Orleans. He'd tapped into the soul of New Orleans, too. I think he just thought that the business was shitty."

Ivan Bodley says he found it hard to make a living as a musician in New Orleans when he was in town in the early-to-mid-'80s, when the business might certainly have been shitty.

"There just didn't seem to be a way to make money as a musician in New Orleans the way

I saw it," Bodley said. "Bands were playing five sets a night on Bourbon Street for $75 or something, if you could even get those gigs.

"There was also a joke that I heard in those days that all of the best musicians in the world lived in New Orleans, but none of them were in the same band together. Until Continental Drifters, that edict seemed to ring true."

Surely, the business *was* different there. Shitty? Maybe, maybe not. But certainly different from what someone accustomed to L.A. might expect. As former Atlantic Records A&R rep, MTV personality, and veteran musician Tim Sommer says, New Orleans musicians can get tied down to the never-ending well of gig opportunities.

Said Sommer: "There was a peculiar ethos—very, very common to New Orleans musicians. I could find a New Orleans musician who was incredibly, incredibly talented. Let's say I found a New Orleans musician who was the next Sam Cooke, and I said to that New Orleans musician… let's call him Mike:

"'Mike, I think you should be on a major label, and I'm going to arrange for you to go to New York and showcase for three different major labels. And in fact, I'll buy your plane ticket. We're going to showcase for these major labels, and you might get a million dollar contract out of it. Or at least get a hundred thousand dollar contract.'

"And Mike would say to me, 'But I'm getting $75 to play on Rampart Street on Monday night. I don't want to miss that gig.' *That* is the New Orleans way of thinking."

Did a bit of that ethos rub off on the Drifters? It depends which way you look at it. On one hand, they were certainly motivated by the fact that they knew what they were doing was great. They wanted their work to be heard by a larger audience.

At the same time, though, there's no question that they wanted it on their terms. There was no desire to kowtow to the major label dollar, especially because almost everyone in the band had been there before.

Sommer looks at that as the most endearing thing about the Drifters.

"They all knew that wasn't the path to happiness. They all knew that wasn't the path to making wonderful music, and making music for the right reasons," he said. "In the history of pop music—since, say, 1965—I'd be hard pressed to find a band whose talent and abilities were greater in proportion to their lack of desire for fame."

It wasn't that they weren't interested in taking opportunities to broaden their reach, it's simply that they were aware of the avenues they *weren't* willing to go down in order to achieve that.

In many ways, that's what led the band to Monkey Hill—a small label that could put some money, clout, and motivation behind them but weren't interested for reasons beyond a belief in what they were doing.

And so, what happens when you owe that label an album and nearly half the band leaves before it sees the light of day? Some bands might just put it out and deal with the consequences, but not the Continental Drifters.

They scrapped the whole thing.

What was to have been the Drifters' debut album was no longer relevant or representative of the band that existed, so they decided to start from square one. Luckily for the Drifters, they'd just inherited the Psychos and the duo's many songs.

So they weren't exactly wanting for material. They were, however, unsure about how the

Monkey Hill deal was shaking out. The band was generally wary of the label, but they also had an obligation to fulfill.

Contractually, the Drifters needed to get something going. They hadn't been in New Orleans for very long, though, and had just experienced a rather seismic personnel shift. On top of that, there was just a lot going on elsewhere.

The newlywed Holsapples welcomed their daughter, Miranda Victoria, into the world in September of 1993. Vicki was there to help the parents-to-be, and so were Carlo and Mark—totally drunk in the waiting room.

Susan recalls the Drifters standing by while she stayed in a birthing room.

"Carlo and Mark kept going to the bar across the street because it was taking too long," she said. "They would come back a little [more drunk] every time."

At the time, Susan was allowed to have anyone she wanted in the room with her up to a certain point in the labor process. Mark and Carlo ultimately ended up in the room with Susan as she endured hours of labor.

"The last thing I really remember before the room got cleared was literally Mark in the chair, and Carlo laying on the floor with his hands crossed in his chest; just kind of relaxingly laying there, and one of the nurses opening the door and going, 'You have got to be kidding me,'" Susan recalled.

"Do you want that fool on the floor?"

"I said, 'I don't care.' And she said, 'Well, then, I don't either.'"

The nurse proceeded to step over Carlo to get to the other side of the room.

"And Carlo said something like, 'Hey, baby,' as she walked over,' Susan said with a laugh. "It was such a New Orleans thing."

These waiting room shenanigans became tradition in the band; for every Drifter baby that came after, the band hung around the waiting room, singing or generally causing a ruckus.

That only emphasizes just how tight knit this group of people was. They were a family, more so than most bands are—even some actual family bands. As Susan puts it, Los Angeles was where the "adoption papers" were signed, and New Orleans was where they got "the big emotional house."

So if the Drifters were a family, then Vicki would logically be the Auntie. And she was, of course, but she was much more than that, too. She was, in many ways, Miranda's third parent.

"I could never, ever in a million years express my eternal gratitude for her help on every imaginable level, and some unimaginable ones. She was remarkable," Peter recalled.

The unimaginable did happen that day, when Susan and Peter were told that the baby was in distress and she'd have to forgo her plan to deliver naturally. That was the moment that, in Susan's words, Vicki "bought in" to the family.

"I had a C-section at the last minute and we didn't have any money," Susan recalled. "And [Vicki] was in a corner knitting, and they're coming in telling me, 'The baby's in trouble; in distress. And we need to get her out of there.' And I started crying."

Peter, having done due diligence by reading the baby books, was certain he understood why Susan was upset about the C-section.

"He had done so much reading about what to do, that when I started bawling, he leans over and he goes, 'You're upset because as a woman, you think you've failed by not giving a natural birth. But that is not the case,'" Susan said. "I'm hearing him reading a quote from a book. And

I'm going, 'That is not why I am crying! I'm crying because it's going to cost another $2,100 fucking dollars and we don't have it!'

"[Vicki] wasn't allowed to look at me, she could only sit there and knit. And she goes, 'I'm not looking up, I'm just putting up my hand. I'm in for $2,100.' And put her hand back down and went back to knitting."

Susan looked at Vicki to make sure she hadn't looked at her, and the deal was done. Vicki was in.

And, in true Drifters fashion, Susan's first night home from the hospital was a celebration.

"All I can remember is me being in my bedroom with Mook [Miranda's nickname], finally. We're settled and I'm good," Susan said. "I do not need these people around me, and they want to help. And I go, 'You guys, we made it! Yay! Look at me and the baby! Get back in the kitchen and crack a bottle. Let's do this thing!' And they got so drunk, and I could hear them all night," she said. "It was beautiful. There they were; my buddies, in a victory lap at the table."

The birth of Susan and Peter's daughter symbolized, in many ways, a new beginning of sorts for the band; solidifying their bond and emphasizing that they really just had each other in the unknown world of New Orleans, Louisiana.

And so, they moved forward. Without a designated lead guitar player, they plotted their next move thoughtfully. And within that came the idea that it might behoove them to save their originals for a future project once they fulfilled their obligation to Monkey Hill.

Mark explains: "We were concerned. We were like, 'Well, if we give them our best songs it'll just disappear and nobody will ever hear it.' We felt like, 'Let's not give them everything that will tie [the songs] up. That way we can come back [to them]."

This was an idea that didn't land with Monkey Hill, so they settled on a compromise: half originals, half covers. Picking the originals was relatively easy; or, rather, picking which songs *wouldn't* make the record was easy. Carlo was especially set on keeping certain songs tucked away, like his "Side Steppin' the Fire," which was originally slated for the previous lineup's album, and the yet-to-be-recorded "Long While."

In terms of the covers, the list of songs they had to choose from was long. Raji's afforded them hours worth of time to try out basically anything they wanted, and as a result they built a deep well of music that spanned genres. Covers were arguably as important to the Drifters' repertoire as any original song would have been.

Some of the most notable covers the band ever did? Tyrone Davis' hit "If I Could Turn Back the Hands of Time" stands out, as do the Dusty Springfield classic "I Can't Make It Alone" and the Beach Boys' "The Farmer's Daughter" (also covered by Fleetwood Mac).

For this project, though, they landed on "I Can't Make It Alone," Pat McLaughlin's "Highway of the Saints," the Box Tops' "Soul Deep," Michael Nesmith's "Some of Shelly's Blues," and, of course, "A Song for You."

"Highway of the Saints" was a song that the band had been playing since their first New Orleans trip in 1992, when they sat in with McLaughlin at a gig. "I Can't Make It Alone" goes even further back, to a time when Mark would play Springfield's *Dusty in Memphis* constantly.

"I was kind of sad; I was staying with Kevin Jarvis and his girlfriend, and I would wake up and I would put on that record," he said. "And it was just such a lovely experience. So when the Drifters started going I said, 'I really want to hear you sing this song, Susan.' It was magic to me."

On the 'originals' side of things, the band introduced quite a few new compositions into the mix for this revamped project—including a song of Mark's called "Get Over It," which dated back to the Raji's days and started as a demo with Gary singing.

"I programmed all the drums, played the guitar, played the bass. Robert Lloyd put some keyboards on it, and Gary sang," Mark said.

Unbeknownst to Mark, Gary was also a proficient flutist, and presented the idea of putting it on the demo.

"He was like, 'Hey, let me try this.' I was like, 'What?! You play the flute?" Mark recalled with a laugh.

The song ultimately went in a different direction after Gary left the band, and by the time they decided to bring it to what would become their first record, Susan had stepped up to the vocal mic. The flute solo didn't stick, though.

"Flutes in bands, they're kind of like Birkenstocks. You just don't show up with one," Robert Maché said with a laugh.

Other newer songs in the mix were Susan's "Desperate Love," Carlo's "New York," and Vicki's "Mixed Messages." The latter song was written from the perspective of Gary, during his and Vicki's relationship. A new version of "Invisible Boyfriend," with Peter on vocals, was thrown into the mix as well.

Notably missing from the planned tracklisting were songs like "Who We Are" and "The Rain Song," which understandably didn't go over too well at Monkey Hill.

"The only thing I'll say is, the record that they did for Monkey Hill, I wish they would've put 'The Rain Song' on it. That's all I'm going to say about that," Jimmy Ford said.

Tucking their best songs away, the band convened at the Egyptian Room, a studio owned by engineer Robinson Mills—a 20-something who'd previously interned at the famed Power Station in New York, engineered records for Rick Rubin, and worked on hits by Blues Traveler and the Spin Doctors.

Mills had just purchased the API console that Guns N' Roses recorded their landmark *Appetite For Destruction* album on, and the tape machine used to record John Lennon's *Imagine*, and moved into an office building on 333 St. Charles Avenue.

"I had a bunch of money, and I was stupid and I was in my twenties," Mills said. "I should have bought a bunch of properties in the Irish channel or something."

The room, true to its name and Egyptian-themed, was 75 feet long, 35 feet wide, and 35 feet tall—perfect for a band recording in a room together with limited time. The space had previously been the ballroom for the Daughters of Isis; the female auxiliary to Prince Hall Shriners.

"It had this sunken floor," Peter recalled. "[It was] just really awesome."

"It was beautiful," Mark added. "We loved it there. It was such a great vibe."

Recorded on ADAT (Alesis Digital Audio Tape, an eight-track machine introduced in the early 1990s), the newly-reworked Continental Drifters—Peter, Susan, Carlo, Mark, and Vicki— spent several days with Mills getting the songs recorded.

The band, Mills recalls, knew just what they were going for and how to get there. As a young engineer at the time, Mills says the band's precision and their comfort level with recording— especially harmonies—made a lasting impression on him.

"They were cocky, don't get me wrong," Mills said. "They were assholes. But they were professional. And I don't mean 'asshole' in a bad way.

"I was probably cocky too, and I probably thought I knew everything sometimes. But then they would sort of bring me back to reality. They just knew exactly what they wanted. They didn't have a lot of time to waste."

With a small budget and limited time, the band plowed through live takes of the songs and pieced the record together from there. Once basic tracking was finished, though, they realized they were missing lead guitar and weren't sure what exactly to do about it.

"We recorded all of this stuff, but it didn't have any guitars on it," Mark recalled. "And we were like, 'Well, Peter can play the guitars! Or, Vicki can play the guitars!' And then I went, 'Well, let me just call Robert and see if he would be interested in joining the band and playing on the record.'"

Robert Maché was living in Tucson, Arizona, at the time—relocating there from Los Angeles after the Steve Wynn Band parted ways. He'd married Giant Sand bassist Paula Jean Brown, but that marriage was over, and he was looking for his next move.

"Mark just rescued my ass, and said, 'Come to New Orleans," Robert said. "This was like a gift from the gods."

Getting him on the record would require getting ADATs to Tucson and overdubbing there. Robert enlisted his friend, an engineer named Harvey Moltz, to record him, and Vicki was tasked with bringing the tapes to Tucson. They met up at Moltz' studio and tracked the songs—almost all of which Robert already knew from his days subbing with the band in L.A.

It was a perfect match; an easy fit that made sense for where the band was at creatively and where they wanted to go. Robert made the move to New Orleans soon after, and the lineup was complete.

With Robert in the fold and recording wrapped, the band was finally ready to release their official debut , simply titled, *Continental Drifters*. But this moment wouldn't come without its detours, which by now were to be expected in Drifter world.

Carlo, who had continued session and touring work while with the Drifters, got a call some months earlier to work with Tori Amos on what was to be her second album for Atlantic Records, *Under the Pink*. It was the second time he'd worked with Amos, after being hired by producer Eric Rosse to play drums on her previous album *Little Earthquakes*.

Carlo got the call for *Little Earthquakes* back in 1991, after Amos had completed the record but was told she needed more songs or the album wouldn't be released.

Steve Caton, Amos' collaborator at the time, knew Carlo through their mutual friend Will McGregor, who had been playing with Carlo in Pat McLaughin's band.

Caton got a call from Amos, who wanted him to put together a band to record four more songs, which would be used as demos to present to the label.

"She said, 'I've got $4,000 to do four more tracks—demos. So I called Will, and I called Carlo," Caton said.

Little Earthquakes yielded two Carlo-backed songs, including an especially notable performance on "Precious Things."

"Without those four 'demos,' that record would have never been released," Caton said. "Carlo obviously was a huge part of that, because the drum tracks are phenomenal."

The album proved successful enough that Carlo was tapped for the entirety of its follow up, which was recorded in New Mexico throughout 1993. Caton says that Carlo laid the foundation for the record to become what it was, with his endless swagger and undeniable character as a drummer.

"You know how I always know when a drummer is really good?" Caton said. "When I go to record something and the drum tracks are already on there, and [they're] really easy to play to."

The recording of *Under the Pink* kept Carlo busy when he wasn't working with the Drifters, and he wasn't the only Drifter hustling inside and outside of New Orleans.

Mark had been recording and touring sporadically with Giant Sand, and Peter was taking session jobs too. He, Susan, and Vicki all contributed to Melissa Ferrick's debut album *Massive Blur*—at the request of that album's producer Gavin MacKillop, and all three were also popping up on Giant Sand releases during this time period.

It was in 1994, though, when Peter got a call that changed his career trajectory for years to come. He'd been asked by Tim Sommer to fly up to Reflection Studios in Charlotte, North Carolina, and contribute mandolin and Hammond organ to a Led Zeppelin cover being recorded by a band called Hootie and the Blowfish, who was on the come up at the time. Sommer discovered and signed the band—who, like him, were disciples of R.E.M.

The friendship between Peter and Sommer went back many years, when both were living in New York City and Sommer was a 17-year-old contributor to *Trouser Press*, listing The dB's "Black and White" as a top ten song of the year. Sommer, also a disc jockey at WNYU and a friend of Peter's roommate Naomi Regelson, was a major dB's fan and a student of R.E.M.

"I was always in awe of Peter, and this was even before Peter became involved with R.E.M.," Sommer said.

By the time the Zeppelin tribute came about, Hootie had just recently released their Atlantic Records debut, *Cracked Rear View*. Upon its release in July of 1994, the album had flown largely under the radar and was initially in danger of languishing in obscurity. The band, Sommer, and Atlantic had modest objectives for the record, especially given the state of mainstream rock at the time. Sommer says the goal was to be "as big as The Jayhawks."

An appearance on *The Late Show with David Letterman* quickly moved those goalposts, though, catapulting them from college rock band with a major label deal to overnight success.

By the time the band was tapped to record a tune for the Atlantic-curated *Encomium: A Tribute to Led Zeppelin*, they were quickly becoming one of the biggest bands in the world.

Sommer suggested that they hire an auxiliary player to heighten their live sound, and being the R.E.M. nerds they were, they thought of Peter (having seen him with their heroes at Carolina Coliseum in Columbia, South Carolina, in April of 1989). It was actually an idea that Sommer previously had himself, while the band was working on *Cracked Rear View*.

"I sent a cassette of *Cracked Rear View* to Peter with a note that said, 'I want you to hear this. If this band can ever afford a fifth player on the road, I want you to do it,'" he said. "It did not occur to us that we would ever necessarily be able to afford a fifth player on the road. So I had Peter in mind for Hootie & the Blowfish before the record even came out."

The band was more than excited by the notion of bringing Peter in for the session.

"In my head I'm like, 'Dude, I could play the mandolin part. But shit, if Peter Holsapple wants to come in and play it, that's okay with me,'" Hootie guitarist and songwriter Mark Bryan recalled.

The session went swimmingly, and everyone convened back at their hotel to have dinner and to hang together.

Said Bryan: "He and I sat up in a hotel room and drank, played guitar, and talked until we passed out. We totally hit it off. We both had that geeky musician thing going, and I was already in awe of him. So I was just sitting and listening to him tell stories, and then trying to impress him with what little bit of stories I had at that point."

There was, indeed, a serious musical kinship forged between Mark Bryan and Peter Holsapple that night, with both musicians leaving a lasting impression on the other.

"Mark I loved, because Mark, I immediately knew, was like Pete Buck. Just this unquenchable thirst for playing rock and roll with everybody at all hours of the night and day. He just wants to play," Peter said. "He's got that really great rock and roll spirit."

Peter quickly became the band's de-facto mentor (or, as he would say, their "avuncular presence").

"He was that guy," Bryan said. "Any time something would come up—everybody in the band was just feeding off of it. I remember him turning us on to the Louvin Brothers and all this stuff we had never heard of. He heard us listening to Doc Watson and New Grass [Revival] and he was like, 'Well have you heard the Louvins? This is where all that shit comes from.' He was like a musical history professor for us. We soaked it up."

The Zeppelin session and subsequent hang session confirmed that Sommer's instincts were spot on, and that Peter was the right guy for the job.

"When it was presented to me, I was like, 'I think I should do this, because we have this baby,'" Peter said.

It was a job offer that made sense both artistically and financially. It wasn't a decision he took lightly, though. Taking on a full-time touring gig with a high-level artist at the height of their demand meant that he'd have to sacrifice time with his wife and daughter and the Drifters to make it work.

"I was grateful for an opportunity to play with Hootie & the Blowfish, but my heart of hearts was always with the Drifters," Peter said.

The rest of the Drifters were all fully supportive of the idea and willing to work around it in order to keep the band moving. Vicki says it was a sensible move for Peter—one that they all understood was necessary for him at the time.

"It's not just like you hang out with your friends, make music, and make grocery money on the weekends," she said. "He's an actual professional musician with a family to support."

And Susan was content with staying home with Miranda while Peter worked, as conflicted as he may have been about leaving.

"I was like, 'Who the fuck are you talking to? I can do baby alone! Go!'" she said.

Said Peter: "She really was great at dealing with our little girl, who was starting life with a father on tour. She spent every ounce of her being trying to make life beautiful and fun and happy for Miranda. I think she really succeeded at that more than anybody could imagine."

And Vicki, of course, was third parenting by then.

"I was literally around the block, so it made it easy for Susan and me to hang out, spend time with Miranda, and write songs a little bit," Vicki said. "But mostly just hang out."

The Drifters came attached to Peter as a sort of bonus for the Hooties, who were also admirers of Vicki.

"They knew that I was in this band when I got involved in them. They're all big Bangles fans, too. They were all very excited at the prospect of meeting Vicki Peterson," Peter said with a laugh.

Vicki had her own Drifter vacation in late 1994 into 1995 when she was asked by her old pals The Go-Go's to fill in for a pregnant Charlotte Caffey on guitar.

There was some connection in the public sphere between The Bangles and The Go-Go's, but it was mostly contained to comparisons in the press starting in the early 1980s. They are still pitted against each other in online musical debates, but in reality they became successful on different timelines and were very different bands musically.

"It was sort of like, 'Beatles and Stones / Bangles, Go-Go's.' I watched The Go-Go's come up through L.A. clubs. My band was already playing in clubs when they were in England. They were sort of the conquering heroes when they came home. I had to love them! I didn't want to love them, but I had to love them," Vicki said with a laugh. "To me, I didn't feel like we were that related. We were from the same town and we were the same gender. And to me, that was really the similarities between the bands."

Vicki befriended The Go-Go's and was delighted when her friend Caffey—who was married to Vicki's ex, Redd Kross frontman Jeff McDonald—needed a sub and the call went to her. She spent six months on and off with the band, touring and doing promotional appearances in the U.S. and England.

"It was fun to observe a band and not be in it. They were absolutely lovely to me, and treated me as equal of a member [as they were] on a lot of levels," she said of the experience. "I wasn't responsible for ticket sales. I didn't have to do press but they invited me to do some press with them. But when you're on the road and you're doing that kind of a promotional tour, the press side of it is exhausting. Especially in England when you have to get up at 4 a.m. to do Breakfast TV. That was optional, so that was exciting for me!"

Musically speaking, it was a new challenge for Vicki, who'd never been in a situation where her job was strictly to learn existing material and recreate parts that were already arranged.

"There were some songs, like 'Head Over Heels,' that have a very prominent piano riff. I'm not really a piano player, and I don't think they even wanted to bring keyboards on this run, so I had to transpose this keyboard riff on guitar," she said. "I kind of just knuckled down and learned the material, which is something that a lot of musicians just do every day. And it was a little more foreign to me as a player, so it was good for me."

Vicki's full-time life in music began around 1983, but she'd been in bands since high school and had been playing guitar since she was in the fourth grade. She became enamored with music at a young age, thanks to her parents and her older sister Pam. Their house had an intercom system that they could pipe radio stations through, meaning that there was always something on.

Vicki's sister and Bangles drummer Debbi Peterson recalled: "Our parents were also fans of calypso and musical soundtracks among other interests, so there was a nice variety of music around us. We would sing into hairbrushes, dance, and even create our own plays for our parents and their friends, in which Vicki was very involved."

On family drives, whoever was in the front passenger's seat would be crowned DJ, and it was often Pam who got to control the radio.

"She did a good job because she loved pop and rock, and she had the record collection," Vicki said. "She had the bigger allowance, so she spent all her money on music as a young teen. We got to benefit from that because Pam had the records."

Like most of the Drifters, Vicki grew up with a bit of a music obsession—starting with a love of The Beatles, as did so many other musicians of that era. But what set her apart from other young female Beatles fans was that she wasn't interested in them as dreamy pop idols or fantasy boyfriends.

"I wanted to *be* them. It wasn't so much that I wanted to be their girlfriend; I wanted to be them," she emphasizes.

Like so many others, Vicki took The Beatles bait and dreamed of a life in music.

"By 11, 12, 13, I was the annoying kid who would bring their guitar to parties and sleepovers," she said.

If The Beatles were the bait, then The Cowsills were unquestionably the hook. Vicki recalls one of those drives being her first introduction to the then hugely popular Cowsills.

"This song came on, and I was sitting in the back seat and I liked it." she said. "And Pam turned around and with a little scornful tone in her voice said, 'Oh, this is that band with the girl *your* age in it.' And I was like, 'Wait, what? What?! There's a band with a girl my age in it?'"

That song was "We Can Fly," and the album of the same name became the first album that Vicki bought with her own money. She, along with Debbi, became huge Cowsills fans and later started a band in high school.

"My initial attraction [to The Cowsills] was the fact that they were young, and they were doing it, and they could play," she recalled. "It was the same structure, in a way, that attracted me [to] The Beatles. It felt like: They're a gang. They're together. It's a group. It was something about the collective that I responded to."

It wasn't long before her band with Debbi, and Vicki's best friend Amanda Hills, started playing around Los Angeles. She didn't look at it as a profession, but she was doing music full time.

"'Career' is always a fancy word," Vicki said. "I don't think I used that concept, necessarily. But by 1978/'79, the band I had with Amanda and Debbi, we were playing clubs regularly. I mean, like, three times a week sometimes."

It was while they were playing in their high school band that the Peterson sisters began hanging around Cowsills rehearsals at a rehearsal studio called Earshot, in Burbank, and seeing them every chance they got in the area.

"We would show up at the rehearsals and we were fans, but as we had our own band, [would act] very cool and nonchalant," Debbi Peterson recalled. "I loved the way John Cowsill played drums! We would always reenact his cymbal technique, and some of their dialogue at rehearsals and shows became hours of in-jokes for us."

The sisters' band eventually morphed into The Colours, and then The Bangs, which was renamed The Bangles and became the band we all know today. Success was gradual and organic; an approach they employed up to the time that they were discovered and signed by Miles Copeland—founder of IRS Records and one of three brothers in the Copeland musical dynasty.

"When [Copeland] signed us as a management client, he had the same philosophy—build slow, get people interested, and not go straight to the executives," Vicki said. "And I liked that. And it worked. It definitely worked."

Perhaps it was that same philosophy that attracted her to the Drifters—no overarching sense of urgency to achieve commercial success. Take a more relaxed approach to building an audience, and let the music be the focus.

That seemed to be what all the Drifters had in common. They were committed to prioritizing the band but were okay with detours and time away when necessary because they weren't desperate for success.

And so with multiple band members pursuing outside opportunities, wedging Drifters gigs in between Hootie gigs didn't ultimately prove to be as much of a challenge as Peter may have worried and the band found time to get on the road and promote *Continental Drifters*. They also, during Mardi Gras 1995, recorded The Hollies' "I Can't Let Go" at the Egyptian Room with Robinson Mills at the helm. That song would be released on eggBERT Records' Hollies tribute album *Sing Hollies in Reverse*.

The band took their eponymous debut to SXSW in March of 1995, where they garnered some buzz from press, played some well-attended showcases, and met Edgar Heckmann, a German label employee and music fan, who had just started working on an idea for his own endeavor.

Heckmann was working at a heavy metal label at the time, and approached the owners about launching another arm of the company that focused on music he was interested in. He'd already known Mark's work in The Dream Syndicate—dating back to the mid-1980s, when he met the band backstage at a show in Germany.

Heckmann introduced himself to Mark and his bandmates by approaching them with a handful of records and giving it to them, one by one.

"It was a live bootleg of The Dream Syndicate that he had manufactured and was selling. And he goes, 'I brought one for you, and one for you. I'm like, 'Well, you've got a lot of balls to just walk in and hand it [to us],'" Mark said with a laugh.

Fast forward to SXSW in 1995, Heckmann approached Frank Quintini about his new label and the two had a meeting where they agreed on Blue Rose picking up a handful of Monkey Hill releases; one being *Continental Drifters*. It ended up being the very first release on Blue Rose Records in the fall of 1995.

Heckmann, for his part, was especially thrilled to bring the Drifters' music to Germany and counted himself as a fan of their work. Picking up the record was a no-brainer.

"The camaraderie in the band, the fun making music together was obvious," Heckmann said.

The band's eponymous album began a long and fruitful relationship with Blue Rose, which ultimately led to solo projects and other bands even after the Drifters broke up. The band says they always had a sense that Heckmann was in it for the right reasons, which made linking with Blue Rose the obvious right choice for them.

It proved to be a wise decision, as the album garnered attention in Germany immediately upon its release, and Heckmann began working with a booking agent named Berthold Seliger— himself a fan of the band—on a tour slated for January and February of 1996.

Continental Drifters ended up selling roughly 3,000 copies in Germany and European territories including the Netherlands, Spain, and Italy, though the bulk of the sales were in Germany due to a limited promotional budget outside of the country. That was certainly a larger figure than they were seeing in the States, where they were slowly building an audience but had trouble catching on like they did in Germany.

Still, the album garnered great reviews upon its domestic release on November 23, 1994, with *Billboard* saying the album "delivers, and then some":

The sound is swaying roots rock cum country Cajun; the harmonies, sweet; and the verdict, killer.

Rolling Stone was equally as kind, praising the set as a "fathomless pool of writing talent" that sounds "graceful and unaffectedly lush."

The Drifters got great critical response and built on their long-maintained buzz band status, but still came up short in crossing over. By the time the record came out in Germany, they'd been touring their debut for nearly two years in the States.

They'd opened for like-minded bands like Wilco, who was also on the come-up under a similar stylistic umbrella. They'd opened for Hootie at amphitheaters across the East coast; shows that were impactful and memorable, and that made an impression on fanboy Mark Bryan.

"I did the whole thing of, like, showing up early and going right to the sound desk. And I cried," he recalled of his first time seeing the band. "Like, the sounds that were coming from that stage. Just the sound of the band makes you cry."

The Drifters had begun to make a small dent outside of New Orleans, where they still played regularly, starting a weekly residency at the Howlin' Wolf after Robert moved to town. Those nights mirrored the Raji's residency in a lot of ways, though the Howlin' Wolf's stature made it a much more sensible home for the band.

"Raji's because it was such a funky, run down old sort of punk rock club, it confused a lot of people who would normally want to come see us," Mark said. "But the Howlin' Wolf was more reputable. It was a better club. It was an easy sell to get people in and out of there."

Original Howlin' Wolf co-owner Jack Groetsch had a history with the Drifters that started with Carlo and Ray well before the band moved to town. When the club opened in 1988, it was a 300-capacity room that Groetsch opened with his brother, Jeff, and it hosted both local and touring acts. They expanded several times to larger capacity rooms over the thirteen years that the Groetsch brothers owned the place, and by the time the Drifters started their residency the club had moved to a significantly larger cotton warehouse on South Peters Street (also where the band parked their RV and slept on "The Vatican" trip in 1992).

The Howlin' Wolf was quick to become not only a popular venue for local acts, but also a welcoming spot for artists of all genres. The Afghan Whigs notably recorded a four-song promo EP there in 1997, aptly titled *Live at the Howlin' Wolf*. In the nineties it was a hotspot for club-level touring acts like the Whigs, Pavement, Wilco, and Sonic Youth.

"We were *the* indie, back when indie was a real thing," Groetsch said of the club's reputation. "I was tethered to the club—we were open seven days a week, had three bands a night, and never got a headliner on before midnight. I'd get home at five in the morning if I was lucky, and I just lived right around the corner."

The club's relationship with the Drifters started with open mic nights, which were not your typical acoustic singer/songwriter showcase.

"We always had an open mic on Mondays, and we kinda did it a different kind of way. To get people out for it, we'd have it hosted by a front person from a band," Groetsch said. "They'd get to play, and people could come up and do their thing."

Those open mics led to the band's regular Tuesday night gig, where they'd play their extensive catalog and have friends swing by for guest sets. Groetsch recalls a notable night during Jazz Fest, when Jackson Browne stopped by after a gig of his own to sit in with the band—a night Groetsch describes as "staggeringly good."

"I was in my office, and I was laying on the couch," Groetsch said. "Vicki and Susan come in and start shaking me and they're like, 'Get up! Get up! We want you to meet Jackson. I remember opening my eyes and I was like, 'Well, are y'all gonna get up and play?'"

The Howlin' Wolf became the band's home base in New Orleans, and Peter was also doing a regular Sunday solo gig at Carrollton Station. It was a good situation that gave the band a chance to play as regularly as they could around Peter's Hootie schedule. Groetsch, and his brother, grew close with the band and became genuine fans.

"Here's the thing about the Drifters—they were undeniable. A cut above, you know?" he said. "They're as good as it gets."

Given the band's inconsistent schedule, building an audience in New Orleans took some work. Sure, they had a residency in town and a product in hand, but they were competing for a crowd in a city where live music is a real economic driver. They also were in a city where individual name recognition would only get you so far.

"People have a lot of options every single night," Keith Spera said. "So you're competing with things.

"[And] as accepting as the New Orleans music community is, you've also got to put in your time. It's not like they were just going to pop in here and all of the sudden have an audience. That wasn't going to just happen; they had to put in their time. It was something that they were going to have to get in the trenches and earn."

While New Orleans is a difficult nut to crack as far as audience-building is concerned, what the Drifters always had going for them was that they were a solid live band with the ability to win over a crowd pretty easily.

That was the reputation that preceded them, and the buzz that followed them—both in and out of New Orleans. And with U.S. touring less sporadic, a record out that was getting some attention, and a warm reception to that record in Germany, they were finally starting to capitalize on the momentum that always seemed to follow them around but never elevate them.

Enter: Scott Aiges, a passionate music fan and veteran *Times-Picayune* music writer.

Aiges started seeing the Drifters after they moved to New Orleans, and he covered them regularly.

"It was right up my alley," Aiges said. "It was like The Band meets the Mamas and the Papas. Somebody my age, of my inclinations, is going to absolutely love that."

At the time, Aiges was disillusioned with his gig at the *Times-Picayune* and needing a change. He and his wife befriended the Drifters and he'd become tight enough that he started helping them load out gear at various gigs as needed.

He found that his job as a journalist was beginning to get in the way of his desire to become more invested in the music he was seeing around New Orleans, including the Drifters.

"As a journalist I had to maintain this, sort of, veneer of objectivity," Aiges said. "Which basically meant that I wasn't allowed to have real relationships and real friendships with these people, because they were people that I covered. And ethically, as a journalist, that's not cool.

"That's not what I wanted. I wanted to really know these people; I wanted them to know me. I wanted to be part of it and have genuine relationships and experiences. I didn't just want to write about what other people were doing. I wanted to do something."

One night after helping the band with a load out from a gig at Carrollton Station, Aiges and his wife were invited to hang out at Mark's house with Vicki, Susan, Peter, Mark, and Robert. They stayed up until the early morning hours drinking wine and talking, and Aiges began venting to them about his frustrations at work and his desire to pursue something entrepreneurial instead.

"It was just a time in my life where I was ready for a change," he said. "I was very burnt out from my job; I really felt like I was really just grinding myself to the bone, and not getting the support that I would have hoped that I would from the powers that be.

"I was becoming unbearable to live with, and my wife was getting really short-tempered with me because I was so miserable."

While sharing his struggle with the Drifters, the discussion was interrupted with an idea from Vicki.

"At one point in the conversation Vicki just says, 'Hey, Scott, why don't you quit your job and be our manager?'" he said. "Susan quickly chimed in with, 'Even though we're *completely unmanageable.*'"

There was zero hesitation—Aiges was in. He quit his day job to manage the Continental Drifters.

"I thought that it was a perfectly rational idea to quit a very well-paying job to manage a rock band for a living," he said with a laugh, adding that he thought managing the Drifters would be a "no-brainer" because of the members' pedigrees and the undeniability of their chemistry and catalog.

He'd quickly discover, though, that it was no easy task taking on a band like this one.

There were, of course, the logistical issues that came with trying to get the band booked regularly—after all, he came into the picture simultaneously with the massive success of Hootie and the Blowfish and Peter's new found place in that organization.

But there were other issues plaguing him on the managerial side—namely, as Aiges claims—the fact that they had a bit of a reputation for having egos attached.

"Yeah, people knew them in the industry, but not everybody loved them," Aiges said. "They had a reputation, as many New Orleans bands did, as being pretty difficult to deal with."

Aiges tried to sell the band to agents and labels, but at that point they didn't have the audience or the sales figures to garner much interest.

"The fact of the matter is, they were an independent band that really wasn't moving any kind of quantities of records, and they weren't really worth any money in any markets in the country as a live hard ticket act, and it was a really tough sell," he said.

By the time they'd embarked on their first European tour, though, the band was picking up steam with *Continental Drifters* and getting enough attention in Germany to translate to well-attended club shows. The first tour took place in January of 1996, a few months after the album's release on Blue Rose, with Miranda Holsapple in tow.

Not having experience with bringing children on tour in Europe, Peter contacted Janet Beveridge Bean, of Chicago bands Eleventh Dream Day and Freakwater, to get her advice.

"She mentioned that it was likely that our vehicle over there would not have the U.S. equivalent of securing a car seat," Peter said. "So we invested in luggage straps, and improvised."

Luggage straps and baby secured, they employed Monica Steward, Miranda's nanny and Carlo's girlfriend at the time, for the duration of the Germany trip. Steward had met Carlo in 1994, and the rest of the band came into her life shortly after. Miranda was not even a year old when Steward was hired to be their nanny, and offered the opportunity to join them on the road. It was a formative experience, she said.

"I was 24, 25, and learning about life and music," Steward recalled. "Just being around Peter and his musical tastes and collection was an educational experience. It was a lot of fun."

The inaugural German tour started as a successful outing with some great shows, and some chaotic, albeit memorable, moments in the van.

Early on in the trip, while traveling through the Netherlands, the band's van broke down and they ended up stranded.

"It's in the middle of winter, and all of the sudden I see this axle and it's passing us on the freeway. All of the sudden our car drops. It's just scraping the ground," Mark said.

Stranded with a toddler in tow, Carlo and Monica Steward decided to go off and find help, while the rest stayed behind. It was January, it was cold, and nobody spoke the language.

"We ended up at some farm house in the Netherlands, and the people who were our age—the kids of the farmers—were leaving, and they left Carlo and me there with these grandparents who spoke no English," Steward recalled.

The others that stayed behind remained with the broken down van, doing their best to stay warm in a bizarrely unlucky situation.

"We were all, like, huddled together in the van, with our arms around each other singing, 'It's a Small World After All,'" Robert said. "And that's how we kept our warmth and energy in the sub-zero German terrain. That's what makes you a family, you know?"

The two eventually returned to the rest of the group to bring them to the house where the elderly couple lived, and they left the freezing cold van for the warmth of the nearby home.

"He finally gets back an hour later and he goes, 'Come on! I found a house, let's go!'" Mark recalled. "So we all hiked, and we got to this house. This older couple invites us in—they can't speak English. They invited us in, they fed us, they took care of us until we could get a roadside van to come and get us."

The Drifters, who were en route to Amsterdam at this point, waited with the elderly couple until a van could come and take them to a local airport where they would fly to Amsterdam. The van that arrived wasn't especially passenger friendly, however.

"It was one of those big mechanical vans, right? So, the front seat is just two front seats. And the back is just racks and racks and racks of parts and tools. We had to stand with our guitars in this little tiny aisle up and down the van until we got to the airport," Mark recalled.

A rough start to the tour, but the Drifters were undeterred. They were energized by the warm reception the album was getting and excited about playing to enthusiastic audiences.

A show in Bremen found the band in especially great form—working through a set of songs that started with "A Song for You" and also included new songs like Peter's "Darlin Darlin" and Carlo's "Zoo."

"Zoo" painted the picture of a wild animal escaping from a zoo and running amuck, drinking to excess and causing all sorts of mayhem.

> *That creature tore up my neighborhood bar*
> *It drank up all my favorite brew*
> *That wild thing that got out of the zoo*
> *You could be the victim or the perpetrator, too*
> *Well, best you be careful or that beast might get out of you*

It was a song in which Carlo seemed to be poking fun at himself and his proclivity for drugs and alcohol. And while all of the Drifters liked to drink and—with the exception of Vicki—do drugs, Carlo had gone far beyond using recreationally by the time they got to Germany.

"Heroin, crack, you name it. Lots of alcohol on top of all of it," Mark said. "[It had] gotten to those kinds of points where he should have died himself, probably, a thousand times."

Carlo's addiction had been prevalent in the band in the years leading up to that tour, but reached its breaking point in Germany. Karen Schoemer, who kept in touch with the band and saw them often after profiling them for the *L.A. Weekly* in 1992, recalls going to a show at Maxwell's in Hoboken, New Jersey, in 1995 when she was living there. Carlo's fellow Drifters were concerned enough about him by then that they asked Schoemer and her husband for a favor.

"They asked [my then-husband Dave] and I to 'babysit' Carlo," Schoemer said. "They wanted us to take Carlo home with us after the show to keep him out of trouble.",

It turned out okay, as Schoemer recalls, and they ended up having a nice time together.

"Carlo came back to our house, and we had an amazing time but nobody got into any serious injury, nobody got lost, nobody got mugged," she said. "We kept it kind of safe and clean, and had a great time with Carlo.

"He was kind of a wild man at that time, but that night when he came back to our house he just wanted to talk about music. And he was just fun and sweet and exuberant. We ended up really seeing that side of him."

Carlo's addiction was a going concern for several years by then, and for the Drifters it had gotten to a point where they felt unable to maintain any control over the way Carlo acted when he was high.

One example of note was a gig on September 13, 1995, when the Drifters played Capital City Stadium in Columbia, South Carolina, with Hootie, Edwin McCain, Cravin Melon, Cowboy Mouth, and Dillon Fence. Carlo, Peter recalls, didn't make a good impression on that day; bossing around soundmen and being generally demanding.

It wasn't the first time that'd happened. The magnetism of his songwriting and musicianship was undeniable, so for years his behavior was something his bandmates just had to deal with.

"I don't know what else Carlo was doing," Robert said. "I just know that he drank a lot, and was a belligerent asshole at times. But that's Carlo. And what he'd give you was just fucking beautiful on stage.

"Such a great, soulful musician. And a beautiful, beautiful person, and *such* a pain in the ass. If you want the good, you get the bad."

The darkest parts of Carlo often collided head on with Peter, who recalls one night on the 1996 German tour when Carlo made an arrangement suggestion and Peter's response set him off.

"He said something or other about an arrangement; a change we should make in the song. And I said, 'God, that is so Bourbon Street,'" Peter recalled. "He didn't jump off the drums at me, but I think that was a really turning point in our communications. I think that the lines were drawn."

Throwing in last-minute arrangement and structural changes to songs wasn't typical for Carlo, but Peter remembers that tour being "weird" because of the "arrangement shit" he kept wanting to try.

One issue between the two, which had started all the way back in L.A. and remains a bit of Drifters lore to this day, was a specific cymbal accent Carlo came up with during "Who We Are, Where We Live."

You're headed down the highway, suddenly jackKNIFED

A simple accent on that line, emphasizing the "knifed" in "jackknifed," might seem innocuous enough, but Peter wasn't convinced.

"Carlo, to his credit, only did that accent when he was mad at me," Peter said. "I always thought it was a more elegant song without that. I'm the professor, right? I'm the guy that doesn't like to be wrong."

Well, neither did Carlo. And he was also butting heads with Mark a lot on the German tour—culminating in a pair of disastrous performances that were filmed across two nights for a *Rolling Stone* video feature on the band.

The first night, Carlo was so drunk that he wasn't able to stay on his drum throne.

"He fell off of his chair, literally. Like, in a drunken way. Not, 'Whoops, slipped,'" Susan recalled.

The second night proved to be a huge disaster, and a tipping point for the rest of the band.

Crammed onto a relatively small stage, Mark was positioned right in front of Carlo—blocking cameras from being able to see him. Carlo didn't take this lightly, and kept trying to get Mark to move out of his way, but there was too little space.

"He had drunk maybe four bottles of wine, too, by that point," Mark said. "He had all of these bottles around him. He kept asking for another bottle, and they just kept bringing them."

Mid-song, Carlo had enough and started taking his drunken anger out on Mark.

"He was getting so mad at me that he was just throwing drumsticks at my head and just being belligerent," Mark recalled. "For me it was like, that's all unacceptable. To do that live on a stage, and to get the brunt of that kind of bullshit."

After the gig, as they arrived at their hotel, Carlo got out, vomited, and walked inside.

"Somebody slipped on the puke," Steward recalled. "They were so pissed."

The next morning, as they were leaving the hotel. Carlo noticed a giant red stain on the sidewalk and thought someone had dropped an ICEE on the ground.

"We're like, 'No, Carlo, don't you remember you vomited?'" Mark said. "And he goes, 'I didn't vomit! What are you talking about?' He's getting all pissy and Carlo-like.

"He was just in such denial at that point. Too much alcohol, too many drugs, too much of everything."

When they returned to New Orleans from the tour, Carlo's substance abuse continued to get worse. Finally, the rest of the band decided that enough was enough. It was one thing to party, but Carlo's substance abuse and erratic behavior was another thing entirely.

Mark recalled: "When Carlo and I were roommates back in Los Angeles, we got crazy. We had crazy fun nights doing stupid drugs and doing all kinds of things. Staying up all night for days or whatever. But by the time we got to New Orleans, I felt I had a responsibility. I've left my business with my brother, I'm in a new city where I'm trying to figure out how to fit in and where I belong there.

"I had to be responsible. I just said, 'Okay, that part of my life is behind me.'"

Even Peter acknowledges doing heroin with Carlo when they lived in Los Angeles.

"I can't lie about that," he said.

Despite their indulgences, the band had gotten good at balancing partying with the demands of life. When it was time to sober up, they could and would.

"In reality, everyone else is functional for the most part. Not purely, and not our best selves obviously," Vicki said.

Concerned for Carlo's well-being and needing to make a change, the band gathered at Scott Aiges' house when they returned home from Germany and staged an intervention to get him help and also emphasize where they stood as a band.

"What we brought to Carlo was, 'You're freaking us out. This is not us; this is different,'" Susan recalled.

It was, as Mark describes, a "very uncomfortable" meeting, and Carlo was not at all receptive to the band's outreach.

"We were all just sitting around being very honest and very caring, and all he could say is, 'Fuck y'all. Fuck you,'" he said.

Adds Susan: "His big comeback was, 'Fuck all y'all hypocrites.' Because we're all partying. Sorry, but that's *not* what we're talking about."

Carlo was calling his bandmates out on their own bad habits. But, as they all understood, there was a huge difference at the time.

"He kind of looked around the room and went, 'Are you fucking kidding me?' And he wasn't wrong, but everyone else was functional and able to do their job," Vicki said.

From Carlo's perspective, according to the rest of the band, it felt like they were giving him an ultimatum: get help or leave. Whether they were drawing a definitive line or not remains unclear, but that is how Carlo interpreted the confrontation. He was defiant, bucking their efforts to impart just how worried they were for him.

"At the time, it felt untenable," Peter recalled. "What had been a brotherhood, sisterhood kind of thing was fraying. And it seemed to be coming from Carlo."

This wasn't the first time the band had tried to convince Carlo to get sober. A few years earlier, in L.A., they staged a similar intervention that was also not successful. That intervention inspired Peter's "I Am A Tree," which appeared on his 1997 solo record *Out of My Way*.

"Carlo did say, 'I'm a fuckin' tree. I'm going to outlive all of y'all,'" he said.

The New Orleans meeting, while not intended to be a vehicle for Carlo's dismissal, resulted in just that, with Carlo Nuccio leaving the band he founded some five years earlier.

"We weren't just kicking him out. We were telling him that we were concerned about him," Vicki said. "It couldn't go on as it was, so a change had to be made. You can't just say, 'Oh, I'll be better.' Because it doesn't work that way for most people. Plus, it wasn't the first time we'd had this conversation.

"Nobody wanted him gone, we just wanted him better."

Unfortunately, there would be no way for the Drifters to convince Carlo to get sober, and therefore no way to continue as things were.

By the time Carlo left, the Drifters were already a completely different band from the original lineup. But this was an incomparable loss—some bands would even consider it a death blow. *The* founding member, a principal songwriter, the defining rhythmic element in the group, and one of its most unique voices, was gone.

On a personal level, the family they'd created together was splitting up. It impacted not just the band members, but also people like Monica Steward, who had become a member of the Drifter club as both Carlo's partner and Miranda's nanny.

"It was hard, and I was kind of stuck in the middle because I still wanted to work with Miranda, but I don't think he was happy that I was still working with them," Steward said.

At the end of the day, nobody took this lightly; not just because of what they were losing musically, but also because of what they were losing as a unit. New Orleans made them a family.

"That was heartbreaking and terrifying to me," Susan said. "I was losing a mentor. He was one of the first people who went, 'Fuck your brothers! Pick that guitar up. Fuck you—that's an A [chord]. Do it. Fuckin' pick that thing up.'"

"That was a really, really funky ass time," Robert added. "It was a difficult time. We pretty much cut off a limb when Carlo was gone."

Vicki admits that she was especially skeptical about the future of the Drifters without Carlo, especially when it came to the way they would be perceived going forward.

"I'm a little change-averse, naturally," she said. "And I just couldn't imagine the band without Carlo. He brings all of that New Orleans juiciness and spiciness. His vocal style and the way he plays was just so unique. I was afraid that we were going to turn into a generic pop band if we didn't have that spice.

"Now it's Peter, Susan, and me, and the three of us are graduates of pop bands. That's what we do. So I was a little concerned that it was going to make a huge shift in the band."

The Drifters had come too far at this point to call it a day, but there was no doubt that losing Carlo meant losing a major part of the band's identity. They had some West Coast shows on the books, so they needed to fulfill those obligations. They'd also been preparing material for a follow-up to their debut, and were also pursuing—finally—a demo deal with a major label.

All of that propelled the band forward, ready to face the uncertainty of the Drifters without Carlo.

Chapter Five:
An Energy, Not a Volume

*"Ninety-five out of a hundred gigs, it was nearly, and sometimes
actually, out of body experiences for me. That would last until
the end."*

—Russ Broussard

Part I

Remember that second RV trip that the Drifters took in 1993, right before the band started leaving L.A. and making the move to New Orleans? Well, as we know, Monkey Hill liked to have parties.

And, as with the 1992 NOLA Occupation/Invasion/Conquest, there was enough excitement for the Continental Drifters' arrival in New Orleans that Monkey Hill threw them a welcome party. Other Monkey Hill artists were in attendance too, including The Bluerunners—a Cajun rock band that at the time was prepping the release of *The Chateau Chuck*, which was produced by Peter's dB's bandmate Gene Holder.

The Bluerunners hit it off with the Drifters at the Monkey Hill gathering, and the two bands became fast friends. Bluerunners drummer Russ Broussard seemed to get along especially well with them, though.

"Susan and I were the two that were cut from the most similar cloth," Russ said. "She was the first person I saw when I walked into the party, with a big pregnant belly. And I basically darted across the room and put my hands on her belly."

The friendship between the Drifters and The Bluerunners continued and led to shared gigs around Louisiana. In cities like Baton Rouge and Lafayette, The Bluerunners would headline; selling out 700-capacity clubs. In New Orleans, they would open for the Drifters.

"In New Orleans, we just never had a big following," Russ said "They just didn't jive on us. We'd get the same 30 people every gig."

Peter and Russ had already played together, too, after Peter was asked by Bluerunners' bandleader Mark Meaux to step in for bassist Rob Savoy at a local gig.

"The band had a show at the Howlin' Wolf, and they were like, 'Would you play bass?' And I'm like, 'Oh, fuck yeah. That's going to be easy to play Zydeco bass.' But I was totally out of my depth," Peter recalled in amusement.

Russ had also hit it off personally with Mark, who recalls his first formal hang with Russ happening during the Mardi Gras following his move to town.

"When I first moved there, I was in a Mardi Gras parade and we were both in it together. I was taking mushrooms and just stoned out of my mind," he said. "I didn't know anybody, really. It was just Jimmy Ford and a bunch of his knucklehead friends, and then all of these crazy New Orleans old timers marching in this thing.

"I sort of bonded with this kid [Broussard] because he was laughable, and he had a lot of fun. I was like, 'Oh, I need to be around you!'"

Russ remembers feeling that same gravitation to the Drifters whenever he spent time with them. They seemed to fit together personality-wise; case in point being the band's infamous "drag night" performances, a tradition that started back at Raji's. And it's exactly what it sounds like: The guys would dress in women's clothing, and vice versa.

"Vicki and I had the best time because we would go looking for their clothes and stuff," Susan said. The whole band was game for drag night—though Gary, as Susan notes, was "more prone to the Prince Valiant, 'Prince' look."

Drag nights weren't a constant thing, but they did happen on several occasions in both L.A. and New Orleans.

"I know when I was in the band, at Raji's, I think we did two," Carlo recalled. "Maybe I wasn't even there for one of them, because I only remember my dress for one."

Russ' first drag night experience was a Bluerunners/Drifters date in New Orleans, where he remembers absolutely loving it. His bandmates? Not so much.

"I just thought it was so fun, and my fellow Bluerunner mates were just, like, mortified," he said. "That's how I started to get the clue, like, 'I'm in the wrong band. I need to be in that band!'"

While the Drifters/Bluerunners friendship thrived, both bands' relationships with Monkey Hill did not. By the mid-1990s, the label was not picking up much steam despite its best intentions.

"What the plan seemed to be was to make Monkey Hill a viable custom label for another concern," Peter said. "Which is what people did at that point. [There were] a lot of regional labels. And there was a move to try to establish New Orleans as a rock and roll place. They wanted to be taken seriously that way."

The plan for the Drifters was always to find "something bigger," as Peter said, hence the decision to withhold material from the eponymous record. Ultimately, there really was no desire or plan to make another record for the label. Monkey Hill had also just partnered with a distributor out of Atlanta called Ichiban Records, which Peter was openly skeptical of.

"I remember distinctly having a conversation at the table downstairs at Monkey Hill with Jimmy when he said that Ichiban was going to be the distributor for Monkey Hill," he said. "I was like, 'Really?' And Jimmy was incensed. He was really mad because he felt like this was the best opportunity for the label. It was really about the first time in our long relationship that I had kind of run up against him about something.

"I think that was sort of the beginning of the end of that."

With the Monkey Hill relationship dissolving, the band was ready for something new. Suffering the major blow of losing Carlo would have been the breaking point for other bands, but the Drifters knew they still had something to offer.

They made a decision not to try and replace Carlo directly, i.e. bringing another songwriting drummer and vocalist into the fold to make up for the material that they no longer had at their disposal. Instead, they doubled down on their own songwriting output.

Peter, Susan, and Vicki, all made it a point to write more songs after Carlo's departure;

woodshedding and demoing them over the course of several months. Robert and Mark also started bringing songs and ideas to the table. Robert's contribution to the pool, the tender and vulnerable "Heart, Home," was especially popular among the rest of the band.

"We were all duly knocked out by that [song]," Peter recalled.

There was a rehearsal room in Mark's house in Lakeview, adjacent to his garage, where the Drifters got together and demoed the songs they were working on in the immediate post-Carlo months. Songs like "Heart, Home" were demoed to cassette during these sessions, as were some new compositions from all three primary writers. Peter said these demos gave the band "courage and hope" to move forward as a unit.

By mid-'96, they had garnered some buzz in the States around their self-titled debut, done some sizable domestic touring, and garnered a significant club following in Germany. They also, notably, were named one of the top two unsigned bands in America that year by *Rolling Stone*. All the more reason to keep it going.

There were other reasons for them to stick with it, too—namely, more dates with Hootie on the books as well as other shows they'd already committed to when Carlo was in the band.

The gigs were keeping them focused, but the songwriting was truly what kept the band hungry for more.

"That just, once again, kind of drew us together in a moment of crisis. Do we continue? How do we continue?" Peter said.

Their biggest opportunity yet came in the summer of '96, when they were offered a demo deal from Mercury Records courtesy of Jim Fouratt, noted gay rights activist, nightclub impresario, and—from 1995 to 1999—Vice President of A&R at Mercury.

Fouratt was a friend of Peter, who even knew his brother Curtis in the 1970s when they ran in the same New York City circles. He also knew Mark from the early-'80s Paisley Underground scene in Los Angeles, through The Dream Syndicate.

Fouratt first saw the Drifters at Raji's early on.

"At that point I was working at Rhino [with] Gary Stewart—a wonderful person who absolutely and truly loved music and loved independent artists," Fouratt said, emphasizing that seeing the Drifters was like "musical church."

"Those nights, once a week, were salvation for me."

Fouratt started at Mercury in 1995, and soon got the label interested enough in the Drifters to record a handful of songs in the hopes that they would offer an album deal. Demo deals, in those days, weren't uncommon but are almost unheard of in today's bedroom studio landscape.

"I gave them a demo deal because I wanted to find a way to convince Danny Goldberg, who was the President of Mercury, that they had the potential of bringing forward the craft of songwriting in contemporary music," Fouratt said.

While several Drifters had experience recording demos for writing and production purposes, Vicki said she actively avoided doing demos as much as possible in her Bangles years.

She explains: "In my experience, if you demoed a song, one of two things happened: Either you never achieve what you got in that demo when you go in to re-record it, or it kills the song and you don't want to re-record it

"I was in a band, and in my philosophy, the band grows the song. In the early days of The Bangles, formally demoing songs never happened. Later on it did, when people were writing with other writers. But I kind of chafed against that, personally."

The Mercury deal was a crossroads moment for the band, and they were ready to finally get the offer they'd been hoping for and ultimately find the audience their music needed. They enlisted Kevin Salem, former guitarist for Boston-based college rock stalwarts Dumptruck, to produce a set of songs that including "The Rain Song," "Who We Are, Where We Live," and new songs like Peter's "Darlin Darlin," and Susan's autobiographical "Spring Day in Ohio."

Salem, a solo artist and songwriter who also played guitar with Yo La Tengo, knew Peter from coming up in the 1980s. By the time he got the Drifters' call, he had already released two albums for Roadrunner Records. He was friendly with the band already, seeing them at Maxwell's in Hoboken, New Jersey. He recalls being "blown away" by what they did.

"There were other people approaching Americana [at the time], but were a little less talented," Salem said and laughed.

After seeing an especially great show at the Mercury Lounge in New York, Salem says he decided then and there that he wanted to produce the band.

"The thing I really wanted to do was to walk up to Susan Cowsill and say, 'I'm going to be the next person who records your voice,'" he said, calling her voice "astonishing."

"It is so rich, and has so much in it. When I heard Susan's voice, I was like, 'Holy shit,'" Salem added. "I think I kind of lobbied Vicki and was like, 'I have to record you guys.'"

Fouratt also cites Susan's voice as a major attraction in what made him a genuine fan of the band.

"Susan's voice, unlike Fleetwood Mac—who they sometimes get compared to—is so distinctively American," he said. "And the clarity of her voice, which comes out of The Cowsills, always sets the stage for the Continental Drifters. That pull towards, if I may use this word, a more commercial sense of the songwriting than not."

Fouratt says the distinct combination of Susan and Vicki's vocals was also a selling point.

"I had a sense that they trusted each other as two women in this band, with very complicated males," he laughed.

When Salem got involved, the band had already gotten the wheels in motion with Fouratt—who says he was convinced by the Drifters to work with Salem on the demos.

"With the Drifters, I had to deal with the experience of the people in that band. They weren't a little indie rock band that I had found that would do anything I said or suggested. And they wanted Kevin Salem," Fouratt recalled. "Now, I respected Kevin Salem as an artist. I didn't know him as a producer, but I thought the relationships with the members of the band, and their desire, was important to give recognition to."

Salem says he had muted expectations about what would come from the session, based on his experience with and understanding of these sort of demo contracts.

"I'm not really aware of anyone ever having gotten signed from one of their demo deals," he said. "It's like a way for an A&R person to express love for something that is probably too good to be on a major label."

By the time the session came around, Salem had become close with Vicki, and had seen multiple Drifters shows. He noticed immediately that there was a dynamic and an intimacy that went beyond any band he'd ever seen.

"They really knew each other on every level; cared about each other on so many levels," he said. "That is a really challenging thing to step into as a producer."

They'd also found a drummer in Rob Ladd, a North Carolina session and touring player who was an old acquaintence of Peter's. He'd thought of Ladd for the job when he was out with Hootie, and Ladd was playing drums for Peter's longtime friend Don Dixon, who was opening those shows.

"I was like, 'You know, Rob Ladd is really great. Let's get him down—we need a drummer, and he's a fast study," Peter recalled.

If Ladd was indeed a fast study, it's because by 1996 he'd become a prominent session player after spending years in his own projects and touring in smaller bands. He grew up in Chapel Hill, and got started in bands in high school. He formed acclaimed Carolinas ska band The Pressure Boys in 1981.

"We just fell in love with the ska thing that had started happening," he said. "I saw The Specials on *Saturday Night Live* and lost my shit. I went to school on Monday and some of my friends had seen it, too. We started investigating and we found all these bands like Madness and The Selecter."

The Pressure Boys' first recordings were recorded with R.E.M. producer and Let's Active frontman Mitch Easter, at the insistence of Let's Active drummer Sara Romweber—a personal hero of Ladd's.

"She didn't know it, of course, but she taught me how to play drums," he said.

Through Easter, Ladd met Dixon (Easter's co-producer on the first two R.E.M. albums), as well as Peter and his dB's bandmate Chris Stamey.

"We just instantly found access. We had access to this whole, sort of, North Carolina/Athens/ New York music scene," Ladd said. "It's not like we were part of it, but we had access to it."

Dixon soon began hiring Ladd for sessions, and Ladd would run into Peter at sessions and gigs. He moved to L.A. in 1988, where he swore off of bands and record deals and began trying to get more session work.

"Everyone said, 'Well, you've got to go to either New York or L.A. to do that," he said of his decision to go west.

While in Los Angeles, Ladd saw the Drifters at Raji's a few times. At the time he was playing with Vicki's fellow Bangle Susanna Hoffs on her first solo tour, and was also playing with Go-Go's guitarist Charlotte Caffey in the band The Graces. That band, he says, actually played at Raji's on the same night as the Drifters, albeit on a separate bill.

Despite all of that cross pollination, Ladd says, he didn't see Peter much during his L.A. years.

"You can get in your own world out there," he said. "Peter and I were in different worlds."

Ladd got his biggest break in 1994 when he was hired by producer Glen Ballard to play on an album he was doing for Canadian singer Alanis Morrissette. That album, *Jagged Little Pill*, featured a song called "Ironic," which Ladd played drums and percussion on. The album and the song were both massive hits, and *Jagged Little Pill* still stands as one of the best-selling albums of all time.

And so, when Carlo left the band, Rob Ladd got the call.

"I don't really know why Peter wanted me to do it, because I don't play like Carlo did," he said. "But I was, of course, excited and thrilled."

It was an exciting time, but also a "turbulent" time for Ladd, he says, because his wife was just about to have their daughter and they were moving into a new house. Still, he made the trip to New Orleans for an audition and some gigs.

When it came time to record, the band holed up in a small studio in New Orleans with

Salem to knock out the demos and submit them to Mercury. The studio, described by Salem as "a bunker," was hot, the band was anxious to get the songs recorded, and there were two new people in the fold who hadn't worked with them in a studio setting before.

While the sessions were friendly and everyone got along, there was some concern about how things would pan out.

"It was very tight and under the gun, and they were very tense about the whole thing," Scott Aiges said. "The sessions ended up being something of a disappointment."

As Peter puts it, these post-Carlo sessions meant there were "two new personalities added on to the five-piece hydra of the Continental Drifters." That was no easy thing, by any means.

What was Ladd's biggest takeaway from the session?

"They hated me," he said with a laugh.

For the record, nobody in the band recalls "hating" Ladd as a drummer. He is, as everyone notes, an incredible talent and versatile drummer. But there was definitely a feeling that it wasn't the right fit.

"My recollection is that he was a little bit more overtly 'technician' than them," Salem said. "When you put somebody under a microscope, which was my job, you discover things about players."

Salem says he quickly discovered a lot about the Drifters and the way they work, making the session easy to navigate from a workflow perspective.

"First of all, nobody plays tambourine better than Susan Cowsill," he said. "But also for her, [as a vocalist] it was systematic. Here are three takes: Take one, which is going to make us wonder why we're going to do take two. Take two, which might be somebody suggesting stuff; me or another band member, or her looking for something in her performance. And take three, which is just, let's make sure we're not leaving anything on the table."

Salem also discovered that Peter had a fairly unusual way of keeping himself in pitch as a singer.

"I look up at one point and Peter's got a tuner in his hand. He's overdubbing a vocal and he's got a tuner! Autotune was invented to help people sound like the Continental Drifters."

Essentially, Salem says, the Drifters "needed a lot less direction" than some of the other bands he'd been working with as a producer. That made for an easy session in some respects, but there was, still, the feeling all around that Rob Ladd wasn't a great fit for the band.

"I don't think they were super happy with my feel, and that is to be expected because they'd been playing with Carlo," Ladd said. "He had the greatest feel. It was perfect."

Ladd says that this concern wasn't just coming from the band—he himself also felt like he wasn't vibing with them on a musical level. And, of course, there was the non-musical dynamic; the oft-impenetrable wall that separated the Drifters from many on the outside.

"I didn't feel like I fit into that family," he said. "Not because of them; they were extremely welcoming, and extremely gracious and beautiful. I just didn't feel like I was a good fit for them. More than any group that I've ever worked with, that was a family."

Aiges also points to the closeness in the band as a roadblock between the band members and Ladd.

"It wasn't that *he* wasn't gelling," he said. "They knew him and loved him, and he loved them, and it was wonderful. But it was also under the circumstances of, 'We need a sub drummer for these sessions.' And coming in as a hired gun, he was not part of the family.

"One of the things about that band is, it was very much family. That was one of the things that made it kind of difficult for me. You're expected to be there at Thanksgiving; you're expected to be there at Christmas."

Salem says he didn't think about whether he'd end up getting a job with them if they got an album deal out of the demo sessions. His primary objective, he says, was to "get them a recording that they could use, regardless of whether they got signed to Mercury or not."

"I would have recommended to them that they work with Brendan O'Brien or somebody that was making hit records," he added. "I looked at that as the document. That was the record."

After a whirlwind session and a quick mixing process, the band sent the six-song demo to Mercury and waited to hear back. Despite the tension and the feeling that things weren't feeling exactly right with Ladd, Aiges says the band still had hope that the songs would stand out.

Ultimately, as demo deals often go, Mercury wasn't interested in going any further. The nail in the demo coffin, though, was Jim Fouratt's lack of enthusiasm.

"When we finally sent them, with much fanfare, up to Jim, what he told me is, 'I don't love 'em,'" Aiges recalled.

Fouratt confirms: "I sensed that there was something, when they got in the studio, that wasn't clicking. They weren't in that comfortable pool of members together trusting each other enough to be wildly open in their expression."

There was also a sense, as Fouratt admits, that Kevin Salem was too close a friend to be the kind of producer the band needed.

"They respected him as an artist, he respected them as a friend," Fouratt said. "He could not say, 'What the fuck are you doing? Can you please get it together? Your ass is on the line here, and you are capable of doing what you do best. And it's not happening.'"

Fouratt's approach during the session was to remain hands off, because he doesn't believe that encroaching on the process is "the role of the A&R person." Years later, he questions that approach and wonders if he should have done something different.

"Maybe I should have gone in and said, 'We're not going to work with Kevin anymore. You're too close to him.'" Fouratt said. "I just was never that kind of guy that would say, 'Fuck it. This money is being spent, my ass is on the line here, and this is what I want you to do. Wake up.' I'm just not that guy. And I think that, maybe, it was a mistake on my part.

"And this has nothing to do with the creative ability of Kevin Salem. He's a crafted song-writer, and he's a sensitive ear. A sensitive man. But they were too close."

The potential deal with Mercury was gone in an instant. Nobody was at fault, the session just didn't yield the results they needed.

"Everybody was very disappointed, you know?" Aiges said. "It was like, 'Well, we had this shot, and we blew it.' There was a lot of heartache and a lot of disappointment. The industry is a dog eat dog place, and if things don't line up for you exactly perfectly, then it ain't happening."

What made the band miss their shot with Mercury? Nobody could argue that it was the songs, and the recordings themselves were sonically well done. The reality is likely that it was a combination of things, but from Salem's perspective, it was also a marketability question on the label's part.

"One of [the Drifters'] greatest attributes is that they had three people; any one of whom was good enough to be a lead singer in a band that could accomplish any level of success," he said. "That is their greatest attribute. It is also probably one of the greatest challenges, at that time, for the record industry. That is a head scratcher, believe it or not.

"I do remember people saying at the time, 'Well, we don't know who the lead singer would be.'"

Aiges said he'd tried not only to make the Mercury deal happen, but also spent time in New York attempting to make connections and get some traction; efforts that proved unsuccessful. The demo deal with Mercury, he says, was the best they'd been able to do.

"It was like a mercy deal from Jim Fouratt. Jim, god bless him, managed to get a demo deal out of Mercury, but they weren't ready to offer a regular record deal. And nobody else was offering [anything]," he recalled.

Labels not quite knowing what to do with the Continental Drifters wasn't an entirely new phenomenon at this juncture. In fact, Mark McKenna recalls showing colleagues at A&M Records the band's shelved debut in the hopes that they'd be interested, but they didn't bite.

"I was disappointed that it didn't really happen for that record," McKenna said. "I remember playing it for people at A&M, and I couldn't get them interested. I just could *not* get them interested in it. It was a let down. I was a bit surprised that people were not interested.

"It could've been simply due to lack of organization. I would've thought that there could've been a home for them. But a lot of that comes down to organization. And these guys weren't particularly organized. They were kind of living at Raji's, and I don't know how cohesive their vision was for working."

Whatever reasons A&M might have had in 1993, and Mercury had in 1996, the Drifters were stuck in a frustrating position. They had a lot going for them and yet they couldn't get all of that to translate to a viable record contract.

Certainly some of this can be attributed to the level of ambition that being in a full-scale upstart band requires. They'd all had a decade, at least, of that kind of sacrifice before the Drifters. And as we know, the concessions that inevitably come with most record contracts were not the kind of things that the band members were interested in—stretching all the way back to that very first unreleased record.

For those who loved the band, that sort of thing would often be disappointing at best.

"The Drifters were a reprieve away from major label bullshit," Cheryl Pawelski recalled. "You had several members who had some pretty good bullshitty major label experiences, and there's a trade off in all of that. So I felt like they should be putting out their own records. That's why I was so frustrated, like, why are you waiting around?

"I was always wondering 'Where the hell is the record?' You could feel like there was hesitation. A lot of them had been through it and didn't want to make those same trade-offs."

Scott Aiges eventually found himself feeling burnout from the barriers that he was facing while trying to make things happen for the band; not to mention the fact that he was managing the self-proclaimed "unmanageable." The band's personalities were challenging for him as well (a sizable group of opinionated people who sometimes had an aversion to outsider input would certainly be a challenge to wrangle), and all of this created a perfect storm. It had become so taxing, in fact, that he'd begun seeing a therapist to deal with it.

"The story we tell in my house is that my wife fired them. She saw what it was doing to me," he said of his breaking business ties with the Drifters. "At a certain point my wife just put her foot down and said, 'Nope, they're fired.'"

Looking back on his year with the band, Aiges says he still wonders what exactly it was that was holding the band back on the business side.

"Of course you can't help but wonder if the reason that they didn't become rich and famous is because I was a bad manager, or I was too young and inexperienced to be able to understand opportunities that might have been there and take advantage of them, or just didn't have enough clout," he said. "Susan was the first person to volunteer, 'We're completely unmanageable.' And I think that may be true. And, frankly, I don't think that's a bad thing. I think that they are who they are, and whatever it is that makes them who they are is the same thing that makes them so fantastic."

Part II

There was perhaps no stranger, yet more crucial, year for the Continental Drifters than 1996. They'd started it off with strong international reception to their debut, received major critical notice as a top unsigned band in the country, parted ways with their drummer and founding member, and then had to essentially audition for a major label with a sub drummer. Losing Carlo was beyond monumental, and they had become an entirely new band without him.

It was a year to figure things out, and they decided that the best way forward with the drummer situation was to use hired players—hence Rob Ladd's addition. They had gigs with Hootie lined up for the summer, and a pair of West coast dates in the fall.

Right after the session with Salem and Ladd, on March 24, 1996, Mark got married in New Orleans with his Drifters bandmates—and Ladd—in attendance. His wife, Dana, wanted a gypsy jazz band to play so they hired a local group called the Tony Green Trio.

On the day, when the wedding band was loading in, Mark happened to run into their drummer outside of the venue.

"I went, 'Holy shit!'" Mark said.

The drummer was Russ Broussard.

"I show up at this beautiful house, a mansion in the Garden District," Russ said. "I'm loading in, and I run right smack into Mark Walton! And I'm like, 'Mark!' And he goes, 'Russ!' And we give each other a big hug

"I'm like, 'What are you doing here?' He's like, 'What are *you* doing here?' I barely played a note on that gig. I was visiting and dancing with them the whole time."

At the wedding, Mark came to the realization that the band might be better off playing with a local drummer instead of flying Ladd in and out of New Orleans whenever there were gigs. Russ had left the Bluerunners and was freelancing, so the chance to play together virtually fell into their laps.

"Ahh, *this* is the guy we should be asking to play!" Mark remembers thinking.

It was Scott Aiges, in fact, who called Russ and asked if he'd join the band as a live drummer. Aiges parted ways with the band soon after.

Russ was thrilled by the invitation, and the band set up an audition at the Mermaid Lounge where they ran through a handful of songs. Everyone hit it off instantly.

"My initial feeling was, he was obviously a technically brilliant player," Vicki recalled. "I could tell he had chops, as opposed to being a completely instinctive player as Carlo was, in a way.

"Russ was more thoughtful in what he was playing, which I thought was really interesting and different for us."

Peter also found Russ' musicality to be a good fit for the Drifters, as well as his willingness to collaborate and take feedback.

"He swung in a different way from Carlo's swing," he explained. "It's just a different thing; the vibe is different, and I think his willingness to try stuff and his interest in fitting into what the band was—yet knowing that his addition would change the complexion of it.

"He just knew how to fit in. He really had the gift of listening and finding the spaces to play in and not play in."

There was also a major personality difference from Carlo, which the band welcomed. Where Carlo could be brash and confrontational, Russ was bright and bubbly, if not a tad hyperactive.

"I remember me and Vicki going, 'Well, I don't know. If he can calm down enough…'" Susan laughed. "Russ was a pretty bright little shining star in the night."

"[Russ was] a whole lot of fun and had a positive attitude, which is really, really what we needed," Robert said. "He was totally game. He infused a lot of enthusiasm into the band.

"Carlo came to us fully formed; [Russ] was just that stray that showed up on the porch. And with Russ, we adopted a puppy. He grew up into his paws quite quickly. He was pretty adorable."

The success of the audition led to a festival appearance just a short time later, where Russ made his debut with the Continental Drifters. Aiges, who was still managing the band when Russ was hired, prepped him for the gig, and provided recordings and a master list of songs to learn from.

"It was DATs, a shit ton of cassettes, and a list of about 75 songs," Russ said. "And I had, like, four days to learn them."

His career as a freelancer prepared Russ for the quick turnaround and enabled him to learn all of the band's material in time for his first show. There was just one problem, though.

"The funny thing that Scott Aiges didn't do is tell me to disregard any of Carlo's songs, and give me the titles. Or to disregard any of Gary's songs, and give me the titles," Russ recalled. "We're talking on the drive up and they're like, 'Oh, no no no. We're not doing *that*. We won't do *that*.'"

As it turns out, Russ had learned not just songs from Peter, Susan, Vicki, Mark, and Robert, but also Carlo, Gary, and Ray. Because of this, he had a lot of trouble on that first gig keeping song titles straight.

He explained: "I could see something like 'Mixed Messages,' that title, and I would register a different song. I haven't listened thoroughly enough to even know what they're singing about. I'm just trying to get a basic drum idea and tempo.

"The first time that happened, I was so mortified. Oh my god, it's a drummer's worst nightmare. I was all fuckin' hung up on that kind of shit. But I realized, they're not. It's no big deal. Then I realized it could happen to anyone.

"That's the thing about that fucking band: Music was paramount. We would all give ourselves to the song. The goal was, get out of the way. Get out of the way of the song."

Taking a hired gun approach to the drummer dilemma seemed to be the way forward for the Drifters, at least for the time being. They did gigs with Russ where it made sense, but also followed through on commitments with Rob Ladd on a string of summer Hootie dates in the Northeast.

And in October of 1996, they flew to L.A. for two California gigs, where they hired DJ Bonebrake—drummer for the legendary punk band X—to fill in on drums. It was an experiment, so to speak, to try and see what the right way forward was as a band.

"We were just trying to find what could work and what couldn't work," Mark said. "And DJ was totally up for helping us do that."

Bonebrake knew a few of the Drifters from Los Angeles, but was mainly acquainted with Mark. He also met Robert while playing drums on Steve Wynn's *Kerosene Man* record.

"I just love his playing; he's one of those unique players," Bonebrake said of Robert. "He's got the mojo."

Bonebrake had actually worked with Gary Eaton about a month prior to the shows, when they both took part in a Beach Boys tribute at the El Rey Theatre in L.A., which benefitted an Autism awareness organization called the Wild Honey Foundation.

"I was playing mostly mallets, vibes, and marimba [that night]," he said.

While there was some crossover between the Drifters and Bonebrake, they didn't know each other especially well. Bonebrake suspects that there likely wasn't much lead time after he was hired for the gigs, meaning that the whole thing would have been a bit of a whirlwind.

They rehearsed for two days—an evening rehearsal on Wednesday, October 2, and an early morning rehearsal the following day. The shows took place across two consecutive nights—the first being at The Foothill in Long Beach on that Friday.

"It was an old country and western bar, and I think it opened in the late '40s or something," Bonebrake said. "They had big old photographs of famous Country and Western stars. It was that kind of place."

The next night, the band played at the Alligator Lounge on Pico Boulevard in Los Angeles, opening for Tito and Tarantula.

"I was probably furiously taking notes," Bonebrake said. "I do a lot of these things, and sometimes it works out great. And I'm sure they thought I did okay, but I know I didn't feel totally comfortable."

Being the professional he was, Bonebrake made the gig happen. But as he takes care to note, there's a difference between filling in and fitting in.

"I'm sitting in with this great group, and I'm going to do my best to try to make it sound like I know what I'm doing," he said. "I'm not being humble—I probably did as well as a lot of people, because I'm good at taking notes. I read and write music, so I probably caught all the accents. But that's a whole different thing than when you're feeling comfortable."

With both Ladd and Bonebrake, there just wasn't the chemistry that band was looking for. But with Russ, something was different. The more they were around each other, the more it felt like family. And, as with Susan and Peter before him, the band was even there for Russ when his and his wife Mary's son, Nick, was born.

"When his kid was on the way, we all went over to his house and cleaned it up," Robert recalled. "I remember painting rooms and redoing something in the kitchen. Every time somebody had a kid, we would all be asleep on the waiting room floor in the hospital. We'd just be camped out in the waiting room."

Of course, it was the musical connection that made things so easy and fun with Russ in the fold. He understood how the band operated creatively, and was willing to go on the ride—however it panned out.

"What other band goes on tour for seventeen days, and they come back and the songs have all gotten slower?" Russ said. "Most bands, they leave and by the time they get home the tempos have all jumped up a little bit.

"The Drifters would just settle in. It would just be this spacious, euphoric ride, you know? I might start the tour playing eighth notes on the hi hat, and by the end it's like, I'm not even playing the hi hat. We would have those magical kinds of nights the majority of the time."

There were, understandably, some small concerns at the beginning of the relationship;

notably, Vicki's concerns over whether Russ would be able to play the harder-hitting rock songs like "Who We Are, Where We Live."

"I felt like he was playing too carefully, and not rock enough," she said.

Russ internalized the critique at first, interpreting it as him needing to play louder.

"But at a certain point, it started to sink in that it's an energy," he explained. "Rock is an energy, not a volume. Yeah, it needs some volume, but it's not relative to that. And I can be my dynamic self."

Vicki was ultimately pleased to learn that Russ could, indeed, "rock" as she'd hoped. In fact, as she says, he "absolutely can knock the place over."

"He was so good, and it was so clear that he was good," she said.

Of this, the Drifters had no doubt: Russ was *the guy*. They were ready to make him a full-time offer and bring him on as a legitimate Continental Drifter. To make it official, Vicki, Susan, and Mark took Russ and Mary out for dinner where they asked him to join full time.

It was supposed to be a surprise, Susan says, but there wasn't much about the invitation that was surprising aside from the fact that it hadn't come sooner. Russ was the missing piece; a part of the club.

What does it mean to be an official part of the Continental Drifters? Russ says it was all pretty simple.

"It means now I have a voice in the band besides just drumming. It means I'm getting every call. Every gig is mine. There's not a chance that they go with another drummer," he said. "It's like signing adoption papers, you know? And it was not just for me, but it included my family. Instantly my mom and dad are now a part. I just signed on to be enveloped by, and envelope, them. To merge my sense of family with my blood family and theirs."

That familial embrace had already begun, so Russ says the offer was "almost an admittance."

"We would get home from a run and what's the first thing we do? We would all get together the next day on the lake and barbecue and play frisbee and shit. We don't need a break from one another," he said.

On a musical level, joining the band as a full-on member meant that Russ could have creative input as he saw fit, as the other Drifters did. There was no "session player" mentality required; no predetermined parts to replicate. The drums were his territory to explore.

"They invited me to be in the band, so now I can be free," he said. "But it already felt that way; that I could try things. I could play how I was hearing it. My background—at that point—is pretty diverse, you know? From Cajun music to playing in the Winston-Salem Symphony. And punk. I just felt like I could just be me there."

Let's get into a little bit of that background he speaks of, shall we?

"[I got my] first drum kit when I was two, from my grandmother," Russ said. "Most kids have a toy that they gravitate to; mine was a toy drum. It was like a stuffed animal to me. I never let it go. In the crib, as soon as I could sit up, I started playing it."

Russ' grandmother, he says, was extremely perceptive about the things her grandkids were interested in—even at extremely young ages. She always told them about Russ playing his toy drum or his sister, Kelly, pretending to read books before she actually could. Kelly went on to be a writer and English literature major.

"In the time it took me to read *Catcher in the Rye*, she had read *The Shining* and two other novels. Like, big fuckin' novels!" Russ said.

Nanny, as she was called, was spot on about her grandchildren. That first drum of Russ' didn't last long before he upgraded the next year. His first real snare drum came along when he was 6 years old.

"I still have it. I use it as my Mardi Gras marching snare," he said.

For the next few years after that, he "begged and pleaded" to get a full kit to go with his snare. His mom finally asked him, after about two years, if he'd compromise with one additional piece of a kit added.

"I was like, 'Ugh, it's gotta be either the kick or the hi hat.' I was just torn. I changed my mind a thousand times," he said. "On my ninth Christmas, the day before I turned 9, they got me my 1965 White Marine Pearl Ludwig kit, which is what I would play with the Drifters."

When it comes to that gut feeling musicians and creatives get, that moment where they know they've found their thing, Russ says he doesn't remember a time in his life where he *didn't* feel it. He's always been a drummer.

"I did have a number of naysayers; family members, you know? Not necessarily my immediate family. But my other grandmother and grandfather said that it was a nice hobby to have, and I had an uncle who was a real dick about it," he said. "'Don't be irresponsible. You need to develop a trade.' And I'm like, 'This *is* my trade."

There were times, he said, where he'd go a month without a gig or a short period when he couldn't find a job playing drums.

"Every time it wasn't working out, I'd panic and [say], 'Fuck, I should have listened to him.' And I'd go out and get another job. And would suck at it—horribly. It would be a waste of time and money," Russ said. "And then, surprisingly, a gig would come my way. Like a nice paying gig, or a steady gig. Out of the blue. I didn't go hunting for it. I never said I was giving up music; I needed to survive. So it was like, 'I'm going to wait tables. I have a friend who does that and he does really, really well. He's making $200 a day.' And I'd go in and I'd come away with $13."

Charting a career path was something that became possible at a relatively young age for Russ, with some of his first steady gigs including playing with legendary Cajun fiddler Hadley Castille and gigging with cover bands in Opelousas, Louisiana, where he lived.

"Cover bands back then, there was very little current music," he said. "In 1982, we probably were playing maybe one or two songs that were on the radio in the last five years. It was mostly early rock n' roll—the shit that was influencing The Beatles."

He left Opelousas to attend the University of North Carolina School of the Arts (coincidentally, in Peter's hometown of Winston-Salem), where he landed a paying gig with the Winston-Salem Symphony on pieces that required multiple percussionists.

"That was like a union gig," he said. "You'd get paid for the rehearsals—I was like, 'Wow!' I was just floored. And a performance, I'd walk away with $500. In 1983!"

He moved to San Francisco after that, where he played in bands, and also played for a time in Boulder, Colorado. Those bands were more rock and pop oriented, but he'd also get gigs playing with zydeco greats like Al Rapone and Queen Ida.

He ultimately moved back home, where he landed his "first real road gig" playing with Terence Simien.

"With Al Rapone, I think the longest we went out for was maybe two weeks," he said. "But the first year [with Terence], I think we did 315 dates."

While he enjoyed his time with Simien, Russ felt restricted by how rigid and cemented the set lists were, and there wasn't much fraternity among the band. When the opportunity came to join The Bluerunners after their drummer John Maloney left, he jumped in. They wanted him to join as a full member; giving him the chance to write and contribute creatively.

"I was just starved for *that,*" he said.

The band, he says, was ultimately "not a good match," and he left after a year-and-a-half. Free agency ultimately led him to the Tony Green Trio, playing Mark Walton's wedding, and hooking up with the Continental Drifters.

Russ fit like a glove with the Drifters, found that personal and creative spark he was looking for, and fell into the fold pretty quickly, but that doesn't mean it was an easy time for the others. Carlo had just left the band not even a year earlier, and not on good terms. To them, they'd lost a brother. Russ, a friend of Carlo's himself, says he understood that it would take time for the other Drifters to adjust to Carlo not being in the family anymore.

He recalled: "I heard all the stories. A person that is part of the family is out, so oftentimes they're in the van and they're getting through all of that shit. So I'm hearing a lot of Carlo stories. I would just sit. It's not my place. I just knew that this is a process that they have to do. And it's hard. Grief is complicated.

"There was a lot of that, and that goes on for a while. I'm the new guy; I'm the baby. I would say it had to take nearly a year—Carlo's name just stopped coming up. Something didn't trigger them; some memory or some incident."

For a band with a lot of baggage, it seemed like Russ had entered the fold with virtually none—something that was welcome to them, but didn't happen without personal work on his part.

"Before I got there, I did extensive therapy on myself," he said. "Lots of different types of therapy. I was unpacking my bags, per say. As soon as we enter adulthood, we're carrying all of that baggage from whatever we perceived in childhood. True or not, our perception of it can be misaligned or not good for us. We have to come to terms with it if it's not. So I did a lot of that work."

Getting to 1997 with the band still intact and a new drummer in the fold was an accomplishment in itself. For all their talent, the band had been a creatively emotional rollercoaster that reached dizzying heights and extreme lows. Pushing forward became an exercise in determination, as Susan says.

"It's like a dysfunctional family that won't break up," she asserted. "There is something palpable here, there is something valid here. There is something legit here. But it's wonky and it's not healthy."

When Russ joined, the band didn't realistically have much to hang onto—no label, several consequential lineup changes, no management. But what they did have was a deep love for what they'd created, and a deep affinity for each other on virtually every level.

And, obviously, there was the music—the songwriting, the chemistry, the spark. This was the thing that enabled them to get past the critical point of Carlo's departure, but also what brought them there in the first place. The music was what united them, but was so often also the catalyst for their most dysfunctional moments both artistically and personally.

In short, it took serious dedication to make it to 1997, and this was a pivotal moment for the future of the band.

Scott Aiges sums it up best: "They used to say about The Who that it was like a battery, and the acids have to mix in order for that particular spark to come together.

"[The Drifters] argued a lot, they kissed and hugged a lot. And somehow they managed to bring it together, write those great songs, and play them together on stage. But it took a lot to get there."

Chapter Six: Vermilion

"I've said this a million times, but: We're going to be in our 80s on somebody's front porch playing music."

— Vicki Peterson

Losing Carlo and gaining Russ put the Drifters in the unique position of, once again, starting anew. From a purely musical perspective, what they lost in Carlo's singular vocal style and swaggeringly groove-centric songs, they figured out how to compensate for with a more focused and streamlined emphasis on classic pop sensibility.

And luckily for them, in regard to "the family," they didn't lose anything—in fact, they found a different, but equally as fitting, personality in Russ. The tight bond of lineups past was not lost.

"We wanted that. That was part of who the band was," Mark said. "Even from the very beginning, everybody would come to Carlo's and my Batch Pad. We'd sit there and make dinner all day, and drink a lot and talk and tell jokes and have fun. It's just part and parcel to the whole community aspect of what we were and are."

It's amazing Russ fit in as well as he did with the Drifters, even though the writing was on the wall years earlier when he'd first become friendly with them. In truth, Drifter history has proven that fitting in wasn't easy. Mark remembers calling Wilco drummer Ken Coomer after Carlo left to see if he'd be interested in playing with the Drifters.

"I just thought he was a great drummer," he recalled. "So I called him and said, 'Hey, we're looking for a drummer.' And he just went, 'Ah, no thank you. Nope.' He saw the dynamic."

The fortuitous addition of Russ to the Drifters dynamic immediately started paying dividends musically, but in true Drifters fashion, their lives also began to overlap in ways that were just plain strange—like Mark and Russ' wives both giving birth to their sons a day apart, and the two families literally passing each other in the hospital.

"We were just being discharged as they were being wheeled in," Mark said. "We saw them. That was pretty bizarre."

Capitalizing on this meant one thing for the Drifters: Getting into a studio immediately and doing *something*.

"The first album that they put out was basically dead in the water, because it was [on] Monkey Hill. So the first thing that they wanted was to get me on record with them," Russ recalled.

As it happens, at the same time the band was looking to record with Russ, a small local label out of Oxford, Mississippi, was getting going. Black Dog Records was owned by Cary Hudson and Laurie Stirratt, guitarist/singer and bassist/singer, respectively, for Oxford band Blue Mountain, and Hudson's cousin Chris.

Blue Mountain had been friends with the Drifters for a few years, but Hudson and Stirratt—married at the time—first saw the band in Los Angeles when they were living there in the early 1990s. They'd read an article about the band and felt compelled to check them out at Raji's.

"Laurie was from New Orleans, and I'm from South Mississippi, about a hundred miles from New Orleans," Hudson said. "So it felt like we were reading about some people from back home. We went out to hear them and I just loved them."

After formally meeting the Drifters a few years later, the two bands started crossing paths when the Drifters drove up to Oxford for gigs. At the time, Oxford had a pretty thriving music community that was extremely welcoming to New Orleans artists.

"It wasn't as big as Athens, but it was one of those towns that had a scene. A lot of people came through; a lot of good bands," Hudson said.

Oxford had become something of a "second home" for the band, as Peter describes, after they moved to New Orleans. Not only did they open for Wilco there when Carlo was still in the band, they also went there often for smaller gigs.

"My god, one night the Drifters stayed in the home of the mayor of Oxford. With a big wrap-around antebellum porch at our disposal," Peter recalled. "We made friends immediately. We loved playing there."

Russ also had an Oxford connection in John Stirratt, Laurie's twin brother, who he'd played with in The Bluerunners. Stirratt left that band and started working for Uncle Tupelo, before following that band's co-founder Jeff Tweedy on to his new project, Wilco. He remains Wilco's bassist and longest serving member behind Tweedy.

Before joining the Drifters, Russ and John Stirratt were catching up one day and reminiscing about their time with The Bluerunners. Russ mentioned that he'd been playing with the Continental Drifters, and Stirratt was elated.

"He said, 'Oh my god. What a great fucking band. Boy, we [Wilco] made the mistake of okaying them opening up for us in Oxford. And we didn't want to take the stage; they were so fucking good!'" Russ recalled.

This was the reputation the Drifters were getting in Oxford, thanks to higher-profile opening slots but also due to the friends they made there. One of those friends was Mitch Ulrich, owner of Oxford record store Uncle Buck's, and a local talent buyer who would often book the band around town and even hired the Psycho Sisters to open for Fairport Convention's Richard Thompson.

They'd also befriended Garrison Starr, an upstart singer/songwriter at the time who was originally from Hernando, Mississippi, about an hour from Oxford. Starr was living in Los Angeles by the mid-1990s, having been signed by Geffen Records to record what would become her 1997 debut LP *Eighteen Over Me*.

Starr grew up a huge Bangles fan, and in particular, a massive fan of Vicki as a writer and guitar player.

"I really gravitated towards The Bangles," Starr said. "I just thought it was rad that they were four hot chicks playing guitars—electric guitars—and playing drums. I just loved it.

"Vicki was my favorite. I thought she was so badass. And I think, probably, being a young girl and feeling like there were certain expectations of me, I knew I wanted to play music but I didn't know how that was going to happen. So I think I was living a dream vicariously through them."

When she started working on her record for Geffen, which she recorded partly in Oxford, Starr had Vicki in mind to sing on the album and decided to reach out. Vicki agreed, and the two became fast friends.

"Really, we became friendly when she came to Oxford to sing on the record. She was, like, the first vegetarian that I'd ever met," Starr laughed.

Starr says that her attraction to Vicki's musicianship and songwriting was likely formed by a mutual affinity for the pop music of the 1960s that shaped so much of what The Bangles' original music was, especially in the early part of their career.

"There was an aesthetic and an authenticity about Vicki that I gravitated towards. There's a real authenticity in her playing, and in her writing and singing. She's very honest. It's just her," she said.

After befriending Vicki, Starr ended up in the Drifters' orbit for a time, opening for the band in Oxford and guesting with them at the Howlin' Wolf.

With their many connections to the city, recording in Oxford seemed a no-brainer for the band, so they took Russ up to Mississippi and got to work. The Black Dog session took place at Route 1 Studio, the label's in-house studio which was situated on farmland owned by Chris Hudson—a chicken farmer by day.

"[He] wanted to do something in the creative world, other than just slaughtering chickens," Russ said.

Chris Hudson enlisted engineer Jeffrey Reed to work on the session, who was connected to Black Dog through his work with Blue Mountain. Reed was an engineer at Ardent Studios in Memphis when he first began working with Blue Mountain, ultimately engineering and co-producing their 1997 release *Home Grown*. It was around this time that Reed says he was approached to work with the Drifters—a band he didn't know by name.

"I had never heard of the band before, but when Chris started rattling off names, my jaw kind of dropped," Reed, a longtime fan of individual Drifters' previous endeavors, recalled.

For this session, the band chose to record Vicki's as-yet-unrecorded "Christopher Columbus Transcontinental Highway," a song that recounted a tense roadtrip with Gary Eaton from New Orleans to L.A.

> *Driving by that detour we took*
> *To watch the sunset at the scenic overlook*
> *The light was lovely but to my surprise*
> *The most violent colors were in your eyes*
> *All the reds and yellows, black and blue*
> *It's what I remember from driving with you on the 10*

"We were in the process of breaking up," Vicki explained. "I was staying in New Orleans for the summer. I rented a place for the month of August, and I was going to drive back home. And for some reason all of the sudden he was like, 'You can't drive across the country by yourself!' So he literally flew out and was going to drive back with me, and it was just the most horrific journey you can imagine. On so many levels."

The flip side to "Christopher Columbus" (called Side: One, with "Columbus" dubbed Side: A) was, appropriately, a cover; this time, a spirited version of Fairport Convention's "Meet on the Ledge."

What's important about this was that it largely marked the greatest stylistic pivot of the band's career, as they began to fully embrace and explore the seminal work of Sandy Denny, Richard Thompson, and the groundbreaking British folk rock collective that was Fairport.

The relevance of Fairport in regard to the Drifters' post-Carlo years cannot be overstated; some Fairport songs had been in the ether since the days of the Batch Pad, but were never properly integrated into a Drifters set in the Carlo years. "Meet on the Ledge" was the first time they'd put that influence on record.

In keeping with the structure of sessions previous, the two songs were tracked as live as possible and done rather expeditiously.

"When it came time for overdubs, that's when the real magic started happening," Reed said. "If I recall correctly, the lead vocal was laid down in probably one take and the background vocals were added as a group, not individually. One microphone, working out parts on the fly and fun stuff like that. It was just a joy to watch some people I looked up to put together some music in such a laid back yet professional way. The talent present was undeniable."

The session at Route 1 for Black Dog was enough to motivate the band to get on the road again, so they teamed up with Steve Wynn and put together a tour where they'd swap headlining spots. The premise of this next outing was simple, as Mark said.

"We have to get together, go out there, and show that we're still a viable band."

The run with Wynn took place across the Northeast and through the Midwest, with stops in Boston, Chicago, D.C., and other major markets. It was a unique tour, as Wynn's usual band was unavailable so he and his drummer/wife, Linda Pitmon, capitalized on having the Drifters along by putting Mark, Robert, and Peter in the band and inviting the other Drifters up as guests in their set.

The Drifters and Wynn swapped headlining duties, depending on the market, and the tour was a successful showcase for the band's vast repertoire and a solid springboard for the Black Dog single.

Wynn remembers the Drifters playing three hour sets every night; not unlike a typical Raji's or Howlin' Wolf gig.

He recalled: "On a tour *that* grueling, their insistence on playing three hours every night, whether there were 400 people or 40, was trying sometimes. I say that laughing because we loved every minute of it.

"But it was like, 'Wow, they are here to *play*. They're not here to play a short little tight set. They're here to make as much music as they possibly can.' Even if they're going to be exhausted the next day, it doesn't matter."

Just after the Drifters/Wynn roadshow was complete, Peter jumped into his next project: An evening of music in the nave of St. Ann's and the Holy Trinity Church on Montague Street in Brooklyn, New York, paying tribute to the legendary folk singer and songwriter Nick Drake as part of The Arts at St. Ann's programming.

It was to be a memorable night of music with a cast that included Susan Cowsill as well as names like Terre Roche, Duncan Sheik, Syd Straw, Sloan Wainwright, Peter Blegvad, and more.

But it was also a day forever marked by tragedy.

Peter Holsapple is the younger of two boys; his brother, Curtis, was 11 years older. As Peter says, he didn't have an especially close relationship with his brother because of their age difference.

"We referred to ourselves as two only children, which I think is pretty apt," he said.

Their father, a banker and retired U.S. Navy commander, moved the family from Greenwich, Connecticut, to Winston-Salem, North Carolina, in 1962 when Curtis was 17 years old and Peter was six. His parents, Peter says, had their sights set on in-state tuition for the college-bound Curtis.

"He had had sort of a checkered prep school career," Peter said, adding that *The Catcher in the Rye*'s seminal narrator and main character Holden Caulfield had a major impact on Curtis as a teen.

"I know it absolutely informed his desire to be a New Yorker, which in turn influenced my desire to be a New Yorker," Peter said. "Even though in New York we weren't particularly close, either. We ran in different circles."

Curtis was a club manager around New York in the 1970s and '80s, as well as a choir director and a trained organist who played in churches.

"One of the few memories I have of living in Old Greenwich is riding with my mom to pick Curtis up from his organ lesson, and we'd get there a little bit early so we could hear a little bit of what he was doing," Peter said. "I see how people can see god through music sometimes, I guess. That made a huge impression on his little brother, to say the least."

The two stayed in touch through their adult years but always remained in different crowds.

Curtis did see his brother play in New York, though, and in the early nineties he showed up to a show in New York with Chris Stamey and Ilene Markell, when they were promoting the *Mavericks* album. Curtis, Peter says, looked "really gaunt."

"I went back to where I was staying with Ilene, and she said, 'He looks bad,'" Peter said. The Holsapple brothers got together at Curtis' apartment the next day, where in their "traditional Holsapple-ian dialogue that skates around using the words," Curtis made a revelation.

"Everything you think is happening with me right now is happening with me," he told Peter.

What Peter assumed, and Curtis confirmed, was that Curtis had AIDS. This was the era just following the height of the AIDS epidemic but still at a time when the virus was disproportionately impacting gay men in major metropolitan areas.

Curtis was an active part of the community in New York City, dating back to the 1970s, though was not openly gay to many, including his family.

"I knew when I moved to New York, because I just knew," Peter said. "I knew what he was doing, and I knew the people he was working with. And it was fine. It made no difference to me; it was my brother, who I loved and I respected and worshiped. And it also wasn't any of my fucking business."

Fast forward to 1997, when Peter was hired to be musical director for "Bryter Layter: The Music of Nick Drake." He planned to stay with his brother during his time in New York, but his parents advised him to check in because they'd gotten word that Curtis was being admitted to the hospital.

He rearranged his plans and found a place to stay with a friend, and went to visit Curtis when he and Susan arrived in New York.

"There was a big article on [the Nick Drake show] in the *New York Times*; a preview, I think. And he had it in his room in the hospital, but he wasn't able to read it," Peter said. "I could tell he was just hurting so badly. He couldn't talk. He was aching; every time he moved, he just groaned."

Susan, Peter says, was his "rock" through the entire ordeal.

They stayed with a friend during their time in NYC for the show, going back and forth between rehearsals, the hospital, and the house where they were crashing.

"I was, like, doing this for days on end, the minute I got up there. Because I had to," he said.

The day of the show—November 8, 1997—arrived, and it proved to be a major success. When Peter and Susan returned to the apartment where they were staying, though, they were met with a voicemail from Peter's father on the answering machine.

Curtis had died earlier that night.

"It's the first time I ever heard my father cry," he said.

Today, Peter remembers his brother as a central force in his early life and in his career path from an early age; someone who encouraged and fostered his innate piano skills.

Curtis, he says, even wrote out numbers that corresponded to the notes of "Twinkle Twinkle, Little Star" on onion skin paper, mounted it to shirt cardboard, and numbered a section of their upright piano accordingly so that Peter could figure it out.

"My brother was, alongside my choir director, Helen Cornwall, and my band director, John Shelton—that's the holy trinity for me, that made me feel like I could do this music shit," Peter said.

He certainly did do the music shit, starting in his first band—Dana and the Blue Jays—when he was just 8 years old. And yes, he considers it a real band.

"We were 8 and we didn't know what you did to be in a band," Peter said. "You just got a couple of people together, played some songs together, and you gave it a name. But we didn't know. How do you get to be The Beatles? That was a mystery to me, for many, many years."

As Peter came up through the teenage band ranks in Winston Salem, there were, it seemed, camps forming among the young musicians: Some, like Chris Stamey and Mitch Easter, were more fascinated with record making; the recording and engineering side of it all. Others, like Peter, were much more enamored with the craft of songwriting and the thrill of gigging in bands.

"They were the science guys," Peter said of Easter and Stamey. "They were the kids with tape recorders and model rockets and stuff like that. I made model cars, but it was a different kind of discipline than the science of recording and stuff like that."

Before that, Peter had attended Phillips Exeter Academy, a prep school in New Hampshire. It was there that he met and befriended Benjamin Montmorency Tench III, a keyboard prodigy who would, of course, go on to be a founding member of Tom Petty and the Heartbreakers.

"I found myself on the same floor as Benmont and a guy named Will Magoon, who had a huge collection of the newsprint editions of *CREEM* magazine," he said. "He had a voluminous knowledge of all things Detroit rock and roll, and he and Benmont had been friends since they were freshmen four years before. And so I was like, 'Wow, okay. I play guitar, by the way!'"

They started a band together, Oirolf P. Florio Memorial Blues Band, working up songs by Mott the Hoople and The Stooges. That band ended after Magoon graduated mid-year, and Peter and Tench started another band—with Tench switching to bass—called R.I.P. Snizz, in honor of a student at the school who'd been "let go" during his senior year.

Peter left Exeter and returned to Winston-Salem, where Rittenhouse Square—a band that featured Mitch Easter and Chris Stamey—was formed soon after.

Easter remembers knowing Peter from school, but points out that he was one grade ahead

Sean Kelly

of Peter, "at a time when that stuff actually mattered." He'd heard about Peter from friends, and they ultimately started working together when a session (attended by Benmont Tench who went to North Carolina to visit Peter) was organized at Chris Stamey's house—which Easter likens to the Al Kooper album *Super Session*—"except that we were, you know, children."

Regardless of their age, that session would prove to be significant in the history of the Peter/Mitch Easter relationship, as it spawned a friendship that led to the formation of Rittenhouse Square.

"It was a really stupid band in a lot of ways," Easter said of Rittenhouse, "but it was [formative]. I feel like I learned a lot of stuff in that band. And we had this kind of unbelievable setlist, looking back at it. It was all covers, but the songs are just hilarious.

"None of us could really sing at all. Chris and I had just started singing, and it was just abysmal. It was shocking."

One of the standout memories of Peter's teen years was being present for the recording of a live show by an earlier incarnation of Rittenhouse Square, recorded by Chris Stamey at RJ Reynolds High School's auditorium.

"I stood with him down in the pit, where we were looking up at the band. And it's, you know, six feet above, right? And Mitch Easter looks gigantic!" he said. "And I was like, 'Okay, I think I get it now.' As I said earlier—that disconnect between what The Beatles were doing on Ed Sullivan and what I was plinking on with *The Golden Beatles* songbook; suddenly, it all became clear. And it also became evident that I can do this."

He would later form the H-Bombs with Easter, after the two had been recording together when they were both in college.

"I was just recording my brains out, it felt like, when I was in college," Easter said. "And Peter was a person who would come over to my house and we would just do stuff. And that was really fun, and I felt like it was really creative."

After college, Peter moved to Memphis following a trip there with his bandmates (where they infamously met Big Star's Chris Bell, but you can find that story in the Big Star documentary *Big Star: Nothing Can Hurt Me*) that inspired him to give it a go.

While living in Memphis, he kept getting haunted by ads in the *Village Voice* for a band called Chris Stamey & the dB's, who were looking for a keyboard player in New York.

"And then I was like, 'Okay, I'm gonna move to New York.'"

Peter ventured to New York City, where he joined The dB's, intent on solely being their keyboard player and not writing any songs. Sound familiar?

And so continued the music shit.

After his brother's death, Peter returned to New Orleans where the Drifters wrote songs and plotted their next move.

They had garnered some recognition in New Orleans by this point, building up goodwill as a solid live band and making friends and connections in the process.

Annie Clements, a New Orleans-born musician best known for her long tenure as bassist for country group Sugarland, and more recently with singer/songwriter Maren Morris, recalls Susan getting some local attention pretty immediately after they moved to town.

"The Drifters show up in New Orleans, and up until this point, Li'l Queenie has been the reigning female vocalist in the city," Clements said. "And then it was like this big thing when the Drifters came to town and suddenly, like, Susan is winning the [female vocalist] awards in the local paper.

"I remember Susan joking and saying 'Me and Li'l Queenie are both going to put on roller skates and skate arm and arm up the center aisle to accept the award together.'"

At the same time the band was pushing the Black Dog single on the road with Steve Wynn, they were also making plans for what would be their second full-length. They'd already decided on a studio; Dockside Studio, a picturesque remote facility situated on several acres of land in the small town of Maurice, Louisiana. The studio is owned by Steve and Cezanne "Wish" Nails.

Maurice, in Vermilion Parish, is about ten miles from Lafayette, and the perfect place for a band like the Drifters. It's the kind of studio you go to when you want to create without the allure of a city around you. Steve Nails, his wife says, always knew he'd end up on that big piece of land in Maurice.

"We lived on the same river, Vermilion River, in Lafayette about fifteen minutes away and Steve had a party barge," Wish Nails recalled. "Steve and his friends would always ride down the river to this property and tell everyone that was where he was going to live.

"You could see the big South Louisiana style home, the pool and the building that the studio is in now, all from the river. One day he took me and he said the same thing: 'That's the house I'm going to live in.' I told him he was crazy; it's a generational estate. Their kids are going to live there and their kids' kids. We already had a nice home and thought of no reason to even move.

"It was probably three months later that I was looking for a little rental to purchase and fix up and said, 'Oh my god, there is a big house on the river for sale.' He said, 'Let's go look and just see what it is.' The second we turned onto the long oak tree-lined driveway he said, 'Call the bank. This is our house.' It was the same house he had been looking at!"

The band was first invited to check it out after Peter discovered an ad for the studio and called to inquire. He spoke with Steve and Wish, who welcomed the Drifters down to take a tour.

Steve Nails also saw an ad in the paper for the band's show at Grant Street Dance Hall in Lafayette. When he noticed that the listing mentioned Susan Cowsill as a member of the band, he was floored.

"I said, 'Oh, no,'" he amusedly recalled. "Because Susan, John, and Barry [Cowsill] are the reason that I got into music. So this is really LSD psychotic."

Unbeknownst to Nails, both Susan *and* Barry Cowsill were living just three hours away from him. Needless to say, he was thrilled.

At this point, Carlo was still in the band and they were scouting for their next record, so after the gig at Grant Street, they made plans to stop by.

They arrived in the middle of the night, intrigued by the long stretches of dirt road and the sheer size of the property.

They were given instructions for accessing the place on their own, since they'd arrived at an ungodly hour and the proprietors were fast asleep.

"We drunk-ass pull up, it's probably 4 a.m., and we're instructed to go down to the studio and sleep there and we'll see them in the morning," Susan said.

"We got there in the pitch black, in the middle of the night," Mark added. "We had no idea where we were or what we were doing, but we got there and were like, 'Wow, this is amazing. What a cool barn, what a great studio, what a great board. What a great vibe.'"

They woke up the next morning and were greeted by Steve and Wish, who gave them a proper tour of the studio and its surrounding pool house and barn.

"They came over looking like a bunch of gypsies, mostly because of Susan Cowsill and her hat and no shoes," Wish Nails recalled.

Steve Nails says he remembers the moment he met Susan, one of his childhood heroes, for the first time; summing that moment up rather simply: "Vicki and Susan have a five dollar club for everyone that gives them a look," he said. "And I'm the president of the five dollar club."

The band hit it off immediately with the Nails, and they pretty much knew right then that they'd found the right spot.

"Steve was a wise ass, and Wish was just this beautiful figure sort of drifting around, showing us everything," Peter recalled.

Susan remembers a moment during the first night at Dockside when she and Vicki were laying outside and looking at the sky, basking in the beautiful and slightly strange surrealness of where they were—not unlike their first middle-of-the-night arrival in New Orleans some three years earlier.

"Vicki and I were laying on our backs out in the woods in Louisiana going, 'Where are we now? What's happening now?'" she laughed.

Dockside had everything the band needed to make a record, but also offered them the opportunity to actually stay on the property while they made the record. They were sold; to say they were enamored is putting it mildly.

"I think on the ride back, I don't know if we'd even made it out of the driveway after that when we said, 'We need to find a way to do this record *here*,'" Peter said.

Wish Nails said the feeling was mutual; there was a connection made that day that everyone says was undeniable.

"We felt a connection with them right off because they were all different," she recalled. "They just drug themselves early in the morning to our house after having coffee overlooking the bayou at the studio deck.

"They said they didn't know what good fortune had brought them to such a relaxing place, with an invitation from people they didn't know. We were all equally curious."

Fast-forward to the next year, and Russ is in the band. They'd just done the Black Dog single and made plans to decamp to Maurice in March of 1998 and record a full-length. With the Black Dog single being a one-off release, the band was without a U.S. label and had ultimately no funding behind them to get a project off the ground. They decided to turn to Edgar Heckmann at Blue Rose, who agreed to put up some money for the record.

They'd also gotten a bit of money from Hootie & the Blowfish, who at the time had a label called Breaking Records; a subsidiary of Atlantic Records then owned by the Warner-Elektra-Atlantic label group (known as WEA).

Peter explains that the Hootie camp gave the Drifters a deal with Breaking Records, but that there was an understanding it wouldn't be a fully funded and released project. In a way, it was similar to the demo deal from Mercury.

"I assume it was perceived by the powers at WEA as being a write off of some sort. It was almost like demo money," he said. "Which was an incredibly, incredibly generous thing to do. [Hootie] basically paid for the recording. Mensches, what can I say?"

Between that funding and the Blue Rose money, the band had enough to pay for studio time and personnel, tape ($400 per roll, as Russ recalls), and a basic salary of $300 a week per band member.

At this point, Russ had not only become an official member of the band, but he also joined Mark in handling much of the band's business.

The two primarily took care of booking shows, and while they tried to delegate business and promotional tasks amongst the rest of the band—who were, as Russ stresses, eager to help—the Mark/Russ duo had become so well-oiled that they ultimately determined it was easiest if they did things themselves.

"It's just easier, more efficient, faster," Russ laughed.

They'd developed a routine, of sorts, in terms of how they'd fit Drifters activity around everyone's lives and especially Peter's commitments with Hootie. Essentially, Peter would show the band his schedule, and it would be Mark and Russ' job to fill any time off from Hootie with as much as they could.

"And Peter would say, 'I'm good,' you know? When he would come off the road, he didn't need to be home, per say, because his family was going to travel with us," Russ said.

Just prior to recording what would become *Vermilion*—named after Vermilion Parish—the Drifters worked a lot. There was a 'Continental Drifters and Friends' residency at the Howlin' Wolf, as well as plenty of weekend runs and longer bursts of touring that kept the band active.

Russ recalled: "I remember [the residency] being very consistent, and us hitting weekends consistently. Even a ten-day run or something, and then getting home Sunday. Monday we'd have our familial barbecue with everyone, and then Tuesday we'd be doing a rehearsal run-through with a guest artist, either in Mark's or my living room. And then we'd go to soundcheck."

All of that activity fueled the band for the impending recording. With some money behind them, the Drifters enlisted New Orleans producer and engineer Mike Mayeux to co-produce and made plans for an intense seventeen-day recording session, where they'd track and mix fourteen songs.

Some songs would finally see the light of day after being kept from the first album—namely, "The Rain Song" and "Who We Are, Where We Live," two staples of their live sets that the band finally felt ready to put properly on record.

Other songs had been floating around for some time, like "Meet Me in the Middle," which was later included on Peter's solo release *Out of My Way* (1997, Monkey Hill). The album featured Carlo, Ilene Markell, and Peter's old school pal Benmont Tench, among others.

"Meet Me in the Middle" is an example of how two drummers could interpret the same song in vastly different ways. The solo version with Carlo was much straighter and almost more of a rock song in how he approached the groove. With Russ, the song swung a lot more.

"It's like a '50s, almost rockabilly, early rock and roll thing," Russ said of his interpretation.

Mark recalls hearing "Meet Me in the Middle" for the first time at one of Peter's solo gigs at Carrollton Station, where he went as a (drunk) spectator but was coaxed into jumping on stage to play it with Peter.

"He's like, 'Hey, Mark, play this song!' I was like, 'I don't know that song,'" Mark laughed. "I had no idea at the time what the feel was."

Another unreleased song from Peter's pre-Drifters session in Los Angeles with Carlo, Benmont, and Ilene, "I Want to Learn to Waltz With You," was reworked for the Drifters as well.

Unlike most of the rest of the songs the band planned to record, "Waltz" wasn't one that everyone was solid on—in fact, they weren't convinced they could capture it.

"We were all really really nervous about how the fuck we were going to get 'Waltz With You' down right," Robert said. "We would trainwreck it live because nobody could remember how the end went and shit like that. I just remember we set up, and the hair on my arms stood up. And we nailed it in one take."

Peter emphasizes that both "Waltz" and "Meet Me in the Middle" were songs of his that he handed to Susan to take over lead vocals for the *Vermilion* arrangements.

"[Susan] did a far better and more emotional job on both songs," he said.

From Vicki came the previously-released "Christopher Columbus Transcontinental Highway," which would be freshly recorded for the sessions, in addition to "Who We Are." She also contributed a new song, called "Watermark," which she says was influenced heavily by Louisiana and Russ' introduction of the rubboard to the Drifters sound.

"I wanted to do something that was a little Zydeco flavored," she said. "That was inspired, again, by boys. You know how they do! That was sort of a combination of moments I'd had with Tim Cohn, who was a dear, dear friend of ours, and also Kevin Salem."

It's a song that she says is more hopeful and optimistic in regard to love and relationships than some of her other songs; there are tears, but they've dried. The watermark aspect, while emblematic of healing in a relationship, was inspired by a real watermark on the ceiling of her home in Louisiana.

"I remember I was just kind of laying there looking up at the ceiling, and there was a water stain on the ceiling," she recalled. "And I started thinking about what that meant. With Louisiana with flooding and all of that, you look for the watermark on the buildings. It tells you how high the water got. It tells you how bad it got. So it kind of was a symbol of that, in a way."

"Watermark" started with lyrical ideas, but took off musically when Vicki tuned the high E string on a guitar down to a D.

"I did the drop D on the E string, and the riff just kind of happened," she said. "And as soon as the riff came I realized, 'Okay, this needs to have a little bit of a zydeco, swamp feel to it. And of course it's also got the Celtic thing—because they're the same thing!"

There was also a Vicki/Susan co-write in the mix; a new song called "Way of the World," which they wrote on the road. With Robert jangling along on twelve-string and Russ channeling a charging, upbeat 1960s pattern in the choruses, "Way of the World" was as psychedelic as the band had ever been.

> *It's the way of the world, say a prayer and it all comes true*
> *Cross your heart, hold your breath, touch the wall, you might make it through*
>
> *Oh Lord, please let the landing gears come down*
> *It's a cry in the dark*
> *And you know you don't make a sound*
> *It's the way of the world*

One of the key lines in the song's chorus, Vicki says, was inspired by Elvis Presley; and also found Susan taking artistic license with grammar, as songwriters sometimes do.

"When we wrote, 'Way of the World,' [Susan] was quoting Elvis—when he would talk about his fear of flying, and he would pray, 'Oh lord, let the landing gear come down,'" Vicki said. "She read that somewhere and wanted to use it, but she'd always sing, 'Let the landing gears come down.' And Peter would say, 'It's not plural—it's landing gear. It's a collective noun!' And she'd go, 'I don't care. I'm singing gears.'"

"Way of the World" is a notable song on *Vermilion* because it, perhaps more than any other song in the collection, shows the most distinct difference between Russ and Carlo's playing. It also was, for Peter, a moment that showed how this lineup was able to sync with each other and arrange interesting deviations from an otherwise straight ahead pop song template.

"That last verse after the solo, when we have those little extended bars—I can't remember where it came from, but it's one of the most brilliant moments on a song on this record, in my estimation," he said. "It is the sound of one band breathing together, and one heartbeat through there. That's the indescribable part of being in this band, is that when that happens organically, it's just the greatest thing. Things just happen the right way."

Peter also contributed some more recent songs, including "Darlin Darlin," which presents a Meters-meets-acoustic guitar groove and a melody that finds Peter reaching to the top of his range. "Darlin Darlin" had previously been recorded for the Mercury demos.

As he explains, it was a song that wasn't actually intended for the Drifters originally, save for a demo a couple of years earlier. He'd been approached to submit the song for a film, but the filmmakers had a pretty big caveat—he'd have to record it with Hootie and the Blowfish as his backing band.

Peter asked the band's management about the idea, but it was taking a while to get a response.

"Finally, after waiting and waiting and waiting, and watching the window shutting, I was thinking, 'Who else do I know that could do a good version of it? What about the Black Crowes? I can approach them!' So I wrote to Chris [Robinson] and Steve [Gorman], and I sent them a copy of the Drifters version of it," he said. 'And [the filmmakers] were like, 'Nah, if it's not Hootie and the Blowfish, I guess we really don't want it.' I was like, 'Fuck!'"

While the song didn't end up being licensed for film, with the Drifters, "Darlin Darlin" found a good home.

Another Peter song brought in was the ambitious and sprawling "Daddy Just Wants It To Rain," a nearly eight-minute story about a couple that met and married at the start of World War II, had children and lived a modest life throughout the 1950s and '60s. It follows the family through decades of hardship, including a drought that led to the father's beloved farm—where they lived and worked—being foreclosed on him.

"I wrote that song in the 'control room' area of the studio behind our house on Paris Avenue," Peter recalled, adding that he remembers it being "blisteringly hot" when he wrote it. The lyrics, he says, came together "from whole cloth."

Lyrically, it was a song that felt so personal that Peter says people would often assume it was about him. He'd have to break it to them that it was actually a fictional story, not a story about his father getting his farm foreclosed on.

"Honestly, my dad worked for the bank that probably foreclosed on him," Peter laughed.

Susan was also bringing songs to the table, like "Spring Day in Ohio," an intensely autobiographical song featuring her father, Cowsills manager Bud Cowsill, who died in 1985. In more recent years, Bud has become known as an antagonistic figure in the story of The Cowsills for not only his severe mismanagement of the group (which led to their demise), but also the abuse he inflicted on his family.

Susan describes the writing of "Spring Day" as a natural progression of the healing she found for herself in the Drifters, following the trauma she suffered as a child.

"An unexpected gift from becoming a Continental Drifter was my own brand of self-healing that I tapped into, that I didn't have prior to that, which was writing songs," she explained. "I didn't used to plan, I just kept moving. So when I'd stumble on something beautiful and amazing, it was fun because I never expected it.

"['Spring Day'] was pretty much the tribal cry. If you don't know that it's about my journey with my parental male unit, you can think it's anything because that's the beauty of songs."

There was another new song in the mix as well—a Peter/Susan co-write called "Drifters." In many ways the centerpiece of the album, "Drifters" is declarative as much as it is autobiographical; a true sonic document of a collective feeling, and a moment in time being preserved for all time.

As Peter recalls, he approached Susan with the music fully formed, as well as lyrics and melody for the chorus. Those parts, he said, fell right out in very little time. The rest of it he was struggling with, so he gave it to Susan to work on.

"She locked herself in the back bedroom with a six-pack of beer and a guitar and a cassette recorder and a pad and a pencil, and I didn't see her for hours," he recalled.

What emerged was something Peter says he could never have done alone, but also something that fulfilled an ambition he'd had in both his musical and personal relationship with Susan.

"Some of the things that I had hoped for in my musical relationship with Susan in a band were realized in that song. The collaborative nature of that, the selfless aspect to the creation of it, the final product," he said.

And, yes, there's a not-very-subtle reference to the band's many arguments—especially ones in the L.A. era when things would get heated between band members at rehearsal: three overlapping voices swirling thru a flanger, carrying a brief bridge with a line that is half inside joke, half mantra.

You don't understand.

"At the end of the day, what I meant was—and to this day, I get a lump in my throat—for reasons unknown and untold, certain humans make that undeniable connection with one another that sticks out in their life amongst them, individually and collectively," Peter said.

"Drifters" embodied the spirit of the band; the unity, the joy, the chaos—all of it. But what of its self-referential nature? Are "theme songs" cool? Historically, it probably depends on the song, or the artist, even. The Drifters were immediately hooked on theirs.

"I loved it. This is our 'Creeque Alley.' They told [the story] beautifully, and we're going to sing it for the rest of our lives," Vicki said.

Russ agrees, and says he looks at the song as being inclusive of not just the band, but also its audience.

"Yes, on a microscopic level, it's our band. But it also speaks as loudly of our audience, and the union there between us and them," he said. "And I can easily make that even more macro and go, 'Fuck, aren't we all related?' To me, it's just a beautiful story of oneness."

Ultimately, "Drifters" was a perfect storm of emotion, and everyone felt they'd landed on a recording that matched the song's gravitas. Mayeux says the song was done in just two takes.

The recording and mixing of what would become *Vermilion* was done at lightning speed in comparison to how most bands make records, and the Drifters make no bones about the fact that this was due largely to Mike Mayeux.

"Mike Mayeux worked really, really, really hard," Robert said. "I just remember him with headphones on, just saying, 'I'm going to take a break. I can't hear anything anymore.' He put in such long hours. He was very, very dedicated, and really fun to work with."

"By the end of it, my ears were ringing," Mayeux confirms.

Mayeux describes the recording process as one where the band tracked basics together in the live room, and then each individual would take turns refining their parts with limited band interaction.

"Basically the way that the Drifters worked is that everybody was pretty self-conscious," he said. "They would play together, but then when people would start listening to their [parts], and I was basically assigned, 'You get an hour with Vicki, and she's going to come in and make herself happy.' And nobody else really would come in there. For the most part, everybody just sort of came in after school and did their parts."

The setup was also pretty straightforward, as Mayeux recalled.

"[Dockside] had the main room, with basically two iso[lation] booths that were next to each other and then a little iso booth," he explained. "And then the bass was in one of the big [rooms], and Robert was in one of the big ones."

The record was tracked mostly live with minimal overdubs aside from punches and re-recording some primary parts. And as with previous sessions, there was no click track/metronome running like the vast majority of artists do today.

This method made some aspects tough on songs like "Darlin Darlin," where Peter had to re-track his acoustic guitar after basic band tracks were done. With nothing keeping time in the drum-less intro or queuing him in, it took some work to get the timing matched up.

Mayeux calls this an example of "Peter being a genius," but also gives credit for this feat to the shorthand that the two had cultivated by the time *Vermilion* was recorded.

He did have some help for these sessions—a young engineer named Jim Watts, who had just been hired to be the in-house engineer at Dockside a few months earlier. As Watts recalls, he was living in Austin when a friend called him from Kingsway Studio in New Orleans to tell him that he heard about an engineer job at Dockside. He called Steve Nails on a Friday for a phone interview.

"By Tuesday, I had moved to Maurice," Watts laughed.

Watts' first record at Dockside was a Derek Trucks record, alongside regular Dockside engineer Tony Daigle. Just a few weeks later, the Drifters arrived for what was Watts' first engineering job at Dockside on his own.

Watts recalls the Drifters record as being one of a constant slew of projects he had at the studio, which continued for his entire run as house engineer.

"In my experience at the time, in the haze of record after record, one of the primary memories I have is of exhaustion," he said.

Watts, while a fan of The dB's, had no prior relationship with anyone in the band before the sessions began. Mayeux, however, had been in their orbit for several years. His relationship with the band started with Peter, when he was working on the demos which became The dB's *Paris Avenue* record.

He'd also worked with Peter and Carlo on the aforementioned Holsapple solo album *Out of My Way*, and did some sessions with the Psycho Sisters.

He was brought on to *Vermilion* after it was determined that they wanted an outside producer to help them steer the songs in the right direction. It was his first time working at Dockside, but he'd already had a lengthy career by this point working at the Egyptian Room, as well as doing sessions at Daniel Lanois' legendary Kingsway Studio. Mayeux was also a singer, songwriter, and guitarist in his own right as part of the band Beatinpath.

Going in, the band did zero pre-production with Mayeux, mostly due to budget constraints. Instead, they used the trip down to Maurice to pile into the van and listen to music. They had one record in mind that was the primary sonic reference point—Rod Stewart's 1971 megahit *Every Picture Tells a Story*.

"When we were going down there, it was two-and-a-half hours to Lafayette, we just played that record over and over again," Mayeux said, pointing to the groove as the focal point in terms of how he interpreted the band's reference.

"How big do things have to be to make that groove work?" he continued. " We didn't want things [to sound] massive. It's not a big rock record. Mark Walton being such a great bass player, it just sort of opens itself up to that, too. He's saying a lot of stuff down there that you want to hear. He's helping drive the groove just as much—in fact, maybe even more than Russ. [Russ] might be keeping time more than anything else, and Mark's doing it the way McCartney does."

In a way, the *Every Picture* reference was a solid reference point for continuing what Carlo had conceptualized for the band sonically years earlier—not utilizing many effects and keeping things relatively dry (i.e. little to no reverb) and up front in a mix.

"The original aesthetic of the sonics of the band when Carlo was at the helm was like a Band record, without a lot of reverb and kind of in your face," Peter said. "And we sort of took it from there, and still kept a, kind of, underproduced record."

Underproducing meant that the various elements could be balanced more easily and there was room for some cohesion in the way things were presented—for example, Vicki's guitars were often situated in a consistent space on each *Vermilion* song, and the listener's ear could reliably and comfortably understand the elements because there wasn't a ton of overdubs hiding or crowding primary instrumentation.

This was crucial on *Vermilion* because, like *Every Picture Tells a Story*, acoustic guitars (and mandolins, for that matter) were central.

"We wanted to make sure that the acoustic guitars spoke," Peter emphasizes.

When all was said and done, the Drifters and their dedicated producer accomplished the recording, overdubbing, editing, and mixing of a fourteen-song record in seventeen days. Everyone emphasizes Mayeux's focus and determination to keep things moving—especially in the mixing process.

"We were trying to keep them away from the mixes as much as possible, so that somebody could walk in and have a clear perspective on what we had," Mayeux said. "We basically allotted four hours per song. This is what we have. If we're going to make it out of here by this day, you have four hours per song."

Some songs, Mayeux says, came together quickly, while others took time. And there were certain songs that he focused on more because he felt strongly about them—"Spring Day" being a prime example.

"I did a lot of extra work on 'Spring Day' because obviously I loved it so much. I was doing a lot of flying fader automation during that song just to make things kind of fly in," he said.

Songs like "Watermark" and "Heart, Home" were much more challenging to get right in the mixing phase.

"They're very vibey songs, you know? They kind of float," Mayeux said. "It was hard to find something to anchor them to in a quick mix."

The Drifters embraced "Heart, Home," turning into a standout moment on the record.

"It's a breathtaking song," Peter said. "The construction of that song is so simple, but just so infallible. The minute that song starts, you know you're in for something."

Even Jim Watts remembers "Heart, Home" making an impression on him, as a new resident of Maurice who was struggling with homesickness.

"From initial conversation to moving to Lafayette, it was three days, and then I was thrown into the fire of nonstop sessions," Watts said. "So I was a little homesick, and out of my depth. That song, at the time, was one that really resonated with me."

The last song on the record, "Anything," was a song that the band labored over, as they couldn't land on a vibe that worked. The song, a Vicki/Peter co-write and duet, became a bit of a mystery for the band, and they even went so far as to set up in the stairwell of the studio to see if a change in scenery and sonics would give the recording what it needed.

That experiment wasn't deemed usable in the end, and they ended up stripping things back to just acoustic guitars and mandolin and tracking in the main room.

"We tried it full band and we didn't like it, so we went up to the stairwell and we sat around with acoustic guitars," Mark said. "We tried it here, we tried it there, and then finally we got it."

Working on *Vermilion* was the first time that Mayeux had been clued in to Susan's three-take vocal approach. It's something everyone who works with her learns quickly, and a method of working that is proof of her singular ability as a singer.

"I like things in quick order, if possible," Susan said. "I move too fast for people sometimes, but as far as singing goes, when I'm in there, then I am now officially checked out [from] you and everybody else. And there are only going to be so many ways I feel about what I'm saying, and I only have the ability in my body to do just that. And I don't need to ask more of it."

Where Susan adopted such a straightforward way of working, she isn't certain, but it's something Mayeux adapted to so that he could connect with her in ways that yielded the best performances. He also learned a technique during the *Vermilion* sessions that he says created a productive working relationship between the two.

"She kind of treats [vocal performances] as personalities," he explained. "If you're looking for something different, you can describe a different girl to her. 'You're not that girl, you're this girl.' She loves to put on characters.

"Most of the time everything she does is awesome, but if I needed to get her to give me more of one thing or another and she was hearing it, I could just tell her, 'Yeah, this chick, she's a boozer. A smoker.' Or, 'This girl's nicer than that. This girl's a little more angelic.'"

The Susan Cowsill approach to recording, Mayeux says, was more or less, "If you don't like it, fuck you." She had a lack of preciousness that most musicians don't, and it came across in the confidence she displayed at a microphone. What you'd get in the end was a voice that is frankly underrepresented in the annals of music history—undoubtedly one of the great voices in music.

"Susan just makes me cry when I listen to her sing," singer/songwriter Amy Rigby said. "It's so raw and feels like it comes from such a real place. And that's just a rare thing."

In the end, the band came away with a record they felt collectively confident in. And after all they'd been through individually and collectively in its first five years, to finally have a record like *Vermilion* in the can was perhaps the most significant moment in their career so far.

While the Drifters were completely different on paper from the band that started at Raji's—with Mark Walton the only original member remaining—the evolution of the Continental Drifters led them to a cohesive lineup and an album that felt like what they'd been working towards all along.

Russ was what they'd been looking for since Carlo left; a way to get the car off the blocks.

"Having that forward impetus and the enthusiasm that went over into recording *Vermilion* was just amazing," Robert said. "Recording *Vermilion* at Dockside was just one of the loveliest experiences I've ever had. It was a really magical time."

Steve Nails also felt the magic. He recalls Peter and Susan's daughter Miranda, and Russ' son Nick sitting on the effects rack in the middle of the control room during recording, and he and Wish coming to a realization just by seeing the families in action.

Indeed, it was the Drifter babies that made the Nails' realize they wanted a kid of their own, and Wish got pregnant with their son, Dylan, soon after.

"[There] was so much love in the air," Nails said. "On the effects rack, we had two babies—Nick and Miranda. And then I said, 'I can do that.' And then Dylan was born."

The experience of recording *Vermilion* was so positive that it shows on the final product. The album is of a piece; it is cohesive. It is all original; a statement if the band ever had one to make. *Vermilion* is concise, intelligent, and emotional. It is well mixed, well produced, and contains all the sonic elements of a classic roots rock record.

They knew it, too.

"I did think that *Vermilion* was a very strong record, and it felt very uniquely 'us' to me," Vicki said.

"We really felt like we caught some stuff," Robert added. "Everybody was just on a high. We were in great, great moods. It was the family band. It was the *good* family band."

Not only was the band thrilled with what they'd done, Edgar Heckmann was floored by what they turned in.

"I will never forget the moment when Peter gave me the master tape of *Vermilion*," Heckmann said. "It was in March 1998 at SXSW, just a few days later after the album had been mixed. It was like getting a long-awaited child, a treasure of gold."

The band was at a high point, creatively speaking. And for Russ, whose marriage was struggling at the time, being in the Drifters also became the defining aspect of his life—the place where he could be fully himself.

"We all had our own issues in our personal lives," he said. "It was like the band was the best reflection of ourselves. The band and its music, and how we could all come together—no words were off limits if we were talking about the music. No one would be offended, no one got agitated. No one got defensive.

"We all were unified in that. And then all else, even *that* was easy. And for me, that was so uncommon. Boy, how liberating."

They were all proud of the record, but Peter looks back with some pause about that particular point in time. It was, he says, a time when "the cracks were starting to show" in his relationship to alcohol.

"There were moments in that band around this record that just felt like, 'Wow, this is happening to us. This is happening for us,'" he said. "Unfortunately, on my part, alcohol really interfered with that for me and for my bandmates."

Peter's relationship with Susan, while creatively thriving in some ways, was starting to suffer on a personal level, and alcohol was a major contributing factor.

"I was drinking a lot," he recalled. "I was not having a fun time, and I was being very—I think I was not a very good partner in that couple, because I couldn't let go of a lot of my preconceptions of how it might play out. Things are not always as they seem, and that's okay too. And I think that I was so self unaware of the chaos that my drinking was creating.

"That I didn't careen into a school bus or drive myself off a road, or fall from a height, or kill somebody accidentally—how did I ever get through all of that?"

Even creatively, Peter says he felt as though he may have taken control too much during the *Vermilion* sessions, referring to himself as a "pushy bastard."

"I see the guy that was kind of directing the show and I think, 'Wow, I wish I had been more pleasant and deferential about it.' I think I just was a guy that didn't know where the brakes were," he said. "I'm a juggernaut in the studio. I move forward and I want to get it done. I think I may have been a dick, and I'm sorry. And maybe I'm just overreacting and over apologizing."

Each one of his bandmates, though, happily and readily dispute Peter's perception of himself as being overly opinionated or pushy. In fact, they affectionately refer to him as "Peter the Leader."

"We needed a leader," Susan said. "All that Peter was, and is, a leader. I never felt he was beating anybody down or upside or anything."

Mark agrees wholeheartedly, disputing Peter's concerns about being a dominant force in the studio.

"Peter is the more eloquent speaker, and he gets his ideas across a lot better," Mark said. "If that's being heavy handed, so be it. But I think Peter always has really good ideas, and they're always worth trying. So I don't think that's a true statement.

"I think ideas are just that—they're ideas. And we're always up to taking somebody's idea and trying it and seeing if it works."

Adds Russ: "It's not often that I'm recording and I don't miss his interjections or his suggestions for songs. He can make a little suggestion that distinguishes a part of a song. Even if it doesn't have a bridge, he can distinguish something that makes it feel like all of the sudden we're playing a bridge."

Personal perceptions aside, what everyone agrees on is that *Vermilion* was a feat—an accomplishment nearly eight years in the making. They were ready for what was next: Getting the record out in Germany, and busting their asses to find a label that would believe in it as much as they did.

"You can't do a history of the Continental Drifters without putting the alcohol in perspective," Peter said. "Because a lot of it was consumed by many of us. Constantly. Repeatedly." From the collection of Robert Maché

(left) Susan and Peter in the 1990s. From the collection of Robert Maché

Robert takes a solo at Summerstage Festival in Central Park, New York City, 1995. Photo by Eric Maché

(right) Susan and Robert at the Summerstage Festival in New York, 1995. Photo by Eric Maché

(bottom) A shot of the Drifters from behind the stage at Summerstage, Central Park, New York City, 1995. Photo by Eric Maché

Mark and Robert share a laugh onstage during the Summerstage Festival, 1995. Photo by Eric Maché

Mark and Peter switch off bass and guitar duties behind Susan and Robert, Summerstage 1995. Photo by Eric Maché

(left) Vicki and Susan lead the Drifters in Central Park in 1995. Photo by Eric Maché

Peter on keys and Vicki on guitar, Summerstage Festival, 1995. Photo by Eric Maché

(left) Vicki, Susan, Mark, Robert, Carlo at Summerstage, Central Park, 1995. Photo by Eric Maché

The Drifters pose at Mark's Wedding, March 24, 1996 (L-R: Robert, Rob Ladd, Susan, Mark, Vicki, Peter). From the collection of Mark Walton

Russ Broussard (right) drumming with the Tony Green Trio at Mark's wedding in spring of 1996, the gig that ultimately led to his invitation to join the Continental Drifters. From the collection of Mark Walton

Adrift in Germany, 1996 (L-R: Carlo, Vicki, Peter, Mark, Susan, Robert). Photo by Siby Weidner from the collection of Robert Maché

Susan on the mic in Germany, 1996. Photo by Siby Weidner from the collection of Robert Maché

Sean Kelly

(right) Mark and Vicki on a balcony in Germany in 1996. Photo by Siby Weidner from the collection of Robert Maché

The Psycho Sisters, Vicki and Susan, onstage with the Continental Drifters in Germany, 1996. Photo by Siby Weidner from the collection of Robert Maché

Peter steps out from behind the keys to play guitar in Germany, 1996. Photo by Siby Weidner from the collection of Robert Maché

Vicki and Mark singing together in Germany in 1996. Photo by Siby Weidner from the collection of Robert Maché

Carlo on the drums in Germany, 1996. Photo by Siby Weidner from the collection of Robert Maché

The whole gang, circa 1996, in Germany (L-R: Susan, Vicki, Carlo, Mark, Robert, Peter). Photo by Siby Weidner from the collection of Robert Maché

Vicki, Peter, and Susan onstage at Jazz Fest, New Orleans 1996. Photo by Eric Maché

Miranda Holsapple grabs Annie Clements' nose at Jazz Fest in New Orleans, mid-1990s. Photo by Vicki Peterson

Mark at Jazz Fest, New Orleans, 1996. Photo by Eric Maché

Robert and Susan at Jazz Fest in New Orleans, 1996.
Photo by Eric Maché

Peter at Jazz Fest, New Orleans 1996. Photo
by Eric Maché

Russ and Miranda Holsapple during a Drifters' German
tour. From the collection of Robert Maché

Drifters in Germany, 1997 (L-R: Vicki,
Robert, Russ, Mark, Peter, Susan, Miranda
Holsapple) From the collection of Vicki
Peterson

Vicki, Susan, and Robert on stage in Germany, 1997. From the collection of Vicki Peterson

(left) Vicki onstage in Germany during a 1997 tour. From the collection of Vicki Peterson

All dressed up and ready to go, the Drifters pose for one of their drag nights in 1997 (L-R: Mark, Robert, Russ, Susan, Peter, Vicki). Photo from the collection of Robert Maché

Robert decked out for a Drifters Drag Night. Photo from the collection of Robert Maché

Drifters and friends backstage at Maxwell's in Hoboken, New Jersey, 1999. (Back row L-R: Freedy Johnston, Russ, Peter, Mark, James McMillan, Kate Jacobs, Vicki, Dave Schramm, Steve Wynn / front row: Linda Pitmon, Robert, Susanna Hoffs, Susan, Alan Bezozi) From the collection of Peter Holsapple

Vicki at World Trade Center, New York City, July 4, 2001. Photo by Arnold Neimanis

Russ behind the kit at the World Trade Center, July 4, 2001. Photo by Arnold Neimanis

Susan and Mark share a mic at the World Trade Center, July 4, 2001. Photo by Arnold Neimanis

The Drifters on stage at the Hynes School Fair in New Orleans, 2001. From the collection of Peter Holsapple

Sean Kelly

Chapter Seven:
Some of Carlo's Blues

When Carlo walked away from the Drifters in early 1996, it was a separation that everyone felt deeply and personally. It took time to adjust to the loss, and to fill the musical void. There was no replacing Carlo the drummer, and there was no replacing Carlo the personality.

But, life moved on and so did Carlo. He began pursuing other projects and job opportunities and was working steadily by the time the Drifters hired Russ and recorded *Vermilion*. And although they all lived in the same city and were all working musicians, the remaining Drifters didn't bump into Carlo as often as you might expect.

"I wouldn't have honestly known quite what to say," Peter said. "You love somebody a lot and you see them doing stuff to themselves that is just hard to sit by and watch, because of the effect that it has on them."

After Carlo left the band, he took some of the songs he'd been working on, including "Zoo," and started on a solo record for Monkey Hill. The album, *Loose Strings*, featured a cast of New Orleans musicians including then-local Bob Andrews—best known for his work with Graham Parker & the Rumour—as well as Anders Osborne's keyboard player Glenn Hartman.

Hartman was already in Osborne's band when Carlo left the Drifters and joined that band in 1996. The two became fast friends and worked together on *Loose Strings*, which was recorded at local musician Buzzy Langford's home studio.

"Carlo is a creative genius," Hartman said of his longtime friend. "Brilliant songwriter, brilliant singer, brilliant player on multiple instruments. People loved a lot of his songs. When he left the Drifters and he became a sideman, he lost that outlet. But he also was not in the healthiest place of his life. So he was, with the help of friends, trying to find his voice."

Hartman said it took "a while" to get the album made, considering the state Carlo was in at the time. Years later, Carlo would confess to Hartman that the album was "a cry for help."

Loose Strings was a heavy record—contextually and musically. Songs like "Church of the Dwindling Spirit" are deeply personal, as is "Sake of the Family," a song written in response to his departure from the Drifters and the loss of the familial bond they shared.

The album was released in 1998, the same year that the Drifters recorded *Vermilion*.

One of the most crucial friendships Carlo made during the *Loose Strings* period was with Alex McMurray, frontman and guitarist for Royal Fingerbowl—a band that garnered a sizable following in New Orleans in the 1990s; enough to land them a deal with TVT Records in 1997. That band was also managed by Scott Aiges.

McMurray first met Carlo a few years prior, when they were both at the Maple Leaf Bar and McMurray got into a confrontation with another patron. Carlo happened to step in and prevent a physical altercation.

"Long story short, Carlo kept a guy from beating my ass," McMurray recalled. "He was this guy in a leather jacket with a cigarette who was obviously on something. I mean, you know, it was three in the morning. We were all on something.

"He was a little scary, but I was pretty wasted and he definitely saved me from getting my ass beaten."

Fast forward to 1997, when Carlo played with Osborne at the House of Blues in New Orleans, with Royal Fingerbowl opening.

"We get done and somebody says, 'Hey, man. Carlo Nuccio just loves your band. He made everybody in the dressing room shut up and listen.' And that kind of stuck with me. I was like, 'Huh. That loudmouth asshole likes this shit,'" McMurray said with a laugh.

Not long after that gig, Royal Fingerbowl's drummer, Kevin O'Day, announced in Austin that he was leaving the band at the end of their current tour. Unsure of what to do, McMurray decided to take a walk and try to clear his head.

Carlo, he says, came to mind immediately as a potential replacement, so he called their mutual friend Glenn Hartman, who was still playing with Carlo in Osborne's band. Hartman offered a wholehearted endorsement of Carlo as a player, but also a warning.

McMurray recalled: "I knew from Glenn somehow that Carlo was not that happy with this Anders situation. So I called Glenn. I said, 'Kevin O'Day just quit my band. What do you think if I called Carlo? What would that look like?'

"He said, 'I'll tell you exactly what it's going to look like. He's a great musician, and he would probably join your band. But if you go on the road with Carlo, this is what's going to happen: X, Y, and Z.' And I was like, 'Huh. Well, I guess I could probably deal with that.'"

McMurray hung up, undeterred by the disclaimer, and immediately rang Carlo to pitch him the idea.

"Carlo picks up, and I say, 'Carlo, it's Alex McMurray.' And he says, 'I'll do it,'" he recalled.

Carlo already knew what McMurray wanted from him, and he didn't need any time to consider.

"As he would put it, he 'sussed it out.' He just knew everything," McMurray laughed.

Carlo had found his next move, and joined Royal Fingerbowl soon after. Scott Aiges, who worked with Carlo when he was managing the Drifters, was not too happy.

"[Alex] calls me up one night and he says, 'Our drummer, Kevin O'Day, has quit the band. And I've hired Carlo.' And I told him on the phone, I said, 'Well, then, I quit,'" Aiges recalled. "He raced over to my house at eleven at night and talked me out of it and convinced me not to quit."

Indeed, Carlo had garnered a reputation for being difficult to work with—evidenced by his time with the Drifters and other projects. But his feel was undeniable, the life he injected into the music he played was almost tangible. As a musician he was the perfect hire, with a freakish ability to serve the song like few other drummers could.

"Personally, I don't think I have a single thing in common with other drummers," Carlo said in a 2008 interview. "What most drummers are missing is a song sensibility. It's like they're up there just to boom, whack, and beat their stuff. They're not thinking about the lyrics or dimension of the song—bringing it up, bringing it down, staying off the lyrics. Most guys just seem to clobber right through.

"When you're just clobbering everything, that's work. But if you're just listening to everybody else in the band, listening to the lyrics and you're not thinking about what you're doing, then it's easy."

Listening. That is perhaps the key to what made Carlo so hireable; desirable, even. He listened. And what that gave him was a sound, a signature, a stamp.

"I don't know who taught him that, or if he just intuited that," Hartman said. "He was such a student of New Orleans music, and pop music. Every New Orleans R&B song, he knew. He just loved music. He wasn't just listening, he was listening to what made it great. And he was kind of able to translate that in a very mature way."

His addiction, though, would prove to be an increasingly intolerable blockade to his creative brilliance. That, combined with an assertive and combative personality, was often a catalyst for the burning of bridges and fractured relationships.

Carlo's longtime friend, Iguanas' bassist Rene Coman said: "Carlo was always Carlo, you know? That was sort of the joke—his justification for anything. 'I'm Carlo, damnit.'

"[But] because he had that kind of built into the mix, in a lot of cases he wouldn't stay somewhere for a whole ton of time."

He stayed in touch with Martha Gehman during this tumultuous period, remaining friends after their relationship ended. She remembers noticing that his addiction seemed to be getting increasingly worse when they would talk.

"He would call me and he would just be drunk, drunk, drunk, and his drinking just really accelerated," Gehman said. "He just—he wasn't able to deal."

As the Drifters did, McMurray ultimately reached a breaking point.

"He put everybody through fucking hell," McMurray said. "The people that ran the clubs we played at, every sound man we ever dealt with, fucking hated his guts. The people at the label were like, 'This guy's a mess.'"

McMurray's relationship with Carlo was both a creative partnership and a deep personal friendship that could sometimes be volatile; similar to the familial dynamic of the Drifters.

"We were like brothers," McMurray said. "I hated his guts half the time, but I loved him. We had a connection that was really strong."

Carlo's addiction, coupled with the reputation he had around New Orleans, proved too much for McMurray—who left the Royal Fingerbowl in 2001. Carlo was on a serious decline, and McMurray says he had no choice but to cut things off.

"After I quit the band, I stayed the fuck away from him," McMurray said. "Number one, he made me crazy. And number two, he was just bad news."

Carlo was, indeed, in a dire situation. He was driving away not just his friends as a result, but family as well. His sister, Lena Nuccio, says she and her brother didn't have a close relationship throughout the 1990s and into the early 2000s because of his addiction.

"I missed out on a lot," she said, adding that she didn't know much about his musical endeavors because of the distance she kept. Lena says she was also raising two kids and working to support them, which meant that attending shows and supporting her brother was not always possible.

"It just didn't happen very often because I was busy working full time and taking care of my kids and just living that life in that capacity," Lena said. "I was oblivious to a lot of his musical world."

The state of things for Carlo, and consequently his family, at this point stood in stark contrast to his upbringing in an Italian family of seven. Carlo and Lena were two of five kids; their father, Joseph Nuccio, a former boxer who owned a bar in the French Quarter called Harry's Place.

Nearly every Nuccio sibling grew up taking dance lessons at Anthony Alexander's School of Dance, including Carlo, and he credited his tap, jazz, and ballet training with giving him the foundation to become a drummer.

As he recalled in a 2019 interview, he would often tap dance outside of Harry's Place and entertain passers by.

"When my father needed me to get out of the bar for a minute, I'd go outside and I'd dance, and I'd make money," Carlo recalled. "That started probably around the age of four or five."

Becoming a drummer, "was a natural progression," Carlo continued. " There was a drum set down the street from my house; this guy Lenny Collata, who was, like, four years my senior. He had this drum set, this old Rogers red sparkle drum set, in there. I used to piss him off because I could get behind him and do stuff that he couldn't do.

"That was all largely due to hoofing. Hoofing, you know, it's all rudiments. It's drumming with your feet, but you even clap your hands in there. You put those beats in between—even grace notes sometimes. Sometimes you can do grace notes inside of the steps."

Lena Nuccio recalls his affinity for rhythm being a constant part of their childhood.

"Carlo beat on everything," she said. "He would beat on anything, and he just always had that rhythm. It used to drive me nuts. It was like he was in another world."

One of Carlo's early claims to fame was coining the now-iconic phrase "Who Dat," which he trademarked, alongside studio owner Steve Monistere, in 1983 after he first heard the phrase used by fans of the St. Augustine High School Purple Knights football team.

It's a saying, though, that has roots even further back to a *Times-Picayune* article in 1852.

Together, Monistere and Carlo created a version of "When the Saints Go Marching In" and recruited revered vocalist and New Orleans native Aaron Neville to sing. That version, with the song's legendary "Who dat say dey gonna beat dem Saints?" chant performed by a group of Saints players that included Dave Waymer, Louis Oubre, and Reggie Hill.

"It was kind of funny. That first couple of passes, they were really kind of wimpy about it," Carlo recalled of the studio session in a 2010 *Times-Picayune* interview. "It led to a minor altercation between me and Dave Waymer, when I said, 'No wonder you guys are losing games.'"

Upon its release, the song was a huge hit and quickly caught on across New Orleans as something of an anthem. It started playing regularly at the Superdome over the next few years, as Lena Nuccio—a former Saintsation dancer who joined the squad in 1987—recalls.

"They played it at the Dome, and I remember saying, 'That's my brother. My brother wrote that song!' I was very, very proud of him for those contributions," she said.

While Carlo and Steve Monistere did own the trademark for the phrase "Who Dat" starting in the early 1980s, it expired in 1993 and was later purchased by the NFL. Today, it's a brand of its own.

The "Who Dat" phenomenon, while a notable addition to Carlo's resume, only scratched the surface of his contribution to New Orleans and its music community. After returning to NOLA in 1993, he began cementing himself more as both a musical fixture and a unique character in the scene—playing on sessions for Osborne, Buckwheat Zydeco, and Theresa Andersson.

He also worked at times for Malcolm Burn, a Canadian-born producer who by this point was best known for his work as engineer and co-conspirator for mega producer Daniel Lanois. When Lanois moved to New Orleans and opened Kingsway Studio, Burn followed—quickly forging a path for himself as a producer of note for artists like Giant Sand, John Mellencamp, and the Neville Brothers.

"You couldn't talk to the guy without busting a gut," Burn recalled of Carlo. "I don't even know how to describe his sense of humor. It was like he'd sort of gone to the other side and come back, and survived. You always had the impression that this guy should be dead already—like ten times over, you know? There was a sort of a dark humor that, of course, does come with the territory if you're from New Orleans anyway."

One of Burn's most famous productions was Emmylou Harris' *Red Dirt Girl*—recorded at Clouet Street Studio in New Orleans in early 2000. That album, which won a Grammy® for Best Contemporary Folk Album, featured a cover of a Patty Griffin song called "One Big Love," with Carlo on percussion.

Jim Watts, who engineered the *Red Dirt Girl* sessions and worked with Burn frequently, recalls Carlo coming in to track on top of a loop that they'd built from drums played by Ethan Johns. Naturally, Carlo's signature style comes through even as his role was only to play flourishes.

"Malcolm and Emmy left for the day and said, 'Here, have at it.' And Carlo came in and did overdub some drums on there," Watts recalled. "There's a lot of little tom fills and extra feel stuff that is him. So he is injecting that *thing* into it."

Carlo worked on some notable records—not just Amos' breakthrough *Under the Pink* or Harris' genre-bending *Red Dirt Girl*, but also Kristin Hersh's acclaimed 1999 album *Sky Motel*. That album was recorded at Kingsway, with Trina Shoemaker producing.

Musically, the 1990s was a fruitful decade for Carlo, despite his troubles. And he was, as always, a generous guy with a big heart.

"Carlo was a big puppy dog. He could do the tough guy shit, but he was a very soulful Sicilian American from the deep South," Matt Piucci said. "He was a very generous guy. When I got married in 1986, we were on tour and we came back. I told Carlo we were going to honeymoon in New Orleans. He goes, 'Oh, you can have my apartment.' He meant *have his apartment*. He left. It was very, very sweet."

Piucci also recalled meeting Carlo's family, who he says reminded him a lot of his father's (very Italian) family. When they were on tour together with the Rain Parade in 1986, the band stopped in Chicago, where Piucci's parents lived, and New Orleans, where they stayed with Carlo's parents. He remembers them being generous people who, of course, always had food at the ready.

"We're in New Orleans, and we stop at Carlo's house," Piucci said. "We had stopped at my parents' house, and my dad, being Italian and all, made a ridiculous amount of food. He got along with Carlo. So [Carlo] wanted to return the favor, and when we went down to New Orleans, I walk into Carlo's kitchen and Carlo's mom says, 'Hiya, hon. Are ya hungry?'"

The Nuccios' Italian generosity and familial spirit was certainly passed down to Carlo, who many say was always willing to step up and make something happen for someone when they needed help or a favor.

Jimmy Ford recalled: "He had this 16-track two-inch [tape] machine that he lugged around in the back of his Bronco, like it was a refrigerator/freezer or something. It was an incredible fucking machine, right? So finally, he calls me and he's like, 'Hey man, you wanna buy this?' I'm thinking if I get one session out of it, it might be worth it. And that was in the ADAT days.

"I said, 'Look, I'll buy that machine for what I would pay for one brand new ADAT.' Motherfucker throws it in the back of his Bronco and drives across the country. And the machine ran for about ten years."

Lenny Zenith, a trailblazer for trans musicians, remembers Carlo defending him from a transphobic audience member at a gig at Jimmy's in New Orleans in the 1980s. Carlo, he says, chased the guy out of the club.

As a drummer, Carlo's idiosyncratic approach made him an asset to so many records and so many live bands. Galactic drummer Stanton Moore even cited Carlo in a video on his Drum Academy YouTube channel as a "master" of what's known as the "swamp shuffle," a groove that Moore describes as living somewhere between straight and swing.

On the more straightforward side, take Tori Amos' hit "Cornflake Girl" as an example. Carlo's propulsive, albeit tame groove grounded Amos' busy piano hook. No fancy fills, nothing flashy, just a simple and solid groove. And yet, it was unmistakably Carlo.

"We both talk about serving the song as being what we're about, and one of our commonalities," Russ said. "But we're both as guilty as anyone else at overplaying, or doing things that didn't necessarily serve the song.

"But, for me… it's his feel. I know that the space is between his kick and snare. The space is between his left hand and his right hand; just from having to study him so in depth."

For producers, his tastefulness and ability to listen and work within the context of the song made him an obvious choice.

"I just remember being blown away because he did everything I liked," Steve Berlin said. "Certainly there was nobody that I knew that played anything like Carlo. Nobody had that feel and that deep, Southern soul. He was certainly the funkiest drummer that I knew of back then."

What about his playing is so unmistakable? Ultimately, it's a combination of factors. Carlo played, and seemed to tune, in such a way that was deeper, looser, and more resonant. More sustain, more low end; a less tight and crisp snare sound. That's not to say he didn't adjust for the song or project—say, for a pop song that called for a certain sound—but his stamp, if you will, had a larger and more resonant sound to it.

There was also his ear for playing behind the beat. In music, playing behind the beat essentially means playing a little late—staying behind the tempo just slightly. There are numerous drummers in all genres that are excellent purveyors of this approach, but Carlo had an instinctive ear for where he wanted to be time-wise, as Rene Coman explains.

"Playing with Carlo as much as I did, I quickly figured out, 'There's only one place he's going to play this stuff.' And either you can go with him or you can try to fight him, but it's a losing battle," Coman said. "Some guys, they want to put [the beat] in a certain place and they want you to counteract that and be on top of it or something. With Carlo it's almost like, if you get on top of where he was he'd put it back even farther."

For Dave Catching, who played with Carlo in not only the Drifters but also in Devil Squares (along with Gary Eaton), Carlo's playing style was completely foreign to him the first time they worked together.

"Most of the bands I played in were either country or punk rock or rock and roll, and I'd never really played with a backbeat drummer from New Orleans that was on the back end of the beat," Catching said. "I remember the first time thinking, 'What the hell is this guy's playing style?' I didn't get it because I was always on the beat or ahead of it, and he was so far behind. The first gig I played with him was at Al's Bar in downtown L.A., and we started the show and I was like, 'Ah, fuck, I finally get it now!' That was a real eye opener, you know?"

He had a playfulness to his style as well, as Danny McGough recalls.

"Carlo typically will fuck with you," he said "When he would play you'd go, 'Oh my god, what is happening?' And then, boom!

"It's kind of like swimming in a vodka tonic or something. There are these bubbles that keep you floating, but every once in a while you get hit by an ice cube."

Keith Morris cites Carlo as one of his favorite drummers he's played with, and they did indeed play together for a spell when Carlo was in Los Angeles. In fact, one of Carlo's many brushes with high-level opportunity came as the drummer for Morris' post-Circle Jerks band Bug Lamp, which the two formed in 1990 with guitarist Rob Stennett and bassist Bruce Duff.

"One of my favorite things about Carlo was that he had, like, a slump and glop," Morris describes.

Playing with Carlo in Bug Lamp was a thrilling but at times frustrating experience for Morris, who says there was a lot of buzz around the band since it was his first band after Circle Jerks went on an extended hiatus. They had major label interest, and were negotiating lucrative offers from labels but Carlo and Stennett, Morris says, were both "impatient" and left the band before a deal could be made. What's more, Morris was several years sober by this point, and playing with an often-intoxicated Carlo proved challenging for achieving the level of focus and attention needed to propel them forward.

Bug Lamp never made a proper record, but worked on so much material (much of it composed by Carlo) that Morris recalls feeling overwhelmed by the sheer amount of ideas going around. They gigged often in their short existence, and were one of those bands that could have been so much more.

Morris remembers a classic Carlo moment at a gig in San Diego: "We had a show down in San Diego at a place called The Casbah. Everybody that plays in San Diego plays there. We pull up, we unload the gear, we do the soundcheck, and then right after we get through doing the soundcheck, Carlo stops the guy that makes sure all the beers are properly stocked. Carlo stops him, and he's got a case of King Cobra [malt liquor]—the stuff is used to remove rust and grease in your car. This stuff is not even fit for human consumption.

"Carlo goes up to the guy and goes, 'So, what are you doing with this?' And the guy says, 'Oh, we can't sell this so I'm getting rid of it.' And Carlo said, 'Just go ahead and give it to me.'

"Before we played, Carlo drank probably 20 of them. His brain was erased. So we played our set, everybody's digging it. A drunken Carlo is better than eighty percent of the drummers out there. It's ridiculous that he could take himself and remove himself that far from reality, and yet sit behind a drum kit and just play like a motherfucker.

"So while we're playing, he finishes up the other four [beers]. We play our last note, and nobody bothers to look at Carlo because of the condition he was in. And all of the sudden, Carlo breaks into a drum solo. And when I say a drum solo, I mean a twelve-to-fifteen minute drum solo. What the fuck?! He's basically riffing on John Bonham's 'Moby Dick.' He's playing it almost note-for-note but he's also adding his little bits and pieces.

"At this point in the evening, the crowd is supposed to be heading out the door. But nobody leaves. The whole room was stupefied. There were jaws on the floor."

Carlo's abilities didn't come from nowhere; he had an array of influences. Coman cites rock standards like Led Zeppelin and The Beatles as Carlo's influences, as well as New Orleans jazz and R'n'B greats like Earl Palmer, who influenced both Carlo and Russ.

"It wasn't just one bag," Coman said. "He kind of had a Carlo bag that he made out of all of that, you know?"

Drawing from influences is one thing, but finding your own approach while taking inspiration from your musical lineage is something else entirely. It's a delicate balance that Carlo managed to strike—finding guidance primarily from drummers like Palmer and legendary New Orleans drummer Big John Thomassie.

"That feel, you can find it historically before him," Russ explained. "You can find the drummers that he was influenced by. In time, I've learned how to play with that and do different things, you know? Like push the snare or have a little control over it. For Carlo, Big John Thomassie was a big one. If you listen to him, he in my opinion is the closest thing to a Carlo groove."

The *Loose Strings* era was a complicated time for Carlo, who was deep in his illness and living on the absolute edge. He was already a larger-than-life character, as many from New Orleans tend to be, but drugs and alcohol heightened that part of him further.

"There's something about people who are actually from New Orleans," Hartman said. "The few in the music scene that are from there are extraordinary in personality and in musical ability. It's kind of like encountering anything from New Orleans—it's ten times more than you could ever imagine. You can't explain it; how over the top it is, any door you walk through.

"That's kind of Carlo, in a way. You take that person and that musicality outside of New Orleans, and you just become… you're so much larger than life."

There are downsides to that sort of personality; namely, for Carlo, it was the way he worked with others in a creative setting when he had an opinion on something. It posed problems with the Drifters often, as Peter recalls.

"I think Carlo and I, and Carlo and Mark, definitely locked horns about stuff. He didn't pull any punches," Peter said. "Understanding, of course, that Carlo is Carlo, and Carlo for good or bad is larger than life. He's the son of a boxer and a bar owner, a tap dancer, and a smart guy."

Steve Berlin recalls hiring Carlo for a session with Buckwheat Zydeco and having no choice but to fire him when Buckwheat could no longer tolerate Carlo's insistence on doing things his way.

"Buck literally wanted to kill him," Berlin said. "That same thing that made him such a character in L.A., literally it drove Buck out of his mind. 'Tell that motherfucker to shut the fuck up. I don't want to hear his opinion about anything.'

"I pulled him aside more than a couple times and just said, 'Look, man, you're pissing Buck off. Just don't say anything. Just shut up and listen to him.' And he literally couldn't do it. He just literally could not shut up."

Most everyone who remembers Carlo's combative nature also notes that he was almost always right. And while some, like Buckwheat Zydeco, weren't particularly receptive to his opinions, others welcomed them and even relied on Carlo's ear for guidance.

"The thing about working with Carlo in the studio was that he was supremely musical," Lenny Zenith said. "He was passionate about the tracks, the takes, the feel. He would not quit until it was done right; it wasn't always easy, but he was always right."

Drug addiction interfered with most aspects of his life, however, and he even nearly squandered a few session opportunities that came his way as a result. Going back to Los Angeles, Martha

Gehman notes that Carlo flaked on an audition for John Hiatt because he was passed out drunk. Similarly, Malcolm Burn recalls hiring Carlo and Rene Coman in 1999 to play on an album he was producing for Swiss singer/songwriter Stephan Eicher, which was to be recorded in Switzerland.

"[Stephan] was a very, very talented guy—very delicate, soft spoken, sensitive artiste, you know? And I decided that it would be interesting to bring my friends from New Orleans over to Switzerland," Burn amusedly recalled. "I was there with my friend, [guitarist] Jeff Treffinger, and Rene showed up, and Carlo showed up about a day and a half later. Somebody said, 'Oh, Carlo's on his way from the airport.'

"It was, like, snow outside, right? There's like half a foot of snow outside. And all of the sudden he's like, 'I'm here! Motherfuckers lost my goddamn luggage.' And Carlo walks in wearing shorts and a t-shirt. And that's the only thing he had. That's all he had for about two days up in the Swiss Alps."

However difficult it was to wrangle him, there was no replacing what you got with a Carlo performance. Even when Eicher brought in the legendary Manu Katché to re-record drums on a few songs, Burn recalls preferring Carlo's playing.

"As great of a drummer as Manu Katché is, he didn't hold a candle to what Carlo did in terms of vibe and feel," Burn said.

Carlo's world progressively grew darker and his circles smaller. He isolated himself from family and friends, falling deeper into drug addiction, and losing out on jobs. Both Lena Nuccio and Alex McMurray recall him at his worst, looking almost unrecognizable and even cheating death on multiple occasions.

"When he was really using hard, he was a skeleton and he just looked like shit," McMurray said. "It was so sad to see him so you didn't even want to see him."

Adds Lena: "He looked so sick. He was on heroin and everything. He looked like a skeleton."

He'd also been arrested several times, asking his mother on one occasion not to bail him out for fear of where that might lead.

"My mother—god love her—she will love you to death," Lena said. "She and my father were so afraid of their boys being in jail. Carlo would tell her, 'Mom, don't get me out. I'm going to die. If you get me out, I'm going to die.'"

Loose Strings was a lot of things for Carlo—a showcase of his songwriting prowess, a vehicle for his incredible voice, and a way for him to keep himself busy musically. It was certainly a feat on many levels, and one deserving of a celebration—which he did with a release show at the Howlin' Wolf. Mark Walton decided to attend despite not having spoken to Carlo at all since their less-than-amicable split two years earlier.

"I thought I'd at least show up and give him my love," Mark said. "I got yanked on stage to play a song, which I hadn't played in years, and I'm like, 'I don't think I should be up here.' He just saw me there and said, 'Mark, get on stage!'"

The two hardly spoke at the show, with Mark quickly thanking Carlo for inviting him up and then leaving after the gig was finished. A brief and distant connection for two fractured friends, over in a blink.

Chapter Eight: Here's a Record… Who Wants It?

"It was just a crazy family. It was really good. Everybody was drinking. We'd all get pretty fucked up, but the shows were great."

—Robert Maché

Part I

Every band wants to make a record they're proud of; something they can use as both a calling card and an artistic proof of concept. *Vermilion* was always intended to be that for the Drifters. After all they'd been through, losing so much of their identity when Carlo left, they needed a win and they felt like they finally had one.

Despite each Drifter's individual takes on the pursuit of "success," they were united in the fact that what they'd created at Dockside was something they'd be proud to shop around and find a home for in the States.

"I had this fantasy that the Continental Drifters were going to be the face of Americana; that we were going to be the standard bearers," Vicki said. "We were going to be the ones who brought that music into the mainstream. As crazy as that all sounds. It's kind of what Wilco ended up doing, in a way, but I felt like that was our role to play at that moment."

With the burgeoning Americana scene taking shape in Germany, the band was riding pretty high there after the album's release—not quite "face of Americana," but they were on the cutting edge of a genre that was just starting to really break there. The Drifters were in Germany just one month after *Vermilion's* release there, seeing great response to the record and doing well in clubs across the country.

Heckmann's estimation is that the album sold roughly 5,000 copies in Germany—considerably more than the eponymous record did a few years earlier. And with audiences showing up and national press interested, Germany seemed to be the place to be for the band.

"People were excited, and I think it was getting some traction here and there," Mark said. "I wish we could have gotten out of Germany a little more. That was the disappointment of it all, but of course it was a German record label and [Edgar] was thinking about Germany."

Mark recalls one show in Germany where the band showed up to play and the venue was closed. They were apparently unaware that a show was booked for that night, but they decided to open their doors and let the band play anyway.

"A couple people showed up, so we had fun and we did what we do when no one shows up," he said with a laugh.

The band was having fun in Germany, and it was evident on stage. They were even letting the inside jokes out. At a show in Göppingen, Peter introduced "Watermark" as being written by Vicki—"the Cajun Boogie swamp queen."

"Or to some of us, she's known as Country Ass Bitch," Susan quipped.

They had moments like that in spades, but also some genuinely moving performances like that of "Drifters" on the very same night, where Susan introduced the then-new composition to the crowd.

"It's a beautiful song," she said, "and it actually is about all of us."

There was some truth to that, undoubtedly. It was a song about everyone; a song about the little world they'd built around them and the people who understood, like their growing German audience. Things were going well there, however gradually the successes were adding up, but in the U.S. there just wasn't the momentum that the band needed to get more ears on the product. Getting a label interested in *Vermilion* was not easy, and frustrations were mounting.

"We were trying—we thought that would be the best calling card: 'Here's a finished record. Who wants it? We like it a lot, we think you'd do good by it.' But nobody was biting. Not one person," Mark said. "After the Mercury demos we thought, 'Okay, maybe Mercury would be interested now that we have it done.' But they turned us down. After the demos, it didn't seem like there was much interest at that point. We just felt like nobody was listening to us."

The years of minimal label interest were frustrating at best, and it's not as if the Drifters had chart topping aspirations or were desperate for a major. Sure, they pursued Mercury, but all they really wanted was a label to enable them to make records and tour. There was no real desire for huge major label machinery behind them. For Vicki and Susan, their prior experiences in the mainstream informed a legitimate lack of interest in that path.

"Both Susan and I are probably not the most pristine examples of somebody coming from the major label world," Vicki said. "Susan, because she was so young, and wasn't involved in any of the imaginations of label life, really, other than going where she was told to go.

"For me, I was coming from a poor experience, actually. Ironically, considering I came from a band with top five hits. But my actual experience of working with major labels was not particularly positive. Suddenly it felt real and honest, and we're not trying to please anybody other than ourselves. It was so strong and powerful and beautiful in that way for me, that the idea of signing with a major label—I probably would've been the one to vote against it."

Still, she admits, having the infrastructure of a major behind the band *could* have benefitted them—with one giant caveat.

"*If*, and it's a big-ass if, we had an advocate at said major label," she said.

Peter, for his part, believed that *Vermilion* was a strong enough record to really make a dent in a way that he hadn't been able to before.

"As the eternal aspirant, I always felt like the Drifters had a wonderful, wonderful shot somehow that the dB's had not been able to muster," he said.

This was a feeling shared among the entire band, and thankfully they did have people in their corner who wanted to help. The band's lawyer, Bob Stein, was a central part of that support system around the giant question mark that was *Vermilion*. Stein was a huge music fan and became devoted to helping to find the band a label.

Stein says his relationship with the Drifters began via phone conversations with Mark, before he finally met them in person after what he describes as an "incendiary" show at the Bowery Ballroom in New York City. Getting Stein into the fold was, for the Drifters, a step in the direction of getting themselves organized enough to find a record contract and keep things straight on the business end.

There became an operational cycle, in a way, where the band would play as much as they could when schedules permitted, and then when Peter was out on a Hootie run, Russ, Mark, and Robert would focus on booking, doing press, and pursuing whatever opportunities they could. They'd also get together on a regular basis for band meetings.

"We would do it weekly; have these business meetings," Russ said. "We would discuss what's going on, and perhaps dole out responsibilities. Everyone had jobs."

He emphasized that while they could get focused once the meetings got started, getting everyone there in the first place was a challenge. A difficult undertaking at the least.

"The other common phrase is that it's like herding cats," Vicki said, more pointedly.

Russ describes getting everyone together on time for band meetings as "slogging through mud."

"We'd show up at the meeting missing a boot because it got stuck in the quicksand," he analogized. "We were trying. We were putting effort in to be business-minded so we weren't just spinning our wheels."

For Russ, this wasn't the most business-minded band he'd been a part of, but it wasn't the worst example. He recalls working for Terrance Simien as an example of having an especially strong business model.

"He had his business shit together. He kept good books, he had management. I was a side guy, but at that time he paid us a percentage. So we got to see the books," he recalled. "We'd settle up each week and he'd show us the numbers. I was making eleven percent of 85 percent.

"That was kind of my schooling of having a business in a band. And then I got with the Bluerunners—their business model was a boat with no rudder, no sail, and three holes in the bottom. It was just like, 'What the fuck.'"

The Drifters didn't want to focus too heavily on mainstream aspirations, so they didn't emphasize the business in the same way more industry-minded artists might.

"We never had conversations [about], like, 'Oh my god, how are we going to make a hit record?' That was just never a part of the plan," Vicki said. "[This] was before the launch of social media where you could promote yourself and find ways to monetize your music without all of those other actors. But still, even in that scenario, you have to be a band who wants to also be a business. Most bands don't want to do that."

Some Drifters were more concerned with finding a label than others, but there ultimately was an overall feeling of not letting commercial ambitions get in the way of what the band was really about.

"Why I joined the Continental Drifters was that there wasn't going to be anything official about it," Susan said. "That was my tribal cry—for *me*, Susan Cowsill, personally. Nothing is expected of me, everything is encouraged of me, and whatever I want is a-okay. I'm invested as *that*."

Susan has one of the great underrated voices of her generation. She's a person bursting with natural creative ability. With her history, you'd assume that music was it for her, from day one. But as she explains, it's never been that simple.

"The secret about me, ultimately, is that my main desire in life has never been to be an artist. Of any kind," she said. "My main desire in life has been to be a mom, and a wife, and a family member, and a community contributor, and a do-gooder, and a baker. And I don't know what that means, because I clearly have this *thing*. And I would also feel like I was being really rude to ignore it."

Don Dixon, a longtime friend of the band who's best known for co-producing R.E.M.'s first two albums, says he understands the Drifters' ambivalence toward commercial success—especially Susan's.

"She dealt with all the horror of being a 12-year-old girl on the fucking *Mike Douglas Show*," Dixon said. "That's the kind of trauma she had, but she ran away from it."

Dixon looks at the state of the industry in the 1990s as an "odd" time for music, especially in L.A., and says he thinks that the Drifters being in New Orleans was a good idea for a band with their particular ethos.

"There weren't these clear, clear trends about what was selling a lot," he said. "New wave and punk had come in and kind of blown up a lot of the paradigms. College radio created these monsters like R.E.M., and that was all out of an underground thing.

"It was not part of what had been the traditional Scotti Brothers mainstream of music, which is where the Hollywood music scene was. I thought [Los Angeles] was an awkward place for the Drifters to be, actually. When they decided to move, that made total sense to me—to get out of Hollywood, where nothing is real."

You could say that everyone in the Drifters was just feeding a muse. It wasn't about money, it wasn't about fame. This was a band all about the intention to make music, and "that was good enough," as Russ explains.

"Whenever we can make it happen, it's fulfilling," he said.

With this, there came a casualness about the way the band operated. Still, they knew that they needed money to get the record released, and that's where a label would come in.

There was also the challenge of, at this point, self-managing. As independent artists know all too well, representing yourself can often work against you.

Vicki explains: "A lot of agents, promoters, label personnel don't want to talk to the band members. First of all, they need to be able to say things like, 'You can't draw [a crowd], so I'm not going to pay you that.'

"They don't want to say that. Unpleasant truths—they don't want to say those things to the artist. But they can say it to the manager."

So, with the help of folks like Bob Stein and with the assistance of a solid booking agent, the band was out on their own, making their way as best they could. And the only thing they really wanted was to play. It got to a point where essentially, when everyone was available, they were gigging. They were committed to being on the road as much as possible in front of audiences. That was largely the motivating factor for finding a label to release *Vermilion*.

"We were just kind of horny to get the record out in the States so we could play," Peter said.

Playing live was the modus operandi of the Continental Drifters; it always had been, but *Vermilion* raised the stakes. As Susan recalls, it was the first Drifters record that, for her, was truly a concerted effort to make something cohesive that they could get behind.

"*Vermilion* was very intentional. *Vermilion* was a collected group of people with a mindset," she said. "And we were well into our 'Club Drifter' way of life. Our own little boat on the island that crashed or not, if we wanted. That kind of vibe. The Mickey Mouse Club had been formed, and we had a theme song and everything."

The band was fired up, and ready to get out and get the record heard, despite a lack of label interest.

"We pulled a million strings to make it happen," Russ said. "All the strings were in front of us and it just felt like the shit's getting done whether we had a label or not."

At the same time this was happening, Peter was tapped to be musical director for another night of music at The Arts at St. Ann's in Brooklyn, New York—this time, he was asked to curate a show paying tribute to the music of Sandy Denny. The wheels were actually in motion immediately following the Nick Drake show, with Peter suggesting it to Arts at St. Ann's program director Janine Nichols. Nichols agreed, and they set off to plan the next year's event.

Denny, today regarded as one of the greatest singers of her generation, was best known for her work in the 1960s with Fairport Convention. She joined that band for their second album, and was credited with steering them in the direction of the traditional British folk music that would dominate their *Liege & Lief* album in 1969.

Following her departure from Fairport, Denny formed the briefly-active Fotheringay before launching a solo career. She also was known for her vocals on Led Zeppelin's "The Battle of Evermore," which gave her the title of being the only guest vocalist ever on a Led Zeppelin recording.

Denny died in 1978 after suffering a brain hemorrhage following multiple severe falls.

Her legacy and influence grew exponentially in the years since her death, thanks to posthumous releases and the influence of her music on the folk rock genre. Peter, a longtime Fairport fan, was largely responsible for the other Drifters becoming fans themselves—to the point where they'd started covering "Meet on the Ledge" and ultimately recorded it for the Black Dog single.

Well, not *everyone* in the band was a Fairport fan.

"Even back when Carlo was in the band, Peter would try to infiltrate some of that [music]," Mark said, admitting that Carlo wasn't much interested in covering Fairport's songs. "Peter would know the exact terminology that Carlo used, but it was something to the effect of, 'I don't want to play that fucking fairy music.' It was something to that effect."

Peter does know. It was actually "leprechaun music."

It's obvious on songs such as "Anything" and "Waltz With You" that the Drifters were veering subtly into folk rock territory when they made *Vermilion*, as the use of folk instrumentation (mandolins, accordions, acoustic guitars) was more prominent than it had been previously.

It only made sense when the idea of a Sandy Denny tribute came to Peter's mind, he thought of the Drifters as the house band.

"Peter was on the road with Hootie all that time," Mark recalled. "He was like, 'I agreed to do this and be the musical director, but I really want you guys to play the music and be the house band. Would you mind doing the heavy lifting and just figure it out yourselves?' We were like, 'Uh, yeah! Sure!'"

Peter did, though, assemble something of an all-star lineup for the show and curate a near-perfect setlist of Denny songs that spanned her career.

"That's sort of my roots, in a lot of ways. As much as the New York Dolls. So it was exciting to me. It was something that struck me as a really fun project that would suit the Drifters particularly well," he said, adding that he discovered both Fairport and Fotheringay on an A&M Records sampler titled *Friends* in 1970.

For the New York show, Peter called on some friends, including R.E.M.'s Mike Mills, Hootie's Darius Rucker, Robyn Hitchcock, Don Dixon and Marti Jones, singer and violinist Deni Bonet, and Jolene frontman John Crooke, among others.

The lineup also featured Welsh singer Katell Keineg, Irish artist Susan McKeown, blackgirls frontwoman Dana Kletter, and singer/songwriter Amanda Thorpe.

Vicki also called in a favor to her fellow Bangle, and auxiliary Drifter, Michael Steele.

"I actually thought of Michael Steele because I knew she was such a huge Fairport fan, and she has just a beautiful voice that I don't think was ever celebrated well enough in The Bangles," Vicki said. "I talked her into doing it, and she took a train across the country."

With that, the band assembled in New York City on November 20, 1998 and rehearsed with the guest stars at SIR Studios for a show the next day.

"Everyone on this show had a time slot to come rehearse for a runthrough. It'd be, like, one or two times through and you may leave. You know, time was limited and it was the day before the show, so we're just knocking it out," Russ recalled.

In a true New York moment, Russ had a memorable encounter during rehearsals with one of his favorite bands.

"I'm strolling down the hall getting some air, and I hear some drums and percussion going on, and the doors open—it's the fucking Beastie Boys!" he said. "They were rehearsing for *Saturday Night Live* the next day."

As was tradition for the Drifters, there wasn't an overwhelming amount of preparation beforehand aside from a day of rehearsal. But there was an energy and excitement about the evening, which was to be broadcast live on WFUV.

One of the performers that evening was Deni Bonet, multi-instrumentalist and singer whose career began in the house band for NPR's long-running Mountain Stage in West Virginia. A prolific session and touring player, Bonet has recorded and/or toured with Cyndi Lauper, Robyn Hitchcock, R.E.M., and Richard Barone, among others.

Bonet met Peter through her Mountain Stage gig, and was ultimately invited to sing a song during the Denny show and contribute on other songs as part of the Drifter-centric house band. Bonet had also performed as part of the Nick Drake tribute the previous year.

"It was just very reverent," Bonet, who sang Denny's solo song "One Way Donkey Ride," taken from her 1977 album *Rendezvous*, recalled of the show. "But backstage, it was all hugs and kisses and love."

Reverence is a near-perfect descriptor for the vibe at St. Ann's that night—emphasized by the fact that there was no speaking in between songs. Save for an introduction by WFUV's Meg Griffin and a short speech from Peter, it flowed from one song to the next. That made for a night that focused on the music rather than the artists involved.

"It wasn't about the individual people singing or the individuals playing," Bonet said. "It was about the collective spirit of the whole thing—to give tribute to Sandy Denny. That's what made it different. I kind of liked that."

The sold-out show began with Griffin calling on the audience to shut their eyes and remember the first time they heard Denny's voice:

When was the first time that you remember hearing the voice of this woman? Try to remember right now how it went through you, and how important it was. Think about that first time, and then realize that tonight so much of that—in a very special way—will be recreated.

Katell Keineg began the show with an a cappella version of "Come All Ye," a signature Denny-fronted Fairport song from *Liege & Lief*, and it only got better from there. Susan McKeown's version of "Tam Lin" remains a standout of the night as well.

"Oh my god, talk about taking no prisoners," Robert said. "She was magical."

John Crooke, whose band Jolene was, at the time, promoting its album *In The Gloaming* for Sire Records, recalls being awestruck by the caliber of talent around him during the Denny tribute.

"For me, it was a bit intimidating," Crooke admitted. "In the highlights of my career, that certainly is one."

Crooke and his Jolene bandmates had gotten to know the Drifters quite well by this point, initially meeting them at a festival they both played in Charleston, South Carolina, but not making much of a connection. They really got to know the band via Peter by way of Hootie— with whom Jolene had toured with for years. Jolene, from Charlotte, North Carolina, was just an hour away from Hootie's hometown of Columbia, South Carolina, so the two bands crossed paths even in Hootie's pre-fame years.

"They took us out on the *Cracked Rear View* tour in the U.S., and a European leg," Crooke said. "And we officially met Peter on that tour. He reached out to Vicki and Susan and said, 'You've got to meet these Jolene guys. They're in the family, so to speak, and they're doing something really great.'"

Susan and Vicki ended up flying out on that tour and hung out with Crooke and his bandmates, and the group hit it off.

"It just blew my mind, just to see the way that they operated first as this wonderful collection of friends and family—first and foremost," Crooke recalled. "This was one of those milestone moments in a series of moments that changed my creative north star."

The friendship between Jolene and the Drifters culminated in Peter, Vicki, and Susan joining them in Quebec, Canada, where they recorded *In The Gloaming*.

Crooke says that Seymour Stein, head of Sire Records, gave Jolene his approval to administer their own budget—meaning they could decide where to go to record and what to do with regard to their album. They chose Canada because, well, it made a hell of a lot of financial sense.

"It was seventy-five cents to the dollar, so with a $125,000 budget we were making a $200,000 record and living like kings," he said. "We could fly in Peter; we could fly in Susan and Vicki. We were able to mix in London and mix in New York, and still come in within ten percent."

Crooke says he "fell in love" with the Drifters and took every chance he could get to be around them—even within Jolene's intense 300-show-per-year touring schedule at the time.

"I would pre-pay my rent at some fleabag in Charlotte for a year, just to get it off my books, and we'd be gone. And every chance I'd get, I'd fly down to New Orleans and go to Vicki's," he recalled. "New Orleans became central to our world."

John Crooke was a music fan and an R.E.M. devotee. So when Peter asked him to partake in the Sandy Denny tribute show alongside that band's bassist/songwriter Mike Mills, he was fairly overwhelmed.

"I was the 'nobody' on that show," he said. "In however modest of a trajectory Jolene had—it felt like there was a lot of momentum, so for [this show] to happen within that, it was sort of affirming in a lot of ways. It felt really fucking good."

Crooke's song was, aptly enough, "John the Gun," which he delivered with a power and ferocity that he'd become known for delivering in Jolene.

"I worked my ass off," he said. "I didn't just pop in and do the song. Man, I was in the woodshed doing the work and putting the work in prior to getting there, because I didn't want to be the one that let Peter and the Drifters down."

Not only did he not let them down, he's cited by many of the Drifters as a highlight of the night.

"He brought his A game for that one," Robert said.

Don Dixon and Marti Jones were two of the other singers that night—joining their many friends in the Drifters and among the lineup of singers. As a producer, Dixon had famously worked with Mills on the first two R.E.M. albums, but was also a longtime friend and collaborator of Darius Rucker and Hootie & the Blowfish.

Peter's connection with both Dixon and Jones went back many years. Dixon was friends with Peter from pre-dB's days in North Carolina (Peter's junior high school days, to be exact, where he saw Dixon's hard rock band Arrogance many times), and Jones—who married Dixon after the two worked together on Jones' records for A&M Records in the 1980s—was a dB's friend who covered a few of Peter's songs.

Not only did Peter have a connection to Dixon and Jones, but Jones actually played a pivotal role at a defining point in Vicki's career.

"She sang on the demo of 'Walk Like An Egyptian,'" Vicki revealed. "It was, I swear to god, one of the reasons why I wanted to do that song. She's like the female John Doe to me. She's just got an iconic American sound."

"Egyptian" was written by Liam Sternberg, who discovered Marti Jones and was having her do multiple demos for him at the time. Interestingly enough, "Egyptian" was initially meant for Toni Basil and not The Bangles.

"He had written another song, which I also did the demo for, called 'Fall to Innocence,' and he had me sing both of those songs in the same session," Jones said. "He meant for 'Fall to Innocence' to go to The Bangles, so he probably just sent both songs."

Similarly, Jones had an interesting connection to Susan, by way of a song called "Chance of a Lifetime"—written by Dwight Twilley. The original demo, which was pitched to Jones by her publisher for her 1986 album *Match Game*, was sung by Susan.

"They sent me the demo and I said, 'Who is singing that?' And they said, 'Well, you're not going to believe this, but it's Susan Cowsill.' And I said, 'You mean, *and spaghetti*?'" Jones recalled, referencing Susan's iconic line from The Cowsills' "Hair."

"To make the circle complete now, Vicki has to do a demo for Susan," Jones jokes.

At the St. Ann's show, Jones and Dixon joined the Drifters for Fotheringay's "Peace in the End," and Dixon also sang Denny's solo song "Gold Dust."

"We rehearsed someplace that was close enough to where we were in Tribeca to walk to," Dixon recalled.

"We walked, like, *miles*. [Dixon] always makes us walk miles! 'It's just up here!'" Jones laughed, ribbing her husband.

They did, indeed, walk with their daughter in the cold from where they were staying to St. Ann's Church—as did Mark Walton.

"I was at my friend's house a few blocks away and I had to run back to get my clothes. And as I was running back, it was really cold. I pulled a muscle in my leg and I couldn't walk, so I got back and I was hobbling," Mark recalled. "So I ended up sitting on a stool the whole show, which kind of bummed me out. But it actually made me focus in a little bit more and actually just play."

Vicki, who'd been assigned the show's titular song "Listen, Listen," was particularly excited not just to be in the backing band for the night, but to sing lead on "Listen, Listen" because it was a rare chance for her to put down a guitar and just be a singer.

"I wasn't normally just a singer, and I didn't even at that point consider myself a singer, really," she said.

The rehearsals went well, but when the day of the show arrived, Vicki says she woke up with no voice. She'd developed what she describes as a "phenomenal" case of bronchitis.

"In the nineties, for whatever reason, it was my disease of choice. I would get it not infrequently, and weirdly haven't had it since," she said. "Susan would accuse me of being a tuberculosis patient because I was always coughing and developing bronchitis."

Devastated, Vicki—with Kevin Salem, who she was dating at the time, along for the ride—decided to try something she'd never done before.

"I always hear, 'Oh, just go get a cortisone shot,'" she said. "So I had Kevin come with me to a clinic, and I saw a physician. She came in and examined me. I had a 103-degree fever. I've played shows with fevers before, it's no big deal. But I couldn't sing.

"And she, as a responsible physician, flat out refused to give me a cortisone shot. She said, 'I cannot give a steroid shot to somebody who has a fever.' And I just burst into tears."

The show—which has since been archived—went on, and Vicki pushed through bronchitis to deliver an objectively beautiful performance of "Listen, Listen," though she doesn't quite see it that way.

"I don't think I've actually ever listened to it," she admits.

The show was a success; a peak moment for so many involved.

"It was magical to me. I thought it was one of the best shows we'd played," Mark said.

Russ agrees, citing the incredible sound at St. Ann's as being one of his personal highlights.

"When we were doing soundcheck, there was this big ass natural reverb in that church. I just had to, like, throw into 'When the Levee Breaks.' you know?" he said. "I played one song with a pencil—a number 2 sharpened pencil. That's how quiet I could be and still be picked up."

That said, having the Drifters in the building made for perhaps one of the louder musical evenings that the church had hosted.

"It's your classic big ol' gothic-style church," Don Dixon said. "Aspects of that are great for recording. It's harder for the sound when we have a huge band like they were. And nobody liked to play soft. I remember it being kind of loud for that kind of building."

"Not all easy music, but what a ride," Russ said of the show. "It was so fun. So many of the artists came out and just floored me. It was just brilliant. I can't speak highly enough about Peter and the job he did, even the setlist. It was just phenomenal."

Notably, legendary producer Joe Boyd, who produced several Fairport albums and was also responsible for producing Nick Drake as well as R.E.M.'s *Fables of the Reconstruction*, was in attendance that night.

"One of the highlights of the whole thing to me was the backstage hang," Robert, who was there with his then-girlfriend/future wife Candace, says of the night. Much of the fun being had backstage could be attributed to Candace, he says, who everyone loved because she provided the much-beloved libations.

Candace Maché readily cops to her role as booze liaison/backstage bestie.

"I was sitting in the church pews and I had a bottle of whiskey, so everybody came to me," she said.

For her part, Vicki says she could appreciate what a memorable night it was, but didn't feel like she was able to be especially present.

"I just remember kind of being in a fog backstage, looking at all of these people and thinking, 'Wow, this is really cool. I wish I was really here.' It's unfortunate that I wasn't able to enjoy it more than I did," she laments.

Part II

The rest of 1998 came and went without a record deal, and it started to feel as though the Drifters had exhausted all of their options. They did finish out the year with a ferocious version of Neil Young's "When You Dance, I Can Really Love" being recorded live at the Howlin' Wolf, mixed by Mike Mayeux, and ultimately released on a compilation called *This Note's For You Too! (A Tribute to Neil Young)*.

They still didn't have a record of their own out in the States, though. And so, determined to make something happen and with the support of their lawyer Bob Stein, the band set their sights on the 1999 South By Southwest (SXSW) music festival in Austin, Texas.

SXSW, they decided, would be the right showcase for them as a band—a place where they knew industry people were congregating and would hopefully be open to seeing them live. They started calling in favors to get showcases, with Susan ultimately calling in perhaps the ultimate friend favor—Lucinda Williams.

"Susan was able to convince Lucinda Williams to let us play on her show that she was doing. So once we got that in place, it was to show labels, 'Hey, we have high caliber friends. They like us; why can't you like us?'" Mark said. "Bob went to town. He just started calling every label and saying, 'Listen, they're playing here. You should come see them.'"

One of the things that Stein says they were up against was the inability to pin the band down stylistically or in terms of songwriting and lead vocal hierarchy. It was something labels had pushed against with the band in years past.

"That was more in play with the very brief, but intense, search for a contract for the Drifters, vis-a-vis the record company A&R guys—more than I'd ever seen it before," Stein said. "And what other band would arouse that question more than the Drifters? Hard to say."

So the band went to Austin and Driftered in front of label execs and enthusiastic crowds. That show, along with other showcases they did throughout the week, had everyone feeling confident and optimistic.

"I remember there was a ton of energy," Vicki recalled. "We're all going, 'Oh my god, this actually might happen. Wow, we might have a home for this. This is incredible."

They'd already found a bit of a home away from home in Austin; like Oxford, Mississippi, it was one of those towns that the Drifters would play in and feel like part of the community—whether it was at SXSW or their own headline gig.

Peter Blackstock, the co-founder of the long-running Americana publication *No Depression*, grew up in Austin and has been involved in SXSW for decades, as an attendee, a showcase host, and supporter. His relationship with the Drifters started as a fan, initially seeing them on February 25, 1993, at their first Austin show (on the second RV trip from L.A.).

The next year, Blackstock says, he attended what remains his favorite Drifters show of the handful he's seen.

"It was the last day of SXSW," Blackstock recalled of the show, which took place at the storied La Zona Rosa on March 19, 1994 with the Ray, Gary, Peter, Carlo, Mark, Susan, and Vicki lineup. "It was specifically billed to be a closing party, meaning after you've seen all your other bands and all the other clubs have closed at two [a.m.], come to La Zona Rosa and the Drifters will go on and play however long they want to."

Blackstock says he'd seen around a dozen bands that day alone, but he arrived at La Zona Rosa for the early morning. show and stayed for their entire two-and-a-half hour set, which ended at 4:45.

"It was one of the best shows I've ever seen of anyone, anywhere," Blackstock said.

The next time he saw the band was at SXSW 1999, the year the *Vermilion* lineup went to pitch their record. *No Depression* hosted a showcase that year at the Broken Spoke, and the Drifters played alongside the great guitar hero Neal Casal, an artist named Hayseed, and former Wilco multi-instrumentalist Bob Egan.

The show with Lucinda Williams, meanwhile, happened at the Austin Music Hall on a lineup that included the Drifters, Williams, Patty Griffin, Jim Lauderdale, and Robert Earl Keen. That gig proved successful enough that the band chatted with a few labels, but only one meeting resulted in anything further.

Razor & Tie Records, at the time experiencing success with artists like Dar Williams and Marshall Crenshaw (the latter being a friend of Peter's), started out as a reissue and compilation label in the early 1990s, but branched out with new artists later in that decade.

One of the label's owners attended the Drifters' showcase at the Austin Music Hall and was impressed by the band. He offered them a deal following that showcase, which Russ says "went to the mat" quickly.

By this point, the band was ready for anything. They needed a label and a U.S. release, and Razor & Tie was offering.

"At the time we felt that they were a really good home for us," Mark said. "They had a lot of really cool artists and we thought, 'Well, we're eclectic. Maybe that'd be a good place for us.'"

None of the band members had high expectations, but were more than eager to get the record released.

"I don't remember feeling like, "These guys get it. They are going to be our machine. They're going to take this music and make the world know it and love it.' I never felt that," Vicki recalled. "They were there because they were the last guys holding the ball when the buzzer went off. The business was already shifting in certain ways. We were perfectly fine and comfortable with the idea of being with a small independent label. I think that was probably preferable to trying to go after any majors."

For Vicki, staying out of the business of the Drifters was always her approach, and it remained that way when it came to getting involved with Razor & Tie.

"I was so intentionally not focused on the business side of things at that point. Just literally was determined to not involve myself in that. And I was successful at that," she said. "It's not like

I didn't care, because I cared, [but] I would have said yes to any label, big or small, if they had said the right things. This is a band that absolutely needed creative control.

"We did not want people in the studio breathing down our necks or watching what we were doing. None of us felt like we needed that. We weren't a baby band. We were a band of people who had been around the block and down the street a few times."

Bob Stein recalls there being some other interest, but largely the concern was that other labels were dragging their feet a bit and might take too long to come to a consensus on a contract and plan for release.

"There was actually some concern, kind of quietly, that if the band didn't get a contract soon, there might be some detrimental or problematic frustration," he said. "[Razor & Tie] was a bit of a victory."

The contract came together quickly, and most of the negotiation was around fairly standard recording contract stipulations that would often prove detrimental in the long run for artists.

"I can say that I fought back, as I would always do, [against] all the boiler plate recording contract things that were really just unfair," Stein said. "The universality of it, the 'this will go on forever and ever' [aspect]. They were what lawyers call contracts of adhesion, in so many ways.

"In a time frame, in a spatial frame, their absolute ability to re-up whenever they wanted. Those were major issues."

Ultimately, it seemed that Razor & Tie understood that the Drifters were experienced artists who'd been down this road before, and were amenable enough to a relatively fair contract. In terms of the amount of money offered to license what was by that point a finished product, Stein doesn't recall specifics but says it was "decided by the band."

The priority was to get a deal for the band that would give them as much flexibility as possible and not keep them languishing in a contract longer than they needed to be or wanted to be, should they need or want to go elsewhere.

"There was little improvement on the original offer, but I was trying to avoid having them stuck for too long," he said. "At the time they talked about doing three or four more records, and we had yet to really know how Razor & Tie would do."

With that, the deal was done on June 17, 1999—well over a year after the album was finished.

By then, the Drifters were riding high on their successful SXSW, the Sandy Denny show months previous, and the experience they had making *Vermilion*. It was largely a fun time for everyone— lots of good times on the road, and lots of shows. It was a time when the band truly was a family.

"There was a time there where we did everything together," Peter said. "Susan and I had that great backyard on Filmore Avenue, and we always had parties back there. We went over to Russ and Mary's; there was an active group of people together."

With a label behind them, the Drifters were serious enough about getting on the road and working *Vermilion* that they brought in Howlin' Wolf front of house engineer Brian "Disco" Oden to tour with them after meeting him at the club and hitting it off. Oden was roughly a decade younger than the band, but became close with the Drifters and was eager to join them on the road.

The pay wasn't great, Disco says, but he didn't care. He just wanted to "be with friends and have fun."

There was a lot of fun to be had at the time, and other bands took notice.

Son Volt, the long-running alt-country band led by Jay Farrar as his post-Uncle Tupelo project, was at this point still riding on the success of its 1995 album *Trace* and promoting the 1998 follow up *Wide Swing Tremolo*. Farrar, living in New Orleans at the time, apparently showed up at several Drifters shows throughout the 1990s— unbeknownst to the band.

The opportunity arose for the Drifters to support Son Volt on a Northeast run in the fall of 1999. That tour included stops at venues such as the 9:30 Club in D.C. and Toad's Place in New Haven, Connecticut. Oden has a distinct memory of playing the final show of a venue in New York City called Tramps, and meeting up with a journalist from *Guitar* magazine after the gig.

"We got smashed, went back to her apartment, I passed out on the couch, woke up, and walked 50 blocks through New York," Oden recalled, noting that he actually ended up walking to the World Trade Center, where he went to the top of one of the towers and took pictures.

For Disco, touring with the band, especially on that run, was as much about the making of memories as it was about the job at hand. It was a joyous time for the Drifters, but not so much for Son Volt.

This was toward the end of Son Volt's initial run, and among the last of that band's shows with original members Jim and Dave Boquist. The brothers were not getting along with Farrar at this point, and could see just how much fun the Drifters were having every day. They ended up approaching the Drifters after a show with a proposition.

"They kind of cornered us one day and said, 'Do you think we could ride with you in the happy bus? We want to ride with you! You guys are having so much more fun than we are,'" Robert recalled. "We were a really tight, fun band. And it showed on stage. We rocked the fuck out of it, and we had the best time. We did more laughing than anything else."

Robert was, and is, a guy who just always wants to play, no matter what. His ongoing affair with the guitar began when he was 14, when he first saw live music. He recalls going to New York for a week and attending the Schaefer Music Festival, witnessing the likes of Tim Buckley, Country Joe and the Fish, and Paul Butterfield Blues Band.

"And then I went to the New York Rock Festival that weekend, and it was the Soft Machine, and the Chambers Brothers. And then Janis Joplin with Big Brother and the Holding Company … and Jimi Hendrix," he recalled. "I was living in Hong Kong at the time, so it was like we got to run free in New York for a week. And that's what we did."

While living in Hong Kong, Robert also got the opportunity to see the Ike and Tina Turner Review—another formative experience, albeit for different reasons.

"I swear I went through puberty in about fifteen seconds," he jokes.

Seeing so many shows so young, Robert discovered that music was the path for him.

"I was just like, 'I love this shit, and this is what I want to do,'" he said.

Robert's first band was called The Electric Chair, which he formed alongside his brother. That lasted just one gig before he moved to New York in 1976. His very first session after relocating was for the legendary German performance artist Klaus Nomi, and he soon joined former Mumps keyboardist/Nomi collaborator Kristian Hoffman in a band called the Swinging Madisons.

That band became popular in the CBGBs scene and around clubs in New York, releasing an EP in the early 1980s. He also worked as a tech for seminal psychobilly band The Cramps in the first four years of their decades-long career—an experience he describes as "fucking amazing."

During the Swinging Madisons era he'd gotten to know Gary Stewart, a fan of the band, and the two became friendly. When Stewart signed Steve Wynn to Rhino as a solo artist and Wynn needed a guitar player, Stewart recommended Robert to audition.

"I was so tired when I got to the audition, I fell asleep playing standing up," he said. "They hired me because I fell asleep."

Joining the Steve Wynn Band alongside Mark Walton paved the way for Robert's earliest Drifters days at Raji's, and the ever-eager guitar player he is, it's no wonder that he eventually got the full-time call.

Vermilion is as good an example as any of just what Robert is capable of as a guitar player—tastefulness being the name of the game. He can rip a staggering rock and roll solo, contribute measured, spacious rhythm parts, throw some fuzz on a twelve-string and bend a mind or two, and bring some Keith Richards swagger to a bottleneck slide. All on the same album.

Robert Maché might be the most underrated Drifter in the bunch—versatile in his playing, willing to shape his contributions to the needs of the song rather than putting an intentional stamp on it, and *never* concerned with taking flashy solos or stealing the spotlight.

"He's probably the first person to underrate himself," New Orleans artist Dayna Kurtz, who presently plays with Robert in Lulu and the Broadsides, said. "He's always kind of stepping aside to let other people shine. He's a generous player and human being."

If versatility and malleability are prerequisites to being a Continental Drifter, Robert has those qualities in spades. His youthful enthusiasm for music doesn't hurt either.

"He's invaluable. He's absolutely invaluable to me," said Kurtz, who also performs with Robert in a duo setting. "He also is just such a fuckin' happy-go-lucky road dog. He'd rather be on the road touring than doing anything else. We've traveled a lot together. We've been to really exotic places. And he's still like a little fucking kid."

It's no wonder, then, that Robert fit in so well to the Drifter family dynamic from his first guest spot at Raji's. His was an energy that lifted the band; his long curly locks flailing around as he himself flailed around during solo sections.

Scott Aiges recalls marveling at Robert's playing often on the occasions he joined the band on the road, alongside their sometime-roadie Tim Cohn.

"There was a moment in the show every night where Robert would go off on this crazy space ride, and me and Tim would look at each other and go, 'Planet Maché. Strap in,'" he said.

In many ways, *Vermilion* was Planet Maché. Not just because of his crucial songwriting contribution in the form of "Heart, Home," but because it was perhaps the ultimate showcase of his capabilities within the Continental Drifters. The songs that preceded his tenure in the band were perhaps more refined with Robert on guitar. Take "The Rain Song," for example. Where the guitar lines in early recordings may have been a bit more unkempt, the album version on *Vermilion* could be seen as more strategic; longer phrases, less fills, wider altogether. Save for the more frantic "Don't Do What I Did" solo, that was the overarching approach to guitar on the album.

On October 12, 1999, *Vermilion* was released on Razor & Tie. The band marked the occasion with a show at the Howlin' Wolf, complete with a movie premiere-esque searchlight out front (provided by a neighbor of Mark's) and a celebratory gala-like party inside.

"We even had one of those hot air blow up men that wave their arms," Vicki said with a laugh. "Mark's neighbor was a promotion dude. We felt very, very, very Hollywood."

Response to *Vermilion* was as good as, if not better than, the eponymous record. Critics loved it—take *Rolling Stone*, whose critic David Fricke offered up particular praise for the songwriting.

"There is a backwoods-Jefferson Airplane feel to the close, lustrous harmonies of primary singer-songwriters Vicki Peterson, Peter Holsapple and his wife Susan Cowsill, and the bayou impressionism of their spins on romance, family and the road is flecked with surprises..."

The Associated Press was even more complimentary in its review.

"Vermilion is not only a great album, it is the kind of rock 'n' roll album rarely made anymore, the product of a collective vision - a real band - rather than the mind of one singer-songwriter."

The album also landed on over a dozen year-end lists around the country. Robert Christgau put the band in his top releases for 1999 in the February 2000 issue of *The Village Voice*, while *Stereo Review*'s *Sound and Vision* called *Vermilion* "pure magic" and placed it at fifth on its top ten albums of the year.

Columbia, South Carolina's *The State* newspaper also placed the album on its year-end list, declaring that "in a perfect world, the Backstreet Boys would be flipping burgers and the Continental Drifters would be at the top of the charts."

Locally, the album got some serious notice in the form of *Gambit Weekly*'s top release of the year. And, quite impressively, the band won *Offbeat*'s award for album of the year in its Best of the Beat Awards.

The most important takeaway from all of this is that, as Russ says, it "validated" the band's feelings on what they made together, and gave them some level of confirmation that what they were doing was working and there were people who got it. Whether it translated to sales was a separate concern altogether—at least they felt seen and heard.

Alt-country monthly *No Depression* was an ally, reviewing the band's releases and live shows as far back as 1994.

"They were certainly part of the thing that was going on when we launched a magazine around 1995," Peter Blackstock said. "Musically, what they were doing fit right in with the younger bands that we saw coming up."

No Depression further elevated the band and the record with a lengthy profile in 1999, written by contributor Neal Weiss. At the time, Weiss had been aware of the Drifters and following them loosely since the L.A. days, when he was a fan of several band members individually and saw them on occasion at Raji's.

"This was an extension of an L.A. scene that meant a lot to me," Weiss said. "Think of it as sort of, like, the family tree of L.A. bands, and you could connect dots.

"That was enough right there for me to want to go check it out. It felt good, it felt honest, and it felt like musicians who were all getting together to play music and share a stage with each other and with an audience."

Fast forward to 1999, and Weiss—a music journalist and audio/video producer who went on to an extensive career in the latter field—was with the publication at a time when they were thriving. The Drifters did, he says, seem to fit in with what they were doing at the magazine.

"No Depression, alt-country, insurgent country, whatever you want to call it [is] one of most vague aggregation names you could ever imagine. It could mean anything to anyone," Weiss said. "It meant some semblance of music that had roots in it; that was out of the mainstream. To me, it hinted at indie rock and all of that eighties college rock that I had experienced. That's really what it was for me.

"My entry point was punk rock, which became a lot of bands getting more rootsy. Which then became Uncle Tupelo. So I came in through a punk [door], whereas a lot of other people came in through country and bluegrass—it's the big umbrella."

While *Vermilion* had enough of the elements that encompassed the alt-country movement, the Drifters were more of a pop band than some of the other like minded bands of the time.

"It was probably more on the fringe of what most people would define as No Depression, which is either some sort of punk-born country-ish rock, or really traditional country folk," Weiss said. "The Drifters are a roots pop band; a little bit more folk rock. And really not all that twangy. But they were roots-based and smart about their history; about their ability to tap into different forms. So, did they fit in? Of course they did, and of course they did not."

Interviewing the band for the *No Depression* story, Weiss remembers the band feeling "really at ease and pleased with the collective that they had become."

"I do think they hit a stride in terms of who they were, how they collaborated, and where they were headed," he said. "Based on my conversations with them, they felt blessed. That's probably the best way to put it. Most if not all of them had done some level of dance with the devil, and then come out the other side with the ability to have careers as musicians. That is a beautiful place, I suspect, to have arrived as a musician."

Like many who followed the Drifters early on have noted, the band that made *Vermilion* was a vastly different band than the one that enamored those in the tight Raji's circle. Weiss counts himself in that group of followers, admitting that while he was a fan of the current lineup when writing the feature, he had an undeniable connection to the L.A. lineup.

"Carlo…holy moly that guy could swing and sing, and do a Levon Helm-esque thing that was fantastic. And Gary Eaton: That guy has soul," he said. "That's the band that really spoke to me. I just want to underscore that. The band that preceded *Vermilion* was very special to me, let's put it that way."

The juxtaposition between the two versions of the band pre and post-Carlo, it seems, created almost two camps within the Drifters' audience. Some were more attuned to the early version and may have even stopped following them altogether after various lineup shifts, while others stayed on board with the direction of the Drifters all along.

Cheryl Pawelski admits that she, too, felt most connected to the earliest version of the band and wasn't as connected to the *Vermilion* lineup, lamenting that the shelving of the first record was frustrating to her as a listener.

"I'm always interested in things becoming things. I would much rather hear somebody's juvenalia. I want to hear your art searching to become. And sometimes when it's fully formed, it's great and it's interesting and it's awesome. But oftentimes I find that I'm less interested," she explained. "What was exciting about the Drifters to me was: What would they become? And that is the frustration with them, because I wanted to hear that first record. I feel like I had the first record, but it only lives in my head."

That was perhaps one of the more unique obstacles that *Vermilion* had in its way–defining the Drifters as a cohesive unit despite the various identity crises along the way, and finding something new and fresh about it that would interest both new listeners and the folks who had followed them from L.A. to LA.

To the band, *Vermilion* seemed their best shot at establishing that and also creating a lasting distinction between what the Drifters were before and what they became.

Boosts from the likes of *No Depression* helped, and the article in question was a forthright look at the band's history centered around their arrival at *Vermilion*. It was certainly their most comprehensive feature since Karen Schoemer's *L.A. Weekly* piece.

With some press and a decent following on their side, the stretch of time between Russ
joining the band and the *Vermilion* release in the U.S. was largely positive for the Drifters. It saw
them finally reaching the goals they'd been aiming for—a label behind them, a solid and consistent lineup, a cohesive record they were proud of, good reviews, people listening at home and
abroad. The goalposts were no longer being moved at nearly every turn.

There wasn't much to complain about on a musical level. They'd had a genuinely wonderful
experience making *Vermilion*, unlike any studio experience they'd had prior.

"There's this purity about it," Russ said. "Going into Dockside to record our album with all
these songs that we all cared so much about already, and all the families are coming and all of
these newborn babies—it was so exciting. It was just bulging with life, and there was no other
agenda other than being together and playing these songs."

"For me, that was the most beautiful record ever made because it was made for every right
reason to make a record," Susan adds.

Following the release of *Vermilion* at the end of 1999, the band returned to Austin for SXSW in
March of 2000 and hosted a "Continental Drifters and Friends" showcase at a venue called Jazz
Upstairs—with a lineup that included Martha Wainwright, The Bottle Rockets' Brian Henneman,
and Kim Richey.

Richey was several years into a successful career as both a recording artist and a songwriter—
most notably for multi-platinum country singer Trisha Yearwood.

Richey was a friend of the band and enlisted them to back her up for her own SXSW showcase the same year on a bill with Lucinda Williams. She doesn't quite recall how she met the
Drifters, but she figures it can likely be attributed to their mutual friend John Crooke. Regardless,
there was mutual admiration from the get go.

"We were supposed to do a tour together," Richey recalled of her early interactions with the
band. "We were gonna do a shared bill and they were going to back me up. But we only did one
show. And the reason for that was because of me—I flaked on it. We had the tour all set up, and
then I got offered to open for Trisha Yearwood."

Richey's management decided it best to take the Yearwood tour dates, especially considering
that she had a record out at the time.

They never toured together, but the Drifters ended up being Richey's band for the Austin
Music Hall gig—which made a huge impression on her. So much so that she, however hyperbolic
it might have been, expressed wanting to quit her own career and join the Drifters.

"I always only wanted to be in a band, and that's like the coolest band ever," she said.

The Drifters felt that love, that's for sure.

"Everybody felt like we were the best; we were unbeatable. That was that whole thing of Kim Richey saying, 'I'm going to quit me and join the Drifters.' Just that feeling of acceptance by our peers, and our rarified view of what the audience might be," Peter said.

"There was a moment of feeling that power on whatever level that exists, and feeling just great about what we were doing. We were united and there was energy," Vicki adds.

This particular point in time was so positive for the band that it was, in a way, contagious, as Kim Richey expresses.

"They all just seemed like friends," she said. "You'd kind of see them all hanging out together when they're not doing shows or rehearsing. Just, like, the belonging—which was really appealing to me, just wanting to belong to something. And they are so musical."

Richey counts herself in a sizable group of people who both understood intimately what the band did well, and couldn't understand whatsoever how they weren't able to make a commercial dent.

"I get so mad sometimes when people say, 'Cream rises to the top.' That's not true," she said. "It's just a crime that some of these artists and bands are never heard, because it's not any lack of anything musically, it's just [that] something didn't line up. There's so much luck involved."

The Drifter bubble was a good place to be, but the real world started to creep in slowly for the band around the end of the decade. Peter and Susan's marriage was declining—a painful experience for all. They separated in 2000 and divorced soon after.

In discussing the circumstances surrounding their separation, both Peter and Susan delicately impart that there were a myriad of things that contributed, yet they both take ownership for their individual roles. That said, the specifics of their breakup remain understandably private.

More than 20 years later, Susan reflects on what allowed things to continue amicably between them in the midst of a difficult split.

"There was lots motivating it that remains. For me and Peter, we really like each other," she said. "And we're both willing to admit we failed. We don't need to hash out the details anymore—we both fucked it up. We both were capable of making it right. It takes both parties or it ain't ever gonna happen."

Specifics aside, it was a time of many unknowns, and everyone dealt in their own way. There was no band breakup after Susan and Peter's split, which made it all the more challenging for everyone to keep it all together.

Peter doesn't hold back on what he was dealing with at the time—his alcoholism was out of control. He was drinking constantly, and more often than not had no recollection the next day of what he might have said to someone the night before.

"After a show, I'd have, sort of, inventory. Whatever it was that I'd been doing, and who I'd talked to. Did I owe somebody an apology? That's kind of a crazy thing," he said. "I never gave it much of a thought. That's the truth. I just did it over and over again. I don't think I did it with anything other than just being ignorant of what was going on. Willfully ignorant."

His drinking, he says, made an impact not just on his marriage but also his other relationships within the band.

"I allowed my drinking to accelerate out of control. It affected my judgment, it affected my state of mind tremendously. It made me into a very suspicious, jealous, internally-raging drunk guy," he said. "I absolutely cop to all of the stuff that I did. I was not a good person at that time. I was hurting. I was hurting other people, and even the ones I wasn't trying to hurt were getting hurt. Collateral damage was the name of the game."

Sean Kelly

Disco admits to struggling with all of this, as the one person outside of the band unit watching the aftermath of the separation. He would try to bite his tongue and not cause trouble; recalling one moment the morning after a show that underlines just how bad things had become.

"Russ and I were sharing a hotel room; we were coming out of the room, and there was so much tension that Peter was causing at that point. And he'd shown up with these flowers that he'd picked. He was desperately trying to pull it back together—the mayhem that he ultimately had caused. And everybody was just biting their tongue to get over it, you know?" he said. "I was riding in the front seat of the van after that with Vicki, and she had set the flowers right in the center of the console, and I have terrible, terrible allergies. The fan is just blowing right on to the flowers, and the room that we'd had the night before had no air conditioning in it. It was so stuffy, and I was dying, and they were sitting there right in front of the air conditioner. And all I could do was see them wavering back and forth with wind passing through them and right onto me.

"I was in so much pain! I was trying so desperately [to ignore it], because I'm the outsider caught up in the middle of all of this shit."

Vicki, he says, noticed he was struggling.

"She grabbed the flowers and rolled the window down and threw them out," he said.

By the end of the 1990s, Susan and Peter were done. With that came some uncertainty about the future of the band—more than there ever had been. Naturally, it made for heavy, uncomfortable moments when the band would get together.

"I remember being at Dockside for New Years Eve with the band, and something was really, really, really off. The energy was just really off," Robert recalled.

The days of the chosen family were gone, and what remained was essentially one big question mark and a lot of pain. Peter conveys that pain succinctly and brutally.

"I would say it'd be hard to imagine, short of [the] death of loved ones, anything that could have been more overwhelming and catastrophic in my life," he said. "And there was nothing I could do about it."

Chapter Nine: Better Day

"I learned so much from everybody, and we all just found common ground—there was something that was just totally unique about the Continental Drifters."

—*Mark Walton*

Susan affectionately refers to the Continental Drifters as a "healing well." And it *was* that for nearly everyone involved. Every Drifter became a Drifter because they were healing from something; to be replenished and made creatively new again. Even if they didn't realize it, they needed the healing, because—as Susan once again says, "everybody came limping from somewhere else."

That's what made every departure so earth-shattering for the remaining members. Someone else was leaving the well. But, in some ways, those who left were leaving because there were new wounds that needed healing. In Ray's case, there were literal physical ailments. In Gary's, there were emotional ones. Carlo's ailments were of the addictive variety.

And maybe Danny was just dumped for Peter. Still, once a Drifter always a Drifter.

There had been so many shakeups within the band, and so many letdowns on the business side, that the sheer fact that *Vermilion* got released was a huge milestone.

The turn of the century and the end of Peter and Susan's marriage could have easily seen the Drifters packing it in and calling it a day. They'd certainly put in a lot of time and effort to try to have a go at it, and they found considerable success for a small band—especially critically. And following *Vermilion*'s release, it did seem like things were starting to come to an end.

Vicki was writing and recording again with Michael Steele, Susanna Hoffs, and her sister Debbi Peterson after The Bangles reunited for a song on the soundtrack for *Austin Powers: The Spy Who Shagged Me* in 1999. That project was taking her back to Los Angeles, which after some time started becoming her primary residence again.

Peter was also once again touring with Hootie & the Blowfish after taking a hiatus from that band to focus on the Drifters.

"It was starting to get a little depressing for me," Mark recalled. "It was always hard because Peter was always going on the road with Hootie. And now Vicki, she's not even in New Orleans anymore; she's back home in L.A. doing a lot of stuff; reviving The Bangles. So we were like, 'Okay, this looks like it's winding down now.'"

Additionally, the Drifters were also having a marketing problem—namely, they just couldn't get away from those Bangles and Cowsills associations. Most everyone had feelings on this that followed them for years. They ranged from slightly annoyed to purely exasperated.

"All of us had overenthusiastic fans who would come to every Drifters show because that's how they could find us," Vicki said. "I did feel bad that when almost every time people talked about the Continental Drifters it was, 'Vicki Peterson from The Bangles, Susan Cowsill from The Cowsills, Mark Walton from The Dream Syndicate.' And maybe they would say, 'Peter Holsapple from The dB's/R.E.M.'

"That was it. Sometimes they would talk about Robert's long and storied career. But usually it was Bangles and Cowsills. I get it. I get it. [But] it's reductionist, and it does not tell the story at all. It just mentions names and history."

Mark recalls hearing a radio ad for a Drifters show at one point after *Vermilion* came out, and in the background of the ad played "Walk Like An Egyptian." It was a constant thing in one way or another, and it was coming from fans, media, and even the label.

"They would put it on the stickers, even, on the fucking albums. I'm proud of Vicki, and I'm proud of everybody. But it's just not what we should have been promoted as," Mark said.

There were also frustrations around the way that the Drifters were always perceived by the general public. Because of how they were marketed and the, at times, sparse touring schedule, the assumption was often that they were a side project; a "supergroup," if you will, whose members had other things going on and made the occasional record together when time permitted.

The Drifters themselves had always fought against that notion.

"We were hell-bent on not seeming like this purported busman's holiday; we were so irked by that description that it was this sort of 'sometime supergroup,'" Peter said. "It was like, 'Fuck. You really are just not getting it, are you? This is a band."

Some notable gigs happened in the face of the continued turbulence within the band, including a Jazz Fest gig in 2000, which featured guest appearances from Drifter pals Adam Duritz and David Immerglück of Counting Crows, and hitmaking songwriter Jules Shear (a friend of Vicki's and writer of The Bangles hit 'If She Knew What She Wants').

"If Nirvana got together with the original members, and The Beatles opened up, it still wouldn't be this good," journalist and longtime fan Brett Milano was quoted as telling a writer for the now-defunct online publication *SonicNet*.

Meanwhile, despite *Vermilion* garnering solid reviews and gaining the band some new fans, it didn't catch on commercially in the States. They were fighting their fair share of ongoing annoyances all around, but they soldiered on and played as much as possible. Gigging was one thing, but would they make another record? Nobody was quite sure. There was still work to be done, though—namely, touring commitments and a planned trip to Germany.

Following Susan and Peter's separation, the band headed up north for a planned run of shows to promote *Vermilion*. They'd been touring the East Coast regularly with each album cycle and in between, and Washington, D.C. was a regular stop (along with surrounding cities in Virginia).

This run found the band in D.C. with a decent crowd—including one fan who by this point was a regular attendee, traveling around the Northeast to see what had become his favorite band. Out of respect for this fan's wishes, we will keep his identity anonymous.

The Fan, as we'll call him, first discovered the Drifters a few years earlier.

"There was—still is, kind of—a local weekly [newspaper] here. Back then in '96, they put out a print issue once a week. One of the things they used to do in these issues was, they featured arts events," The Fan said.

In one issue, The Fan read about a show happening at the 9:30 Club in D.C. by a band he'd never heard of called the Continental Drifters—who was promoting the eponymous record with Carlo in the fold.

"I saw that they listed the members and said, 'Peter Holsapple from The dB's,' and I'd been a dB's fan. And 'Mark Walton from the Dream Syndicate,' and I'd been a Dream Syndicate fan. And 'Vicki Peterson from The Bangles,' and I'd been a Bangles fan. So I was like, 'Oh my god, all of these people in this one band?'"

The Fan attended that 9:30 Club show, in a small secondary room, and says he was "blown away."

"I thought it was one of the greatest shows I'd ever seen," he said. "I went to see a lot of live music, so that's saying something."

What was it about the band that made such an impression on him?

"At the time, I didn't really know about Americana as its own genre," he said. "A lot of the bands that I liked in that era were bands that were influenced by Americana music, but I didn't think of it in those terms. But when I saw the Drifters doing their version of Americana, I was just like, 'This is what music is supposed to be.' At least for me. That was one part of it, but I guess more so it was the energy of the performance, and feeling like, 'This is what *live* music is meant to be.' For me, it was definitely a really eye-opening experience and one of my favorite memories of a live show that I've ever had the pleasure to see."

He remembers the band not actually having any copies of *Continental Drifters* with them at the show because they were "on the outs" with Monkey Hill at the time. He ultimately found a copy at a record store and started "playing it to death" while he waited for the band to come back to the area.

By 1997, The Fan—who worked in the computer industry—had been "on the Internet longer than most people" but the technology hadn't advanced to where he could keep up with the band's happenings. He eventually did discover that they were going to be playing in New York and decided to make the drive.

"I don't remember if I'd ever driven from D.C. to New York prior to that," he said. "Back in those days I didn't really travel much."

The New York trip was for a two-night stand at The Wetlands, where the Drifters played alongside friends including Amy Rigby—noted singer/songwriter who was longtime pals with both Peter and Robert, and formerly married to dB's drummer Will Rigby.

Rigby actually grew up a big fan of The Cowsills, and even briefly had what she calls the "Susan Cowsill cut" as a kid because she wanted her hair to look like Susan's. That was technically her first connection to any of the Drifters, but it really began with Robert, who she dated when they both lived in New York City and he was working for The Cramps.

"That was in 1979/'80," Rigby said. "Like the Susan Cowsill haircut, it was kind of short lived. But we stayed friends, basically."

Rigby kept in touch with Robert after they split, and while in school in England she crossed paths with Peter and Will Rigby when The dB's came to town with the *Taking Liberties* Tour that also included bands like The Fleshtones, The Raybeats, Bush Tetras, Polyrock, and The Bongos.

"I went to see this show because I knew some of the bands that were on it," she said. "I got on this lift to get on the tube, and I was like, 'Oh my god, there's Peter Holsapple and Will Rigby on the elevator with me.' I'm standing behind them, and I know it's them, but I was just so shy."

Amy officially became friends with the dB's a couple of years later, when Peter was room-mates with a friend of hers. Eventually she married Will, and they stayed close in the years that followed. The Drifters ultimately became a band that Rigby connected with as a friend and collaborator; she even became friends with Gary Eaton after he left the Drifters and the two played shows together and co-wrote a song called "What I Need."

Rigby played with the Drifters on multiple occasions after their move to New Orleans, mostly when they'd come to New York and play venues like the Mercury Lounge or the Wetlands. They eventually started backing her up on occasion, most notably at venues like Proud Larry's in Oxford as well as at SXSW.

Rigby gets emotional recalling those particular nights.

"There were two songs in particular that I know we played together a couple times: "Don't Break the Heart" and "All I Want," and I just get chills—it makes me really teary," she said. "[Those songs] had these really defined backing vocals that were always really hard to achieve with just three guys in a band. But to have Vicki, Susan, and Peter singing these intricate harmony parts worked out on the records; it was just so [magical], and always felt like, 'This is so special. This is something to remember.'"

Rigby, like so many friends of the band, sees the Continental Drifters as a unique combination of musical voices that blended in the way that a band like Fleetwood Mac did in their heyday.

"It wasn't this clear delineation of masculine and feminine—who was the guy and who was the woman. The voices had a fluidity to them," she said.

"There's just something about that; I'm not putting my finger on it except to say that it's more fluid. It kind of feels like it gives the women a chance to have a different role in a band than you often see. It seems like it takes a certain kind of male sensitivity or something to make the most of it."

The Fan, who became a big Amy Rigby fan from the Wetlands gigs in New York, says traveling to New York for the Drifters was a pivotal moment for him.

"That trip to New York sort of sparked something in me, and that is the point in my life where I started driving to shows more, up and down the East Coast," The Fan said. "At first it was primarily Drifters shows—when they were playing in Philadelphia or New York, or Boston or North Carolina."

The Fan became friendly with the band at subsequent gigs—especially with Russ, who started recognizing him from seeing him in the front row at shows. He was really invested as someone who understood the music, and the Drifters had become an integral part of his life.

That's why when the band came through D.C. between albums, he knew enough about what they were up against to offer them something unprecedented.

As someone who worked for a major tech company at the onset of the World Wide Web, The Fan had come into some considerable money.

"I'd never had a job prior to that where I had things like stock options or anything," he said. "All of the sudden I discovered I had these stock options. I never thought that I would earn a lot of money. I knew that working in a technical field I'd earn a decent salary, but I never thought I'd be *rich* rich. All of the sudden, I had all of this money. I thought, 'What am I going to do with this?'"

The Fan says he started thinking about "how different" things were for him compared to musicians.

"They weren't on a big label, they didn't have lots of money. They'd been in other bands that were well respected, but I didn't know if they had earned huge amounts of money. I sort of thought that I should support the artists I like," he said.

Approaching the band after the show in D.C., The Fan told them he wanted to give them "a gift" in the amount of $60,000.

"I wasn't really thinking about helping to pay for recording time or anything in particular," he said. "I just wanted to do it out of appreciation for them. I wanted to help them continue to be full-time musicians and not have to call it quits with the band because they couldn't afford it."

Bob Stein, the band's lawyer, happened to be in attendance, and worked with The Fan to draw up a contract and ensure that everything was sound before any money was paid out. The band, understandably, wanted to make sure that he didn't expect anything in return despite him insisting that he didn't.

"I go, 'You don't want anything from the band, right?' And he's like, 'No, I don't want anything,'" Mark recalled.

Stein remembers some of the band being skeptical about The Fan's offer, aside from Russ who had a gut feeling that it was truly the no-strings-attached offer that had been made. Stein backed him up, having navigated similar gift offers for artists before.

"They went, 'Oh, Russ, it's going to be complicated,'" Stein laughed. "But yeah, I take credit for that, and actually, Russ should take the majority of the credit for that."

It was a genuine gift—one that the Drifters all appreciate to this day. They credit the gift from The Fan as one of the foremost reasons they decided to stay together and make a new record, and all consider him a dear friend all these years later.

Motivated by The Fan's gift and always by the music, they started collecting songs and working towards a follow-up to *Vermilion*; their second album for Razor & Tie. This mostly consisted of band members bringing songs to each other when they'd get together at someone's house for a meeting or rehearsal. It was during this time that Robert began to feel like something was up and started worrying that he was about to be let go.

"I totally thought I was about to get canned," he said. "Because every time I'd walk into a room, that part the band would just shut up. *Every single time* I would walk into a room and they were talking, they would just immediately shut up. So what's going on here?"

Unbeknownst to Robert, that half of the band—Peter, Susan, Russ, and Vicki—was dealing with the revelation that Susan and Russ had started dating. It wasn't until a band meeting soon after that all was revealed, when Russ decided it'd be best to talk it over as a unit.

"We thought, 'Okay, here's this change. Everyone's wondering. Let's just go ahead and dialogue on it in the meetings. We can do this like family, the family that we are," he said.

Russ recalls being open with his bandmates during the meeting about his relationship with Susan and the state of his own failed marriage, which he says was "doomed before it started." The news didn't sit particularly well with everyone, despite the couple's intention to air everything out like a family.

"I was just pissed off. I was so fucking pissed off," Robert said.

The band trudged forward after that meeting, but everyone started feeling the stress. There were some of what Mark refers to as "uncomfortable moments," particularly in the van on the way to gigs. Nobody wanted to share rooms with each other on the road, so roommates would alternate each night.

Susan and Russ were falling in love, while others bore witness.

"I just wanted to go back to all the love and all the care and our family," Mark said. "I could see it just getting further and further and further apart, as Susan and Russ became closer and closer."

Brian "Disco" Oden remembers subsequent tours as being extremely tense and fraught with anxiety. Everyone around the trio was hit by the emotional shrapnel of it all.

"Vicki was always just kind of trying to do her best to keep her own emotions in check, because she was so frustrated from the tension. It was very taxing on her. [Susan] was just trying to have a life. Mark was literally scrambling—he wanted so desperately to keep it together," Disco said.

That was the breaking point for Disco, who says he'd had enough of the tension and was especially having trouble with the way Peter was handling it all—in some instances, taking it out on him.

"The man called me a fucking meathead," Disco said. "It was over for me, man. I pulled Mark and Vicki to the side and was like, 'I can't do this anymore. I fucking love you guys so much, but Peter's so volatile. I just can't be here for this. I can't do it.'"

Mark and Vicki, he says, tried to convince him to stay with the band, but he ultimately moved on.

What the Drifters had spent so long cultivating was crumbling, but they all did their best to hang on. From the perspective of Peter, Susan, and Russ, keeping the band going despite their personal turmoil was a priority; especially given the fact that there were children to consider and three other bandmates who'd invested as much as they had.

"The three of us and our 'thing'—and the other three dealing with the three of us and our 'thing,' in various and sundry ways—that's a lot of baggage for everybody," Peter said. "You can only fit so much baggage into a van."

Peter, speaking of vans, started volunteering to drive most of the time the band was on the road, so as to avoid being close to Susan and Russ. There was a lot bubbling up, and that separation on the road made the whole thing a lot easier to deal with. But tensions can bubble over eventually, and they finally did when the band traveled to Germany for a tour in July of 2000. It was their second trip there since *Vermilion*, and the itinerary included a festival in Edgar Heckmann's hometown of Heilbronn.

At the earliest point of their relationship, Russ says, he and Susan did try to keep things muted as a couple, so as to not make the others uncomfortable and as a way to keep the band moving forward.

"In those early days, we were so determined, I think, and we cared because it *is* family," Russ said. "I don't want to cause them grief. We want the band to continue; this is going to require some adjustments. It's big—it's earth shaking, internally. I knew that going in. I knew that as it was all happening. This is going to be big, so you have to cut everyone slack."

This was an extremely delicate balance that everyone tried, but struggled, to keep a hold of. Russ calls it "quiet tension"—the kind that built, and built, and built.

When they got to Europe, the quiet tension had been building for months. Camps had formed, and some were more vocal than others about where they stood on the matter. The day before the festival in Heilbronn, Mark and Russ got into a heated argument in a hotel room—a "tiny" hotel room, as Russ emphasizes. It quickly turned violent.

Mark recalled: "Russ and Susan were trying to say, 'Hey, this is our life. You can't tell us not to do this.' And we're like, 'You can't just shove it in our faces.' It got kind of ugly between Russ and myself that night. It was not good, and I threw my back out because I picked him up and dropped him on his head at one point."

Russ remembers the fight differently.

"He grabbed me in a headlock," he said. "And I just kind of spun him around and flipped him onto his back, and got out of the headlock. And Vicki and Susan were grabbing me. To this day what I'm grateful for is that I didn't punch him, or beat the crap out of him."

They managed to settle down and move forward, but the show the following day was not a good one.

"I was so upset. I stood at the very back of the stage and just played. I didn't want to be part of [the band] at this point," Mark recalled.

There were also moments on the tour of bandmates having to mediate tension between Peter and Susan.

"There was about a two-hour 'Talk Peter and Susan down on the fire escape,'" Robert recalled, with Russ adding that the fighting between them was "so loud, because all of our rooms faced into the atrium."

"It was a small boutique hotel, so on each floor there were maybe eight rooms, if that," Russ said. "Man, it was just going on and on and on."

Vicki pinpoints that tour as the "rotating roommate tour."

The truth was that there was a lot of frustration among Robert and Mark in particular about Susan and Russ' relationship. Whether it was born of being protective of Peter or just being pissed off about the relationship threatening the band, this new partnership threw everyone for a loop.

"We were able to get through it all, but it was really hard during those periods. They were being defiant about their love, and we're like, 'Well this is really fucking hard. Just tone it down a little,'" Mark said. "They just felt they'd finally found each other, and that totally makes sense in the scheme of things—especially looking back on it. But at the time it was like, 'Oh my god, what is going on? Why are they doing this to us?' We were just all mixed up and trying to work it out."

The next show on the tour, in Bremen, wasn't filled with the typical banter of a Drifters show. Mostly silence filled the breaks, and the songs moved relatively quickly between one another. Not to say there wasn't energy in the set; a raging version of "Don't Do What I Did" is the clearest bit of evidence that the Drifters were still capable of doing what they'd always been known to do best, even with so much drama happening off stage.

So the band moved ahead because, at this point, they *had to*, with some funding secured for recording, songs written (and being woodshedded in live shows), and plans being made to record at Dockside. They once again booked a three-week block, in January of 2001, and enlisted Dockside engineer Tony Daigle to record and mix.

Songs this time around were almost all brand new to the Drifters universe, save for Mark's "Tomorrow's Gonna Be," the song that spawned what became the album's title, *Better Day*. Dockside's Steve Nails, by the way, takes credit for coming up with the name of the album—suggesting it to Mark after hearing the recorded version.

"Tomorrow's Gonna Be" was originally written earlier with Mark's friend Tom Boles, and was first recorded for the soundtrack of the 1986 film *Echo Park*. That version featured Concrete

Blonde singer Johnette Napolitano on lead vocals, and was drastically different arrangement-wise than the version the Drifters recorded nearly two decades later.

Mark says the song was about "a depressed person that was trying to find positive in their life," making it particularly fitting for the Drifters at that moment in time.

"Everybody thinks it's a really happy, shiny song. But it's actually like, 'Tomorrow's gonna be a better day. Right, sure it is!'" Mark said. "That's why I suggested 'Tomorrow's Gonna Be' for the record, even though it's sort of a negative song."

The song is "all sarcasm," and weaves between the keys of G minor and G major to demonstrate the bleak outlook that the song's narrator had toward their life.

The original recording with Napolitano has, to this day, remained unheard by pretty much everyone in the band.

"I don't want to give them a preconceived idea of what it should be or shouldn't be," Mark said of his decision to shield his fellow Drifters from the original song. "It should be interpretive. I want to put my own spin on whatever I do. Why just copy it note for note or attitude for attitude?"

The resulting Drifters version swings much more than the original, and has a slight Los Lobos feel to it. It also features Mark on lead vocals, in his first and only turn as vocalist for the band. He played acoustic guitar as well, while Susan played bass and harmonized. Mark ended up singing it at the insistence of Susan.

Going into Dockside to record, while obviously a quite different dynamic from the last time around, wasn't all bad according to most of the band.

"I don't find anything negative about the recording process, personally," Mark said. "Except for the time I came out on the deck out of the kitchen on the balcony, and I got bit by 50 wasps or something. I was in a fuckin' lot of pain. I swung the door and they just all decided to swarm up through the floorboards and just attack me."

That would probably ruin a session for any other musician at any other studio, but not at Dockside.

"Dockside was kind of always this safe haven for all of us, and the vibe of Steve and Wish— it's kind of like you couldn't have a bad day at Dockside. They were just such wonderful, wonderful people," Robert insisted. "I remember just hardly ever getting out of my bathrobe. I had my bench, I had my pedalboard, and I had my bottle of wine next to me."

Russ agrees that it wasn't a bad experience, regardless of what was happening.

"I felt like we did a good job of sidelining the inner shifts and strains that were going down," he said. "And we were giving each other space. Peter was staying up at the big house with Vicki, and then the pool house was Mark and Robert. And me and Susan [stayed] over the studio. Everyone had their own place, in a way. But we were making it."

Things were different this time around, undoubtedly, but Wish Nails also recalls the band simply doing their best to make it all work.

"This group of people all belong naked at Woodstock in the sixties, swimming in the cattle pond and while listening to Jimi Hendrix," she quipped. "There was a bit of hurt and a bit of extra love, but it didn't change what happened and everyone was doing the best they could considering all the love they had for each other. It was almost amazing to watch."

Russ remembers the session as the band at its most experimental—especially with the sonics. And Tony Daigle was on board to explore. They set up an A and B drum kit for the recording—one in the main tracking room and one in the hallway, mic'd more minimally to capture the unique sound of Dockside's tiled hallway between the control and tracking rooms.

The most obvious example of this approach is on Peter's "Live On Love," where they alternated between the two kits at various points in the song.

"Every time I go to [the B] kit, it's a different sound, but I'm going to play it with a different feel, too," Russ said. "I'm going to play a tight shuffle, like hip-hop or something. Sixteenth notes, but it's all swung. And the other kit is playing straight and pretty sparse."

The band used gift funding from The Fan to pay themselves salaries for the duration of the recording, and offset expenses they'd incur while at Dockside. Along with some budget from the label, they spent three weeks recording and mixing a set of songs that were about as fresh as it could get for the band, as opposed to previous records where original songs had been circulating for years.

Naturally, many of the songs were melancholy, and there was certainly a heaviness to the writing that wasn't there before. "Live On Love," while presented with an upbeat groove and a hooky horn line played by Bonerama trombone master Mark Mullins and New Orleans trumpeter Eric Lucero, sounded like a man trying to convince himself to hold onto something; anything.

> *Sometimes I lose my faith, sometimes I lose my way back home*
> *When my communion's done, sometimes my strengths have been atoned*
> *And hardly ever does it feel like the part of it that's real is the part that holds the rope*
> *That's when we live on love, that's when we hold our dreams and hope*

"I think that's probably an attempt at buoying my sagging piece of mind," Peter said. Even Vicki's "Na Na" was defiant but dour—a unquestionable highlight in the set.

> *This is the story of my life*
> *Somebody's little girl to someone else's wife*
> *What happened in between*
> *Is the dying of a dream*
> *And that's the story of my life*

Musically speaking, the highlight of "Na Na" was arguably both Robert's searing solo at the song's midpoint, and his "I Believe in Miracles" lead line in the choruses.

Those moments are often born of amusement for Robert, who likes to sneak in licks that nod to songs he loves and see who catches it.

"When I come up with a part, sometimes it's just for me to make people laugh," he laughed. "In Susan's song 'Desperate Love,' it was like, I wonder how many people are going to realize that this is 'For Your Pleasure' by Roxy Music?"

Vicki also contributed the folk waltz "That Much a Fool," written about an unrequited love.

"'That Much a Fool' is one where I literally woke up with the song. Which has only happened like three times in my life," she recalled, adding that the majority of her contributions were actually written while on the previous German tour.

From Peter came the aforementioned "Live On Love," along with the bouncy "Too Little Too Late."

There's no question that what was happening around them was influencing the songs, albeit indirectly. Even songs from Vicki were hitting emotional points for Susan and Peter.

"I'm remembering a late night when I was playing 'That Much a Fool' to Peter, and Susan walked in and she goes, 'What was that last line?!' I was just like, 'Okay, I think I hit a nerve,'" Vicki recalled. "It was not written about that at all, but that energy was swirling. There was chaos—it was, like, emotional chaos."

If there's one song that could be seen as the addressing of the giant elephant in the room, it would be Peter's "Down By the Great Mistake." He says he originally wrote it with the intention of duetting with Susan, with the two trading lines about their relationship.

"'Down By the Great Mistake' turned into this big imbroglio because I originally thought, 'Hey, you know, me and Susan. Makes sense, right? We're on the outs. We'll sound like fuckin' John and June.' But she had a very sensitive point about stuff with me," he recalled. "I think she absolutely felt—and she was absolutely right, of course—that by singing that song, she would be putting my words in her mouth. The simplest way of addressing it was by not wanting to sing the song. I respected that, and [Vicki] stepped up to the plate and became my comedic foil."

Indeed, Vicki ultimately did agree to be the female voice on the song, and it ended up being a highlight of the recording sessions for Robert in particular, who helped guide the vocal performances.

"I have vivid, vivid memories of being the vocal producer on 'Down By the Great Mistake.' Just like, 'Okay, I totally believe that take,'" he said.

They also kept in some small mistakes in the guitar playing—something Robert says added character to the drunkenness of that song.

"That fractured Doug Sahm kind of thing, and all of my clams on guitar—we just kept all of that shit," he said.

Peter admits to not being fond of the song in the years after the album came out because "it just seemed so ridiculous," but with 20-plus years of hindsight he seems to find the value in its inclusion on such an emotionally heavy album.

"I think all three of us get our yucks in. We're laughing through what we have to laugh through," he said.

For Peter, the recording of *Better Day* is largely a blur due to both his alcohol intake and everything else happening within the group. Looking back, he praises both Susan and Vicki for what they contributed and is not particularly happy with his songs.

"I don't know how I ended up with four songs on there," he said. "I think that Susan and Vicki hit it out of the park with their songs."

Everyone else disagrees with Peter's assessment that his songs weren't especially strong.

"I think the songs on it are fantastic. Peter just downplays it—I think it was because of that negativity, though, that he was experiencing," Mark said.

They're also united in the opinion that Peter's "Where Does the Time Go" is a standout on the album.

"I think "Where Does the Time Go" is the start of my mourning period for my relationship with Susan," Peter said.

The recording of such a delicate song was the only real point where the emotions of the interpersonal chaos was palpable musically, as Russ recalled.

He explains: "I played with brushes—I was hitting hard and on the live kit. And I chose that for the reason of space. That air; to feel the air. Mark was sitting inches away from my bass drum, looking straight at me as we were playing so sparsely. I was playing whole notes, you know? I wouldn't start playing quarter notes, much less eighth notes, until the choruses. There are just gaping holes, and I thought: Hard, confident, and together moving around Peter's vocal.

"During the rough mix listens, Mark and I were jaw dropping, going, 'Holy shit. This is just so painful.' It tickles the stomach, almost, because it's just so open and vulnerable."

They only did one take of that song but worked tirelessly on the arrangement—from the guitar parts all the way up to Vicki and Susan's backing vocals.

"We worked hard on that one. And it wasn't hard work, there was just a lot to do. Peter knew what he wanted and he got it. It was one of the first times I used my Guild Starfire and I played it without a pick. I love the sound of the guitar on that song," Robert said. "That one in particular, we just were in the zone. It's one of my all-time favorite Continental Drifters songs."

That song was about as collaborative as it got for the band (i.e. *very* collaborative) and was a dynamic feat for all involved.

"That was very much Peter's intricacies. We pretty much worked that out while we were recording it," Robert said.

Now, let's talk about the *Better Day* knockouts—namely, Susan's three solo contributions "Snow," "Cousin," and "Someday," as well as "Peaceful Waking," a co-write with Russ.

It's safe to say that these four songs are the most vulnerable on the album. "Someday" finds her waiting for her joy to return—knowing that one day it will.

> *"Someday it'll all come back to me*
> *I'm gonna look for it look for it everyday*
> *I'm gonna climb that tree as far as she goes*
> *Climb a little farther, maybe see some snow*
> *And if that doesn't take away my sorrow*
> *I'm gonna get up again and do it tomorrow*

"Snow" finds Susan reflecting on her childhood, while "Cousin" is probably one of the darker things she's ever written. On that song, the band tried to go for an edgier vibe than they'd previously had.

"We were like, 'Fuck, man, let's go Spooky Tooth meets Led Zeppelin,'" Robert recalled.

"Peaceful Waking" was Russ' first time contributing to a Drifters song as a writer—or any song, for that matter.

"Those are my words that Susan put to music, to show me that I can write," he said. "It was like a journal. I would journal and I'd share it with Susan."

In the earliest points of their relationship, when they were trying to be quieter about it for everyone's sake, they largely communicated by passing their journals back and forth.

"She took my words from the journals, and just put them together into this song format," Russ recalled, adding that the chorus lines were Susan's that she wrote off of what he contributed.

"I would say [the words] to her often. I just wished for her to have peace," he said.

In the recording of that song, Peter says he thought back to the earliest days of the Drifters and his relationship with Susan, where he envisioned them as being one of the great male/female singing duos.

"That, to me, as far as the Peter and Susan singing dynamic that I had always loved so much, that was sort of the final nail in the coffin," he said. "I am very pleased and proud to have been able to sing something that emotionally close with her on that song."

Recording was going well, by all accounts, until the label started interjecting. In an unprecedented move, Razor & Tie sent an A&R representative to Dockside to check in on progress during the recording.

"We wouldn't let fucking A&R people in our doors," Russ said. "It's like, 'No, fuck off. You'll hear it when we're done.'"

Not everyone viewed it as a bad thing, though the majority of the band was not happy about it. For his part, Mark thought it was a good sign that Razor & Tie was invested in the work they were doing.

"I thought it was a positive. I was like. 'Oh man, they're going to fly all the way from New York City to New Orleans, rent a car and drive all the way out to Lafayette? And then stay at a motel because we didn't tell them they could stay with us? That's pretty cool,'" he said.

Robert agrees: "Me personally, I was like, 'Maybe they'll bring us expensive sushi.' Bring me a bottle of booze and some sushi and I'm okay with you."

Sending an A&R rep to the studio would have been bad enough, but things only got more uncomfortable from there. The new guard at Razor & Tie didn't just check in on production, they also started dictating the song sequence and inserting their opinions into the creative process.

The most extreme example of this happened when the A&R rep that visited them started insisting that Vicki's song "Na Na" be the opening song on the album, as opposed to Susan's "Cousin," which the band was in agreement would make a strong statement as an opener.

"Mark was, like, *adamant* that it had to be 'Cousin,'" Russ said.

The A&R rep felt that "Na Na" was the right foot forward for the album, and especially felt strongly that Vicki should be positioned as the "leader" of the band. The band didn't feel right about that being the opener—especially Vicki, who felt she'd need to re-sing her vocal if it was going to start off the record.

They ultimately relented and went with the label's choice.

This was everything the Continental Drifters had tried to avoid.

"I'd been down this road, and I got off this road. This road is bullshit. It's the road to the breaking up of bands," Susan said.

Russ recalls the A&R rep being "googly-eyed" over Vicki, and it became clear in his mind that the rep was there so he could be there with her.

"It was just like, 'What the fuck?!'" he said.

They did leverage Razor & Tie's minimal support as much as possible—enlisting Daigle to remix the eponymous record, which the band was never too happy with in terms of the sonics. That remix was released on Razor & Tie on February 20, 2001, one month after they wrapped the recording of *Better Day*.

When *Better Day* was finally released on June 5, 2001, support from Razor & Tie had become virtually nonexistent. The guys in charge at the label weren't too enthusiastic about the music, and there was enough restructuring happening that the album got lost in the shuffle.

It hadn't always been so bad, though. Prior to their new A&R rep's arrival at the label, they had been working with A&R veteran Mark Lipsitz, who left Razor & Tie after *Vermilion* and went on to work for labels like Bar/None Records.

"He was like a fuckin' little bulldog," Russ recalled. "I talked to Mark [Lipsitz] every day gearing up to promote their release of *Vermilion*."

Lipsitz, Russ says, was invested in helping promote the album and support the band on the road—working with Mark, Russ, and the band's agent to coordinate promotional efforts as much as possible.

This time around, everything was different. Where they once had that support from Lipsitz as their rep, they didn't with the new guy—meaning that the ball started getting dropped more often.

"On paper, we were signed to a record company, but I don't see anything happening," Robert said. "And who are these guys? What are they doing? Do any of them know my name or face?"

During one particularly difficult West Coast tour—their first in several years—the band arrived for a show at Slim's in San Francisco, only to find out that the venue didn't know they were playing. Razor & Tie neglected to do the work it took to advance and promote the show; leaving them feeling frustrated and tired.

"That was kind of the story in virtually every town," Russ said.

Situations like that only added to the enormity of what the band was grappling with, he asserts.

"It's like, 'Okay, so we have a Fleetwood Mac situation here. How was Fleetwood Mac able to do it?' They were fuckin' making millions. This is hard fucking work, and to come all the way out here to promote an album—the venue didn't even know we were playing. They didn't even have us on the calendar.

"So the only people in our audience were people who followed our website. That was a hard fucking tour, and the West Coast is hard because it's long travel days. That's a long time to be in each other's presence, stewing about."

The record company shitstorm that the band experienced at the time certainly isn't a story that's unique to them; almost any artist will tell you their own horror story of industry neglect and inefficiency. For the Drifters, it was just more fuel for a fire that had been spreading for a long time.

As was tradition for the Drifters, they celebrated *Better Day* with a raucous album release show at the Howlin' Wolf. No search lights this time around, but they put on a free show with food and played to a packed room of friends, fans, and family. For this show, the band asked local friends and fans to open the night by performing their own versions of Drifters songs—including a spoken word version of "Daddy Just Wants It to Rain" by NOLA artist Dylan James.

Better Day ended up getting glowing reviews from press following its release, but much of the press they got naturally referenced Peter and Susan's breakup (not Russ and Susan's relationship, however, as it wasn't made public).

A review from a site called *Gallery of Sound* noted the obvious references to the divorce:

It's hard not to read a little fracture into the Drifters' democratic system, with the break-up of Peter Holsapple and Susan Cowsill in the middle of this album--songs like "Too Little, Too Late" and "(Down by The) Great Mistake" seem to detail it.

Thankfully, the Drifters have always been a group of individuals, and their love of the music has transcended the turmoil of the end of Holsapple and Cowsill's marriage. This would be a career album for the Continental Drifters on its own, but considering the emotional upheaval that attended it, Better Day *has all the earmarks of one of the year's best.*

A *Billboard* review also noted the Fleetwood Mac-ian nature of the record:

Mentioning the breakup in a review is one thing—asking about it in interviews is another, and they were getting plenty of that.

One particular radio interview during the *Better Day* press cycle was an example of the questions being asked, but framed from the perspective of the impact the divorce had on the band rather than asking for details.

"Was your splitting up—did it endanger the band initially?" the interviewer asked.

"Of course. Conceptually, it endangers everything," Susan replied. "It endangers your friends, your children's welfare, your band—so you spend a lot of time thinking that over when you're trying to decide how much you want to take on in the world."

Other interviewers would be more direct in their line of questioning, and it was a strange and frustrating thing to navigate for both Susan and Peter. Susan looks back on that press cycle as largely being intensely difficult.

"It was impossible. I'm a human first and a bandmate second and an entertainer third—all that shit," she said. "And so I'm sitting here trying to get up every day and breathe, and try and make a right day out of a wrong situation and this guy wants details out of me while we're promoting a record? It's like, c'mon, buddy."

Peter would ultimately be the one to respond in those situations, he said.

"I think often Susan would not respond. I probably responded because I was an asshole. I think when we were in a public situation with it, we tried to be as circumspect as possible, you know?" he said. "And not publicly make a fuss because privately it was so difficult. When you get back in the van, you better hope there's a case in there, too. That also kind of hastens more alcoholic activity."

Being asked about their breakup in interviews was a painful consequence of keeping the band together and making a record during such a vulnerable time, but it really was the music that made it possible—as Peter says, "that's never anything less than a valid reason."

"The music was always there. There were enough of us where you didn't have to look at the people you didn't want to look at," he said. "I would not have wanted to have been anybody else in that van. I think that it was a really hard way to go promote an album."

The month after the release of *Better Day*, the band was booked in New York City to play an afternoon gig at the World Trade Center (at the same time as Emmylou Harris, who was playing at Battery Park less than a mile away). The show found them much happier and more lively than, say, the previous year's European tour, but they were still dealing with feeling neglected by the label.

While in town, they decided to pay a visit to the Razor & Tie offices, where they hoped to talk with the label heads and figure out how to get the label to pay better attention to them.

"People were perfectly nice. But unless you really have a relationship with somebody there, you're just kind of glad handing and trying to figure out who these people are and do they give a shit?" Vicki said.

At the time, the label was attempting to expand—in fact, the first volume of its immensely popular *Kidz Bop* series was released just two months later to great acclaim. And, as Russ explains, they'd just brought on a new partner to run the company so that the founders could "play golf."

"We said, 'We're trying to do this, but your guy's not listening to us, and he's not talking to us. We're not agreeing here,'" Mark said. "They went, 'Yeah, well, it's just the way it is right now. Sorry.' It's coming from the top down, even though we thought they really, really liked us."

"We got left on the side of the road, essentially," Russ added. "We were putting in this emotional hard work to keep the band together; to keep our relationships, and to stay kind to one another—and going through these major changes in our lives. We needed those wheels to help carry us, and they pulled them.

"We realized during the West Coast tour that we have no wheels. We're Flintstone-running our vehicles, and we're tired of it. We don't have what it takes to carry this vehicle right now."

The pressure mounted as every aspect of the band got more complicated at every turn. Prior to *Better Day*'s release, Vicki had picked back up with The Bangles. With Mark and Russ handling the Drifters' calendar and advising their agent, finding blocks of time to book tours was starting to become a challenge.

In the past, Peter's day job with Hootie & the Blowfish posed the occasional logistical challenge, though the band got better at navigating it over time. With Vicki's increasing Bangles commitments in the mix, however, things were beginning to be as professionally chaotic as they were personally chaotic.

One particularly hectic event during this period involved Vicki playing a Drifters gig, immediately jumping into a car to the airport, getting on a plane to another city, and going right into a Bangles show.

"I was kind of being divided. But my heart was really still with the Drifters. That was the band that had saved my musical life, as far as I was concerned," she said.

To the band's credit, they tried their hardest to keep it together for as long as possible. Given everything that was happening, it's an absolute miracle that they managed to even get a record out. Peter marvels at the "sheer logistics" of it all, but notes that it was always the music that made it work.

The only time in years past that it didn't work was when Carlo derailed the show in Germany because of his aggressive behavior and excessive drinking. Fast forward to 2001, and a show at Grant Street Dance Hall in Lafayette—which was recorded for radio broadcast—proved nearly as threatening to the band's future.

Peter recalls starting to drink the "instant" that he arrived at the venue.

"And so I had a couple of drinks by soundcheck. And I drank after soundcheck. And I drank all through the show, until I was not capable of performing anymore," he said. "I think we soldiered on to the end, but I think they took away any of the songs that I was supposed to sing on, because I don't think I could've sung."

Robert remembers seeing Peter passed out on his keyboard at one point during the night.

"There was a lot of Jagermeister going down Peter's gullet to just escape everything," he said.

After the show was over, a trashed and enraged Peter started taking his anger out.

"I was furious. Drunk and furious. So I was slinging bottles at the back wall of the club," he recalled.

The band managed to calm him down and get him in the van and back to New Orleans.

"I wake up, we're at Mark's house unloading gear, and I decide I'm going to walk home to Filmore," he said.

Mark was incredulous.

"I went, 'That's three miles!'" he said.

Peter walked home and the disastrous night was behind them. A noteworthy anecdote in the band's history, for sure, but over two decades later the others don't remember it as much for what Peter did. Rather, they remember the music they played together.

"There was some weird tension, but there were some really amazing songs from that [show]" Mark said.

"I remember that night being the first night we were trying out 'Snow,'" Russ added. "All of *that*, and what sticks out to me from that show is 'Snow.'"

When things reached their breaking point at the end of 2001, the often-jubilant Drifter environment was already unrecognizable. Tensions were high, and it seemed the fun was over. Following the terrorist attacks of September 11, the band was booked for a European tour just a few months later—in January of 2002.

Touring Europe had become a regular part of the Drifters cycle, though the previous trip in July of 2000 was certainly anything but regular.

Embarking on another European tour, amid the drama the band was experiencing and following the horrific events of September 11, was not an option for Susan and Russ. A meeting took place to discuss it, and everything came to blows.

The band was divided on whether or not to go ahead with the Europe tour. With sound engineers hired, flights booked, dates confirmed, and promo in motion, canceling the run would be a bridge burner. Some were ambivalent, others insisted on going, and the remaining members were adamant about not stepping foot onto an airplane.

With her and Peter's daughter set to go on the trip with them, Susan was particularly against the idea.

"Had we not had all of the personal turmoil, I still was not going to be okay to get on the plane with Miranda," Susan said. "I'm not going to travel to a foreign country after [an] unprecedented attack on the United States had just occurred."

The tour was ultimately canceled—a devastating blow to not just the band but to Edgar Heckmann, who spent time and money putting it together.

"We had laid down everything for the next step for the band in Germany and Europe," Heckmann said. "It wasn't the only tour of Blue Rose artists which had been canceled but this one was like a stitch in my heart. I understood the decision, but on the other hand I was sure that such a terror attack wouldn't happen again. But I wasn't the one who had to get on a plane."

This was a critical point in the division of the band; two distinct camps had been formed, and Robert—who was firmly on one side—felt at the time that the cancellation of their European tour was, for Susan and Russ, a way of leaving the band.

"Me personally, I called bullshit on it," Robert said. "They might have been completely sincere, but to my ears it's like, 'Man, that sounds like an excuse to me.'"

Mark was the one to make the difficult call to Heckmann, informing him of the band's decision to pull out of the tour.

"I was really looking forward to Europe, because I know Edgar was so excited. He spent a lot of money up front to make it happen," Mark said. "That's the hardest call I think I've ever made. I felt really bad. I didn't want to admit that it was over—I was trying to figure out a way to get around it, but I saw that there was no possible way."

In the end, the final straw was broken. Russ and Susan left the Continental Drifters just two days later.

"I could feel that there was a division that was trying to push me out, in a way," Russ said. "I was catching some bad behavior flack. Pointing at me. So the frustration from all of this was starting to be taken out on me. I've done too much personal work in my life to allow [myself] to be doormated. The option I could see, after several band meetings, was to leave."

Just like that, a decade after it began and nearly eight years after packing up and moving to New Orleans, the Continental Drifters were done. It wasn't something anyone took in stride; everyone felt the sting of the loss, and mourned what they were leaving behind.

And yet, there was no fanfare; no public statement. Instead, the band opted to fly under the radar and move on with their lives. The band's last show was a TV broadcast for *Louisiana Jukebox*, which took place on August 9, 2001—one month before 9/11 and five months before they planned to head to Europe.

Just a few days after that final gig, they gathered at Mike Mayeux's studio to record a version of "Listen, Listen" that they planned to include on an EP of Sandy Denny, Richard Thompson, and Fairport Convention covers. The rest of the songs on the collection had been recorded for a radio broadcast in Germany on July 5, 2000. They took the recordings from Hot*FM in Hof, gave them to Mayeux to mix, and compiled the seven songs onto a compilation called *Listen, Listen*.

Listen, Listen was released on CD and vinyl, in Germany only, on November 5, and served as the final Continental Drifters release.

This wasn't necessarily an intentional end point for the Drifters; *Listen, Listen* was intended to be a companion release to *Better Day* that they could sell on the road while in Germany, but that never came to be.

"Honestly, of all the Drifters stuff, that particular morning was one of my favorite Continental Drifters experiences, and it kind of really encapsulated what we were all about," Robert said of the recording, which happened the morning after the gigantic blowout at the hotel.

The show leading up to the fight was an enjoyable one, he recalls, and the band "drank to excess."

He explains the events that followed: "The next morning, we were doing this radio station at ten o'clock in the morning, and the room where the band set up was probably as big as your bathroom. And I was like, 'Oh, shit. They want us to do Continental Drifters songs. I don't wanna do any of that shit. No fuckin' way. It's ten o'clock in the morning and I've got a really bad hangover.

"And everybody else is like, 'You, too? What the fuck are we going to do? What about a Sandy Denny song or a Richard Thompson song? Well let's just do all Sandy Denny and Richard Thompson.'

"Then somebody was like, 'Russ, what are you going to do?' I had turned Russ on to this thing called a laptop, which was a snare drum hoop—just the top hoop—with a metal snare underneath it, but no body. So it was just literally the top head with a metal hoop around it and a snare underneath it, and you could use it for practice sessions and stuff. And they sound fucking great.

"So he got one and loved it, and just brought it on tour for practice and stuff. We thought,

'This will be perfect.' And we go, 'What are you going to do for a kick? Well, what if we put your [kick] pedal under your snare case?'

"It was so immediate—it was so in the moment. We were doing all of these songs that I'd never played on mandolin, and no rehearsal or anything like that. We were like, 'Let's just do this.'"

Robert also notes that their version of "I'm a Dreamer" from *Listen, Listen* was "the first time that Susan had indicated that she was going to go."

"The last line is, 'And the truth is, I don't think I'll ever go.' And Susan just changed it to, 'And the truth is, I know I'm gonna go,'" he said. "And then the shoe dropped right at that minute."

While nobody obviously planned on the band ending, there was simply no point in continuing past the intensity and resentment that resulted from the conversations around canceling Europe.

Russ laments everything that happened, but emphasizes that if things had been different with the label and the business side of things, they could very well have seen the purpose in continuing on and working through the personal stuff.

"Had we had the wheels, I think we would have kept going," he said. "And there would probably have been another record on the tail end of the breakup record. We would've written our experience in the music. That would have been the next record, I assume."

The end of the band was difficult for everyone, regardless of what side of the issue someone was on. And there were two camps being formed as things devolved. Vicki assumed the role of Switzerland in the conflict, but among the rest of the band there was a very painful and almost tangible divide.

"Your identity is wrapped up in it. We were a family. A family, first and foremost, of brothers and sisters. Married or not, it was a total brother-sister family, all around the board," Susan said. "So that was all going away."

For Mark Walton, the man who founded the band ten years earlier, calling it quits was painful and difficult.

"I didn't want to have to say it was over," he lamented. "And it took me a lot to just say, 'No, let it go.'"

When things with the *Vermilion* lineup came to an end in 2001, the Continental Drifters were a band that already looked virtually unrecognizable compared to the one that formed in Los Angeles in 1991, and yet it ended just as it started; a group of like-minded musicians with a palpable chemistry, drifting away from one life and into the next.

Chapter Ten:
I Can't Let Go

"We were a little society unto ourselves, which was really neat.
It was a community of friends."

—Peter Holsapple

Part I

By 2001, Mark Walton was the only original member of the band still there, almost single handedly carrying the Drifters through ten years of lineup changes, drama, drugs, alcohol, relationships, breakups, songs, gigs, feuds, and family. He was the nucleus of the band; the anchor that held it down.

Mark Walton is likely the most internally-beloved Drifter in the bunch, and for many reasons. And those who love Drifters music will tell you that one of the most uniquely defining characteristics of the band no matter the lineup is Mark's bass playing. It's fluid, spacious, elastic, and melodic. The man himself chalks all of that up to feel.

"Bass players, to me, either they're very very over technical, or they're trying to impress or they just play just with the kick drum," he said. "I just wanted to be different and I just wanted to have some sort of stamp. It's all about the feel."

What he had with the Drifters was something Mark says he'd always been looking for in a band since he was a kid—crediting Joe Cocker's 1971 rock doc *Mad Dogs & Englishmen* with lighting a fire.

"That played two blocks from my house—I broke into that theater every day and watched it. I was like, 'That's what I want to do when I grow up.' I swear to god, it stuck with me all my life," he said. "When the Continental Drifters started happening and we started doing stuff like that, it was like I was finally making that dream come true, you know?"

He took what he absorbed from that film and let it inform his attitude on music, hence why he was never concerned with making a living as a musician. It wasn't about that. It was just about the joy of creating art and finding community.

"I don't play for the sake of playing. I like playing originals and doing stuff that makes sense to me. If I want a dollar, I'll go work and make money for a dollar," he said. "I waited tables and tended bar at La Crêpe Nanou, I started building websites for different clubs and art galleries in the city. I'm always that kind of person that can find a way to make money. I've never really made money off of [music]. It's not something that I expect."

As was the case with many musicians his age, Mark's interest in music began with The Beatles on The Ed Sullivan Show.

"There was no question in my mind. It was like, 'Hey that looks like fun!' I don't want to be a plumber, I don't want to do electrician work. I don't want to do manual labor."

His parents, he says, encouraged him and his siblings to do what made them happy. They didn't have any big aspirations of their own—his mother was from a poor part of London and his father was from a poor part of Chicago—so they were generally supportive of whatever path their kids took.

"From their point of view they were like, 'Shit, anything's better than what we did and how we grew up.' So I said, 'Okay, I want to play music,'" he recalled.

Starting around the age of ten, he started playing guitar while living in New Jersey. He and a neighbor friend who played drums got together and tried their hand at songwriting.

"Every song on the radio had the word 'baby' in it, so we wrote a lot of songs with 'baby' in it," he laughed.

When his father, who was in the Air Force, retired, the family moved to Beverly Hills on a whim. He says they "kept driving west until they couldn't go any further, and ended up in Los Angeles."

He attended Beverly Hills High School, and put a band together with a friend from down the block. They started another band once they graduated high school, calling it The Automatics—later renamed The Automatix after they discovered another band with the same name. The Automatix played clubs such as The Troubadour and a defunct room called the Londoner, and were active for a short time before they called it quits. Mark then joined another band with a couple of Automatix bandmates and soon after was fired because they thought he was "too much of a knucklehead" and not a good enough bass player.

"That pissed me off," he said.

By then he'd already started Uncle Studios, the rehearsal studio he founded which was later taken over by his brother Scott—himself a musician who played mostly prog music but also notably toured as a keyboardist with Weird Al Yankovic and played on a Yes album.

Uncle started in 1979, and Mark was fired by his post-Automatix band in 1980.

"They fired me, and I was like, 'Fuck this.' So I was working at the studio and I said, 'Ehh, I don't want to play in a band. That's too emotional for me.' I just didn't want to jump into things," he said.

He was offered some gigs around this time, but mostly turned them down because he wanted to turn his focus to the rehearsal studio and songwriting.

He was living at the Holiday Manor in Studio City, where he says "lots of artists" lived at the time, and remembers it fondly as a great place to live and generally a fruitful time creatively. He was writing and co-writing regularly and Uncle was doing well.

All of that was fine enough for Mark and he pursued those interests for a few years, until May of 1984 when Dream Syndicate guitarist Karl Precoda walked into the studio and asked him to join the band on tour promoting their just-released *Medicine Show* album.

"I thought about it for a day and said, 'Okay, yeah, sure. Let's try it out,'" he said. They toured as support for R.E.M. on his first run with the band, and the rest was Dream Syndicate history.

Mark credits Susan as part of the "equation" that motivated him to pursue music, explaining that the area where he lived as a kid in New Jersey had a big Cowsills fanbase.

"Back then, all radio stations didn't play the same setlist, right? You could be famous in one part of the country and nobody would hear of you on the other side," he said. "There they were huge, and I'd hear them on the radio all the time and see them on TV all the time. I was always really surprised to see this little girl up there doing her thing. I was like, 'See, if she could do it, I could do it! She's my age!'"

Mark's world collided with The Cowsills years later when they started rehearsing at Uncle—which Mark credits to John Cowsill specifically. John, at the time, was playing drums with Tommy Tutone, and that band had been rehearsing at Uncle. When The Cowsills restarted, John recommended Mark's place for rehearsals.

"Once they came, they never left. They always came in every week or every other week and would rehearse," Mark said. "I knew them really well. I wouldn't even have to talk to them. I'd book 'em, I'd set up the room, and they'd just walk in and start playing."

Uncle's origins can actually be tracked to a band called Uncle, which was on the outs and looking for someone to take over their rehearsal space lease. They had a small clientele of artists that would rehearse there already, but it wasn't until a year after Mark took over that things actually took off.

"I did advertising in local papers like the *L.A. Weekly* and the *L.A. Reader*, but it was all word of mouth. I would go to clubs trying to talk up the studio. I did that for a long time," he said.

When he joined the Dream Syndicate, he'd already found modest success with his songwriting, though he says writing was something that never came easy to him; he notes that "Get Over It" is the only song he ever wrote without a co-writer.

That song was written the same weekend that Peter, Vicki, Susan, and Gary got together to record their first single as Double Date.

"They went out of town, and I was all by myself at the Batch Pad. I thought, 'I'm going to write a song.' And I wrote that song," he recalled.

Uncle is perhaps more important to the history of the Drifters than any other location, because not only was it ground zero for the band, it's ultimately the place where most of Mark's musical connections were made and where so much of his life was shaped. He saw it as an opportunity to be around artists he liked, and that approach led to a long and storied career.

"That's why I wanted to start it. I didn't want to go out and be a groupie. Hey, I'll build something, they'll come to me, and I'll pick and choose who I like," he explains.

Some of the most notable artists who were clients of Mark's include Poco, Quiet Riot, Circle Jerks, Bad Religion, and Crazy Horse.

Mark's emotional attachment to bands is what pushed him further with Uncle, what led him to the Dream Syndicate, and then what led him to the Continental Drifters. And so, when Susan and Russ quit the band in 2002, he had a hard time accepting that things were over.

Oddly enough, two gig offers came in after the split—one for a slot at Jazz Fest, and another for Festival International de Louisiane in Lafayette around the same time. The remaining band thought hard about whether they could and should take the gigs, and it was decided that they'd try and put together a lineup as a way to see if it worked.

They enlisted Bluerunners drummer John Maloney on drums, a friend of the band, and also asked their old pal Ray Ganucheau to join them. The rest of the lineup was Vicki, Robert, Mark, and Peter, and together they played the festival dates as well as club gigs at the Howlin' Wolf and Carrollton Station.

Vicki admits to not having any recollection whatsoever of gigs after Susan and Russ' exit. That might be justifiable, as Mark acknowledges that there was just something off about it.

"It didn't have that magic. It didn't feel like The Drifters enough. There's only so many ways you can remove something until it loses the soul," he said. "It probably hurt us not having somebody [on drums] that could just fit in immediately, and knew exactly what we were all about."

Robert is more direct about it, calling the shows "stopgap stuff." He wasn't complaining, though.

"Me, personally, I'll do just about anything to be on stage with Ray's voice," he said. "He's a rock and he's a sweet guy, and that voice, man. God."

Peter says he also doesn't remember anything about those gigs, similarly to Vicki's memory lapse.

"I know they happened, but I share her mass migration of brain cells on that. I can't remember anything about it, either," he said. "It makes me really think that we were probably stunningly ordinary or forgettable, you know?"

And so, after that, things just sort of ended. No formal breakup; they just let it fade.

"It just didn't come up, I don't think. We all just were quiet and didn't say anything. We didn't make any conscious effort to say, 'That's the end of the band,'" Mark said.

The tour cancellation was a major blow for Mark, particularly in terms of his relationship with Susan and Russ. He was hurt by the idea that they were making a choice for the rest of the band that they wouldn't be touring. Leaving just days later deepened that wound.

"What do you mean you're leaving? After everything we've tried to do to keep this going, and you're going to leave because of 9/11? Or maybe they just didn't believe that we'd ever accept them as a couple? I don't know," he said.

The rift that occurred in the Drifters had been coming for a while, and there was not only a falling out between Mark and Russ and Susan, but also a major falling out between Robert and Russ. For Mark, though, it was especially painful.

"To me, a band is a relationship," he recalled. "It just is. And for a subset of that relationship to take precedent over the core kind of just felt weird and wrong and out of place. I didn't know how to handle that, so I just kind of kept it to myself.

"The only time I actually saw Russ and Susan after that was once at La Crêpe Nanou. They walked in halfway through our dinner—I kind of went over and said something to them but it was probably not niceties. I don't remember what I said, but I know it upset them."

He crossed paths with Susan just one other time after that, at the school where Mark's kids and Miranda Holsapple all went. There was a huge storm, and Susan was stranded at the school.

"Susan was stuck at school trying to get Miranda home, so I gave them a ride. And that was it," he said. The two didn't speak at all.

Mark also stopped playing music after the band ended, save for one random gig with none other than Barry Cowsill, who called him out of the blue one day and asked if he'd sit in with him that night.

"Barry just was going crazy playing anything and everything, and I just had to follow along," he recalled.

His friendship with Barry went back decades, and he even remembers running into Barry right after he moved to New Orleans. Unbeknownst to *everyone*, Barry had also moved to NOLA.

"I was half a block from my house, and all of the sudden I bump into him on the street and

I'm like, 'What the fuck are you doing?' He's like, 'Fuck! Fuck! What are you fucking doing here?' I said, 'I moved here! We all moved here.' He goes, 'Fuck! I wanted to get away from all of you motherfuckers."

Following the end of the band, Mark did try to keep it alive in some form or another—calling Edgar Heckmann in 2003 to see if he was interested in releasing the band's shelved first record that they made with Mark McKenna in 1992. Heckmann quickly agreed.

"We were broken up, no band, nothing. I went, 'Edgar, I have this record, and it's never come out. Would you put it out?' And he went, 'Absolutely,'" Mark recalled.

Mark reached out to the others to inform them of the project, and talked to Carlo for the first time in seven years aside from their brief run-in at the Howlin' Wolf five years earlier. It was their first actual conversation since 1996.

"That was the first time I called Carlo. I was actually walking one of my kids in a stroller at the Lakefront, and talking to Carlo. And it was a good conversation," he remembers.

The album, aptly titled *Nineteen Ninety-Three*, was released ten years after originally intended, on May 12, 2003, marked with a reunion of the Holsapple, Ganucheau, Eaton, Nuccio, and Walton lineup at Carrollton Station.

It was the first time that Gary had seen or played with the Drifters since he was fired in 1993, but he remained active in music—perhaps more prolifically than ever—since.

One of the musical constants for Gary after the Drifters ended was his relationship with Lou Adler, who produced the Ringling Sisters' record for A&M. In 1990, when Gary was still with the Ringling Sisters, Adler hired the band to play at a fifteenth anniversary celebration for *The Rocky Horror Picture Show*.

Five years later, Adler hired Gary again to play for the twentieth anniversary, alongside Gary's wife and their bandmates in his post-Ringling group Kingsizemaybe.

During this time he was also working at Uncle Studios, where he met and befriended guitarist Doug Pettibone. Pettibone invited Gary to join him on the road with a band called The Surfers, which included legendary surfers Kelly Slater and Rob Machado.

"We played in Germany, we played in Japan, we played in Puerto Rico, we played all up and down the East Coast," he said.

Gary also toured and recorded with The Rain Parade's Steven Roback in Viva Saturn, which also included Carlo. With Viva Saturn, Gary toured and became "smoking buddies" with Velvet Underground drummer Moe Tucker—who he remembers as being, "fuckin' hella cool."

All that brought him to Carrollton Station in New Orleans, ten years after splitting with the band, standing on stage with his former bandmates to celebrate the recordings they made together eleven years earlier.

Reviews for *Nineteen Ninety-Three* were largely positive, offering a glimpse of what might have been had that lineup managed to stick together and find a home for the record.

As a historical document, *No Depression* praised the album as "an illuminating look back":

A strong album from start to finish, Nineteen Ninety-Three *transcends archival curio status and serves as a terrific showcase for the three men who first led the Continental Drifters.*

Offbeat magazine noted the album's cohesiveness and strong songwriting:

Ray came back to the fold having spent years doing both guitar and studio engineering work
outside of his non-musical career.

"After '93, I did some engineering in a couple different studios. Wasn't really doing much
playing," he said. Ray and his wife formed a rock trio that played around New Orleans for a
short time, before he joined the subdudes who he played with intermittently.

"Subdudes, at that point, had broken up or maybe taken a pause. And they started this band
Tiny Town," he said. "It was Pat McLaughlin, Tommy Malone, Johnnie Ray Allen, and Kenny
Blevins from John Hiatt's band The Goners. I was working for them quite a bit, actually—I
recorded some demos and I was mixing them live."

Some of the work Ray did for Tiny Town ended up on that band's self-titled debut (and their
only album to date), which was produced by The Eagles' Bernie Leadon.

Ray kept in touch with the Drifters after leaving, seeing them on multiple occasions and
remaining friends with everyone, but especially Susan, Carlo, and even Russ who he'd known
from around New Orleans.

He also went on to play in former Cowboy Mouth guitarist Paul Sanchez's band for a time, a
band that would also regularly feature Carlo, Russ, Susan, and Sanchez's former Cowboy Mouth
bandmate-turned-Cowsills bassist Mary Lasseigne.

When the release celebration for *Nineteen Ninety-Three* concluded, Gary, Ray, Carlo, Mark,
and Peter went their separate ways, remaining on friendly terms but ultimately not pursuing
anything further.

Elsewhere, Danny McGough was active in his post-Drifters band Shivaree, which proved to
be his most commercially successful outing as a full-fledged member. Shivaree formed in 1997
and included Danny, singer Ambrosia Parsley, and guitarist Duke McVinnie.

Shivaree was signed to Capitol Records and their debut album, *I Oughtta Give You a Shot in the
Head for Making Me Live in This Dump*, was released in 1999. They had some notable placements
with their best known song, "Goodnight Moon," including on shows like *Dawson's Creek* and
films like *Kill Bill Vol. 2*, but never achieved tangible commercial success in the States.

"The record came out in the States and it sold maybe 20,000 copies or something, and we did
a little tour. The record company gave us a bus, but we're pulling up in a bus to go play a book-
store in Charlotte," he joked. "We'd do, maybe, 500-seater club or something like that. But then
the record kind of died down."

Europe was another story. Shivaree became a huge success overseas, doing considerably well
in Italy, then in France, and even better in Italy after "Goodnight Moon" got placed in a commercial. From there, the band's success expanded to Spain and Portugal, and they started touring in
Europe regularly, for months on end.

"In the commercial it's got these really handsome and beautiful people driving in their
convertible and then they drive off a cliff because they're looking at their watches," he recalls of
the Italian TV spot.

In 1999, Danny also got the opportunity to tour with Tom Waits.

"I was working at a recording studio, and the guy producing answers the phone and he's
talking into the phone and goes, 'Chamberlin? Hmm. Mellotron? Ehhh. Jeez, I can't think of

anybody,'" he recalled. "He hangs up the phone and I go, 'What was that?' And he says, 'Oh, Tom Waits is looking for a keyboard player.' I stood up and I go, 'Fuck you!'"

Danny bombarded everyone he knew who was connected to Waits, and ended up getting the gig. He toured with Waits around his *Mule Variations* record, playing his first show at SXSW in 1999—the same year the Drifters were there and signed with Razor & Tie.

His time in Waits' band was not just musically fruitful but also largely unpredictable.

"By the end of all the touring that we did, we did over 200 songs. Tom really liked changing things up, and he loves the sound of a band tightrope-walking—you don't know if they're exactly going to make it. But we always did," he said.

By 2003, Danny was still active in Shivaree and doing session work in Los Angeles, while his former Drifters bandmates were in New Orleans finally unleashing their long-overdue debut album on the world.

With the conclusion of that *Nineteen Ninety-Three* celebration show, the Drifters were no more. The band was done.

Part II

"Did I mention the four-piece Continental Drifters?" Peter asks, before a lengthy pause.

There was, indeed, a briefly-active version of the band featuring Peter, Mark, Robert, and John Maloney that emerged after the festival shows only to fade after one gig at the Howlin' Wolf. Peter likens the experiment to using music "as a weapon."

"Talk about a product of anger and alcohol," he said. "I wanted it to be like fuckin' Crazy Horse. I think I screamed all the lyrics. I'm sure I was drunk from soundcheck on."

He does have a "very clear recollection of very bad behavior" during that show, channeling the complicated feelings he'd had surrounding the end of the band.

"I was pissed off. I was pissed off at everybody; I was pissed off at the way it shook out for this wonderful band," Peter said. "Because, god almighty, the music was good, you know? And to have the other stuff make it impossible to do that—but it was impossible. There was no way we could do it.

"I wasn't handling it well. I don't know who *was*, exactly. The bottom line for me is—I'm sorry for what I put Robert and Mark and Vicki through, and I'm sorry that that became a situation."

In truth, there was a lot of anger and resentment when the band broke up, coming from everyone. What happened was inevitable, though—to continue the way things were going would be impossible for everyone, and would just invite more pain.

"When Susan and Russ left, I don't think anybody was surprised," Peter said. "It had to happen. The center would not hold, you know? I wish it could have. I think there were too many emotions that were too hard to navigate around."

Decades removed from the end of the Drifters, Peter's perspective on Russ and Susan's split from the group has shifted in some ways. Where he admits he was "being pissy" about their departure and the 9/11 situation at the time, he's "totally on their side now" and can see that there was simply no way to continue the band as it was.

"Something had to give," he admits.

When he and Susan divorced, Peter moved into an apartment above the Circle Bar on St Charles Ave, where he also started a Tuesday night residency.

"I was living upstairs from a bar. What the fuck, you know? I just played and drank all night," he said.

His drinking continued in excess, culminating in a DUI that came from consuming wine after a gig and driving home.

"I got pulled about three blocks away from home, on Catina Street in Lakeview, and I'd had two glasses of wine," Peter recalled. "I spent the night in the drunk tank in Orleans Parish Prison. Had to borrow money from somebody to get out. That was the eye opener. I kept drinking 'til the end of the year, because I thought it'd be easier to remember quitting on New Year's Eve."

Peter says he'd tried to get sober in the past, citing the period following the release of The dB's *Repercussion* album in 1982, when he attempted to go to AA meetings.

"I was a big mess then, but that didn't take," he said. "I think going to jail really was the eye opener. I would like to believe that I could have gotten my shit together had the band been able to continue, but that's a lot of what-ifs. The way everything shook out—I don't know. It's like there's no room for speculation, because everything worked out for a good reason."

New Year's Eve 2002 was, indeed, the date of Peter's last drink. He's been sober since.

"It's the longest I've done anything! Longer than any band I've been in," he says with pride.

On one of the Drifter's last tours, Peter brought his then-girlfriend, Sarah Webb, out with him and the two drove separately rather than join the others in the van.

"I couldn't ride in the van at that point. I didn't want to ride in the van," he said. "And Sarah was great. We stopped at a train museum in Connecticut somewhere on the way to a gig. And we drank a lot and had a lot of fun and laughed, and she kept me buoyant enough to do those shows.

"I can't thank her enough for that, because that's a lot of hard work."

You could look at that tour as transitional for Peter, in a way. He was trying to move forward with his life, and keeping a distance from the others was the best way of doing that. But what of his relationship with Robert, Mark, and Vicki after the band was finished?

Peter doesn't remember much about what transpired immediately after, but he says he feels as though things were "starting to shed oxide and regroup in other forms." That proved to be true both personally and professionally, as everyone really just moved on to other things.

Just when one might assume that the demise of the Drifters would relegate them to the record store discount bins of history, a small but meaningful glimpse of recognition came from none other than Drifter champions Hootie and the Blowfish.

Peter was back at his day job then, as Hootie was prepping their first record in five years, produced by producer/bassist-turned industry executive Don Was. While assembling songs for the album, Darius Rucker—according to guitarist Mark Bryan—was "falling in love" with "The Rain Song" and suggested that the band work up their own version for the album.

Not only did Hootie record "The Rain Song" for their 2003 self-titled album (their final release for Atlantic Records), they also brought in Susan and Vicki—much to Don Was' delight—to sing background vocals.

Hootie was one of the bands that always recognized what the Drifters were doing—whether it was Darius sporting a Drifters t-shirt on television or playing "Darlin Darlin" with Peter during several headlining sets. Covering "The Rain Song" just made sense.

Mark Bryan sums up his and his bandmates' affinity for the Drifters succinctly.

"They all come from the same place musically, to the point where they're not even aware of it. So this thing happens when they start singing and playing together that's old and new at the same time," Bryan said. "It's one of those rare things that few people get to experience, and they found it. It is that sincere, pure thing, and they found it."

One of the most compelling things about the Drifters, aside from that musical purity Bryan describes, is the wide net of people that make up their world; the many musicians and music lovers who were impacted by the Drifters both artistically and personally. It's something that comes up a lot—the "line between band and fan [being] kind of blurry," as Karen Schoemer puts it.

Annie Clements is one of those people.

Clements was just 13 years old when her father, guitar player Cranston Clements, was playing with Li'l Queenie, and Peter, Susan, and Vicki were popping up as backing vocalists at performances around New Orleans. Clements got to join in on the fun as well.

"I was an aspiring musician myself, and they let me come and sing. Which, as a 13-year-old kid, was the biggest thing I'd gotten to do," she said. She actually met Peter and Susan initially when Susan happened upon a flier for a fundraiser organized to help support her father and stepmother financially before the birth of their twin boys. It was right around the time that Susan was expecting Miranda.

"Miranda is two days older than my brothers. That was what compelled Susan to help," Clements said. From there, the families became friends, and when the Holsapples needed a nanny, they asked Annie.

"I had never babysat for anyone outside of my family. It was kind of an easy gig just because she'd already be asleep and they'd be leaving to go play Carrollton Station or whatever. And I would just sit there on the couch until they got back at two in the morning, and then they would drive me home," she recalled.

Quickly, Clements became a close friend, joining the band on the road when needed. She also became a big fan of the Drifters, and immersed herself in all of their musical histories. She pinpoints that—as well as getting to play bass with Peter and Carlo in local performances promoting Peter's solo record—as a huge turning point for her as a musician.

"Being a nanny for them, I became completely obsessed with all of their shit. I got way into The Bangles. Got way into The dB's. At my 16th birthday [party], I sang 'Bad Reputation.' And they got me into Big Star," she said. "Initially I was way into funk and R&B and James Jamerson, and I'm still into all of that stuff. But I would have gone down a very different musical path if I hadn't met the Drifters. And frankly, I could still be kicking around New Orleans playing blues and Motown, which is all great. But they completely broadened my horizons to the singer/song-writer world, which is how I've made a living."

One of the most formative musical experiences for Clements, particularly, was getting to join Susan and Peter on a Hootie tour when she was 16 years old. It was also a monumental moment for her as a teenager; recalling one especially life-changing story.

"My mom had told me, 'I will buy you a car, but you have to save up $2,000 on your own.' And I'm babysitting for the Holsapples, and it's my only income. They paid me $5 an hour, which is huge money for me. I had literally, just through babysitting, saved up like $1,600. And then they tell me they're going to take me on the road with Hootie," she recalled. "They told Darius that I needed however much money to get to my first car, and at the end of the run the guys called me into their dressing room and they handed me an envelope with $400 cash in it."

Clements became a special part of the Drifters world, and those teen-year Hootie tours found Peter and Susan being especially protective of her.

"They smoked a lot of weed, and, to this day, I've never tried it. Never smoked weed, never tried a cigarette. And Susan, I believe, has never smoked a cigarette either. That was, like, her claim to fame. And I wanted to be like her. I just wanted to be her," Clements said. "They were very protective of me, because I was this child in their care. And any time we'd be driving—we were in a van, chasing the bus—and anytime they wanted to smoke a joint, they'd say, 'Okay, Annie, take a nap!'"

The band made an imprint on the folks in their extended universe, even in the years following their breakup. They never garnered a large following or sold many records, but they did make a mark. The Hooties of the world, the Annie Clements of the world, they understood.

And perhaps nobody outside of the band understands it better than Miranda, who grew up alongside the Drifters basically every step of the way. She was still young when the band split up, but says she has distinct memories that stand out to her about life on the road with her family.

"I'll always remember the smell of when my parents came home from a gig. The cigarette hair, just from the smoky club. That was a comforting smell. You would think that a stale bar smell would be the nastiest thing in the world, but to me it meant Mom and Dad were home," she recalled. "And I used to have this thing I did with them—every time we drove into a new town, each time I'd see a water tower, I'd shout 'Water tower!' And they would say, 'What's it say, Miranda?' And we'd try to read whatever town or county we were in.

"And every time we'd see a Waffle House I would say, 'Waffle House!' My dad, or Mark, or one of those corny motherfuckers would say, 'Take the "w" off of Waffle House and you have Awful House!'"

Memories like that are, for Miranda, tantamount to the family vacations and even holiday traditions that families have. They stay with you forever.

"The disbanding, and when everybody moved, that was hard," she admitted. "It was one of the changing points in my life, and I guess I didn't really realize it until later on. Everything I had ever known was Mom and Dad's band, because it was just so much more than a job for them.

"It's my family. They truly are brothers and sisters, and my aunts and uncles—that's how I've always viewed them. They've never been anything different; I don't know a life without them."

The end of the band was painful all around, but the band would live on in small ways in the years that followed. In a moment of happenstance, "The Rain Song" appeared on not one but two albums from reunited hitmakers in 2003. In March, the same month that Hootie's version was released via their self-titled album, The Bangles released *Doll Revolution*, their first record since 1989. That collection featured versions of both "The Rain Song" (with Vicki on lead vocals) and "Mixed Messages"—the latter featuring Peter on mandolin.

Doll Revolution had been in the works for a few years, following The Bangles' initial reunion in 1999. By then, Vicki was managing both Bangles and Drifters commitments and prior to the Drifters' split was planning to continue doing both simultaneously.

"I certainly wasn't going to tell the Drifters, 'No, I'm sorry, I have to go back to my old boyfriend,'" she said. "That was not part of the deal, and I had to make that clear to The Bangles too, that I had a dedication and obligation and *inclination* to continue to work with the Drifters."

Though things had been winding down relatively slowly over the course of their last year as a band, Vicki knew it was over when the 9/11 conversation happened.

"I think we were also feeling kind of battered at that point. It was feeling like, 'Okay, we are battle-scarred people. And maybe it's just time to lay down your arms,'" she said. "That band meant the world to me, really. It did seem really tragic. But at that time it felt mortally wounded."

She'd already been back in Los Angeles when the Drifters ended, and had started seeing Susan's brother John (yes, her childhood crush). They'd been friends for years, and as Vicki jokes he was "always very inconveniently married to other people."

"She was always involved with someone and so was I, and I was always out with the Beach Boys," Cowsill confirmed. "We lived separate lives for so long, and even within our merged lives we lived separate lives. I didn't even catch a Bangles show until we started hanging out."

They went on one rather unserious date before John, who at the time was playing with The Beach Boys, had a gig in Biloxi, Mississippi, and he came in ahead of the show to spend time in New Orleans. Vicki ended up giving him a ride to Biloxi, and she says that's when it "clicked" for John.

"He called me when I got home and said, 'I don't know who else you're seeing or what else you're doing. I don't know how many chin ups I have to do or pushups I have to do to impress you, but I'm going to be your boyfriend,'" she laughed. "Well that was either the sweetest, most romantic, or the creepiest thing I've ever heard. He's either going to be my stalker or my husband."

Vicki and John started dating after that, but it wasn't some quick, locked-in romance.

"I was really cautious. I knew a lot about this guy, and he had to work," Vicki said. "I was keeping him kind of at arm's length for a while. Because the last thing in my life I wanted to have happen was to get seriously involved with him and then have it falter and fall apart.

"I was not up for that, so I just kept him, kind of, at bay for a long period of time. He was working hard."

"There was something about her—I had to fly to New Orleans any time I had a break. I just fell in love with her," Cowsill said. "She made me work."

The hard work paid off, and Vicki and John got married in 2003. You'd think they would have gone right into a musical partnership, but as John explains, they spent years not working together in any way aside from occasions where they'd be guest vocalists on someone else's project.

"We walked around each other like gunslingers, like, 'Well, you go first,'" Cowsill said. "That wasn't our relationship—it wasn't music. And it's so funny because that's what we both do for a living. I wanted to, and she wanted to, but we're both insecure. Somebody needs to take the lead and neither one of us did."

Oddly, 2003 was apparently the year of Drifter weddings. Not only did Vicki get married that year, but Peter did as well, to his girlfriend Sarah Webb.

Susan and Russ also tied the knot that year, in a wedding at—appropriately enough—Dockside Studios, on July 12. It was the first time that Steve and Wish Nails hosted a wedding on the vast Dockside Property.

It was a swelteringly hot day, Russ recalls, but a beautiful celebration with family and friends. Louis Michot, of popular Louisiana cajun rock band Lost Bayou Ramblers, played fiddle during the ceremony (officiated by Russ' former Bluerunners bandmate Rob Savoy), then moved to a setup under the porch where he and his brother/bandmate Andre played for guests during the reception.

"We had a little dance floor, and sometimes I'd sit in, and Susan sang," Russ said. "We cut a rug for a while, and it was fuckin' hot as all hell. One of those really humid, still days that had zero breeze whatsoever. Everyone was drenched—just soaking wet. It was an awesome day."

Most of the one hundred people who attended stayed on the property for the weekend, and it turned into something of a "festival."

"We had people staying in each room in the studio," Russ recalled. "Each bedroom, but then downstairs in the studio—each booth. The bass booth, we had someone in there. We had someone next to that in the vocal booth, and we had somebody in the piano room. They were literally under the piano."

Vicki, who married John just a few months later in a ceremony also officiated by Rob Savoy, was the only Drifters bandmate in attendance. Things were still raw between the others, and the falling out between the Broussards and Mark and Robert was especially severe.

Russ remembers the first time he and Susan bumped into Robert after the band broke up, describing Robert's reaction to seeing them as "ice cold." Ultimately, Robert and Mark were on one side of the divide and, as Russ says, "came as a package on this."

"That was mostly where Peter was going to vent," he said. "I think that Robert was most mad at *me*. He was hurt. We were getting tight—we'd gotten together a few times, just me and him. So I think ultimately maybe he felt betrayed by me because I didn't share all of this with him before it happened or something."

Robert, for his part, jumped right from the Drifters into playing with Swedish-born NOLA musician Theresa Andersson, with whom Carlo also toured for several years.

"She kind of saved my ass for a little while," he said. "I was not a great fit for her, but she was really good to work with. I wanted to go roots and she wanted to go pop, so it was like, 'Okay, see ya.' But she's still a really dear friend."

Ending the Drifters, Robert says, was like "the end of a relationship that had not gone very well at the end."

"There was sadness, there was relief—it was a relief to not be around that energy," he said. "And feed into it and feed off of it. Neither of those were fun."

He says he felt there was a particularly severe rift between him and Susan after everything went down.

"It took Susan and I a long time to become civil," he said.

Susan's next project after the Drifters was a solo career, which began with 2005's *Just Believe It*, but Russ says that doing another record was not the priority for the first couple of years after their exit from the band.

"That was not on the radar," he said. "We were focused on keeping our kids pure and building these new lives with three homes at stake. And Susan and I were fortunate enough to have a Bourbon Street gig.

"It was a matinee gig, and it worked amazingly well with keeping a consistent schedule with the kids. And it paid really well. And for the first time in either of our lives, we weren't really having to worry about money. It was a good time for us."

Their gig on Bourbon Street was an all-afternoon affair, generally four or five hours, and Susan was the bandleader—commanding the stage and entertaining audiences. The venue where they worked gave them free reign to do what they wanted.

"Most clubs would enforce 45 minutes on, 15 minutes off, and keep those drinks rolling. But we were like, 'Man, that makes the day go by way too slow. And if we're bringing people in and they're enjoying themselves, can we just keep playing?'" he said. "I mean, frickin' Soni and Mark Bryan [from Hootie & the Blowfish] sat in for five hours one day. They wouldn't leave! They were enthralled."

Russ says they weren't simply doing run-of-the-mill Bourbon Street numbers—they also threw in some original songs as well as covers that they were interested in trying out. It was both a job and a musical outlet for them, and they enjoyed doing it. It came to a halt, though, when two members of their band left. Susan and Russ had to figure out what happened next.

"Do we want to stay on Bourbon Street? Do we want to keep doing this?" Russ said. "And Susan says, 'It's getting a little old.' It was a piece of cake the first nine months or so—it was a joy to us both. But maybe it has just run its course."

The whole time they were on Bourbon Street, Russ says, they were writing songs together, leading Russ to pitch Susan on the idea of playing a stripped down show and performing some of those songs live. There was no real plan to launch any sort of solo endeavor, and Susan was hesitant to do so at first. But the songs kept lingering, as did the feeling that there was something happening.

"All I could think—and of course it was Russ and I, and he was there to back me up—was, 'I guess it's time for me to do my own thing,'" Susan said. "It wasn't time on a lot of levels, and it was absolutely time on a lot of levels. Change; it's just the toughest thing ever."

Once they decided to jump in, conversations began about what it would take to make a record.

"And then from there, it was like, 'Well, let me see if Edgar Heckmann would be interested in partially financing a solo record like he'd do with the Drifters.' Like giving us an advance," he said. "I just put feelers out like that and got it going."

Heckmann jumped on board, and they booked time at Dockside to record what would become *Just Believe It*. Susan initially wanted to release the record under a new band name, as many of the songs were collaborations between her and Russ, but Russ felt strongly that the name of the project should be Susan Cowsill.

"Just as a concept, like the Drifters had a concept of approach, I think this—even if every song is co-written—it's going to mean something different if it's you," Russ said. "Plus it's going to give us a fighting chance. We won't be starting from zero, you know what I mean? I had to argue that point for a while."

Indeed, Susan Cowsill was really the name of the Susan Cowsill Band—Susan, Russ, his old Bluerunners mate Rob Savoy on bass, and guitarist Chris Knotts.

Just Believe It featured contributions from folks like Mark Bryan (who produced one song on the album), Lucinda Williams, and Adam Duritz. Mixed by producer-to-the-stars Trina Shoemaker, the album was strong, conceptual, and it sounded like a natural next step from the songs she was writing in the Drifters. There was even one song, "Christmastime," that started life as a would-be Drifters song and demoed in one of the band's living room demo sessions.

Ah, yes, and there's another song on *Just Believe It* that's worth noting. "Talkin'," is also often known as "Talkin' Shit," and was written about Peter in their post-divorce world. It's not a subtle take on the breakup, by any means.

> *You should try volunteering*
> *A new hobby or two*
> *Maybe taking up knitting*
> *'Cuz spinning yarn's what you do*

Peter wrote a breakup song as well—called "Lay It On The Line"—but a recording of the song remains unreleased.

"I can say, with hindsight and all that, it's a truly great song," Peter said of Susan's song. "We both wrote our post-breakup songs from our respective perspectives, and then I don't think either of us wrote another one!"

The album was released in Europe in August of 2004, and found a U.S. home on Americana label Blue Corn Music—slated for release in October of 2005. *Just Believe It* could easily have been a springboard for Susan to finally get some notice on a broader scale as a songwriter, but just two months before the album's release date, *everything* changed.

Chapter Eleven:
Katrina...
An Oral History

All of the New Orleans Drifters were impacted by Hurricane Katrina, which made landfall on August 29, 2005. By then, they were three years removed from the band and going about their lives. Everyone was still living in New Orleans except for Vicki, who'd been back in Los Angeles for two years.

Carlo opted not to evacuate, while Susan, Russ, Mark, Robert, and Peter's family (he was on the road at the time) all left. At the time, Peter and his wife had a two-year-old son named Webb, Mark and his wife Dana had three kids, and Robert and his wife Candace had one child.

With the eye of Katrina passing just to the southeast of New Orleans, the storm surge caused over 50 breaches of levees and protection structures across New Orleans. Two days after the storm made landfall, eighty percent of New Orleans was underwater—some areas up to fifteen feet.

Nearly 20 years removed, most New Orleanians agree that the devastation caused by Katrina flooding falls largely on the shoulders of the Army Corps of Engineers' lack of adequate design, construction, and maintenance of the levees and flood protection systems. The consequences of those failures are felt to this day, and for the Drifters, Katrina remains a traumatic and painful experience.

Carlo

(Transcribed from an October 2005 interview with Theresa Andersson and Carlo for the Robert Mugge film 'New Orleans Music in Exile.' Used by permission.)

It was pretty messy. There was a couple of days after the storm where people took on different responsibilities. There was an amazing sense of community, I'll tell you that. People were going into the city and doing this and that; helping rescue people, whatever it may be. And that's kind of where I came into play.

I ended up in Jefferson Parish a couple of days after. Ironically, this old buddy of mine, he's, like, in his eighties and he used to work for Amtrak. His house is all on the same grid as Airline Highway—Airline Drive, now—which is an evacuation route. So they had to get those street lights on. So as a result of getting those street lights on, his power came back on, like, two days after the storm when everybody else around was off.

There was an outcry of neighbors going, 'Please, save my freezer!' We were just, like, loading freezers into his yard and plugging them into his power. We got a bold idea: We'll get some grills over here. We just set up an ocean of grills against the oceans of freezers, and started cooking for oceans of police, firemen, emergency workers. We were just cooking all day and bringing food around to everyone.

It was evident that it was a huge tragedy. Even in Jefferson, where there was no flooding, there was just tremendous devastation. I watched two houses burn with firemen standing in front of them, unable to get water pressure. Just completely at wit's end. The girl at the second house, which wasn't yet on fire, [was] tugging on the police going, 'Tell me my house isn't going to burn.' And they couldn't even look her in the eye.

We watched six fire trucks sit there, idle, and then we watched it catch on fire and just burn to the ground. It was just sickening.

I finally left on the … 16th of September, actually. Which is kind of a long time to stay, but there were a lot of people that needed to be fed. There were probably 30 people showing up to this particular house every night, and on top of that there'd be, like, other people that we'd bring food to. They just didn't have it.

There were some choice meals from the relief systems when they were finally in place days later. But, you know, people had to eat.

The most remarkable thing about the storm for me is that it was this incredible sense of community. People mindlessly getting their boats, putting them on the back of their car and driving them to the Causeway where the water started, and just launching them and letting the emergency services take off in them.

I lost some equipment—nothing like some people I know. I lost a drum kit, a keyboard and a couple things I had at Mark Walton's house. He suffered severe flooding at his house.

Mark

I was doing a lot of work—doing convention work in New Orleans, doing sound and all kinds of different things. And I was setting up for a really big, big show at the Hilton. I was working all day and all night getting it all set up, and I was supposed to be back at nine in the morning.

I wasn't even finished yet—I still had a few hours of work left, but I saw that the hurricane was coming. And I just said to everybody, "I'm leaving. You should go home, too. Take care of your shit."

I went home and I decided to start, sort of, securing things—putting them up high, doing everything I could to protect everything. We've had water in the house before, but it was only a couple inches or up to a foot, maybe. So I put everything in the top shelves of closets, on beds, wherever.

I decided to wake up at three o'clock in the morning to see when the next hurricane advisory was and see what it said. At first it was like, "Eh, it's just going off to the Florida panhandle. Don't worry about it, don't worry about it." And I turned [the TV] on, and it was bullseye on New Orleans.

I woke the family up, did everything I could to protect the house. Of course, my cat was an outdoor cat—Perry—and he didn't come with us. So we set up a bunch of food and protection out in our carport with a bunch of other stuff that shouldn't get destroyed, hopefully.

We woke up, we were on the road by probably six in the morning. There was already this huge line of cars trying to go out. They weren't allowing cars in the city, they were opening all lanes going out of the city. We decided to go as far north as we could and we got to Shreveport, finally, in the middle of the night and got a hotel. It was a Motel 6, which was just nasty as hell. Dana was like, "I am not staying here anymore. That's it." So we got on the road again and continued driving into Texas to try to get as close to Dallas as possible.

But then, of course, our brand new Honda Odyssey van started acting up, and we thought, "Okay, well, we'll bring the car into the shop." And they looked at it and went, "Your transmission is shot. But don't worry, it's under warranty. We'll get you another one." But it took about a week and a half for the new transmission to show up, so we were stuck at this La Quinta Inn. We were just stuck. So we started calling friends and family, and trying to make sure that everybody knew we were okay.

We started having offers from friends—I had a friend whose grandmother died and she had a little house in Baton Rouge; two bedroom, one bath kind of thing. But that was too small. Dana's sister's husband, his mother died and had a house in St. Louis, and we were considering that as a possibility, but we didn't know anyone that lived there, really. So my parents had a big enough house in [Las] Vegas—it was like a four bedroom house. And there's two master suites, too. One wing was not even being used by them.

After the car was fixed we just said, "Okay, fine, we'll just keep driving west and get to Vegas." My wife only took the photo albums, and I took my only favorite bass that I've had since 1979. And that was that. We thought we'd be coming right back.

So we just took over the whole side of the house, and I started getting jobs doing the same kind of work I was getting in New Orleans.

My sister found some friends that had frequent flier mileage and they donated it to me so I could fly out, and I met up with Disco. He's got a big truck and he brought a bunch of stuff. And my brother-in-law is a contractor in New Orleans, so he brought all of his workers. He had this whole crew.

We get up to the house and try to open the front door and I realized I forgot my keys to the house. And my brother-in-law's like, "Mark, the door's jammed. Everything's swollen. You wouldn't have been able to open it anyway." So they just went up there and broke the door down and exposed it to the elements. This was probably about a month after the storm.

So all of the antiques in the house—you know, the glue had dissolved from the brackish water and it all collapsed in place. Anything that was in the china cabinet just kind of fell slowly, somehow, and it disintegrated the wood but everything in it was still fine. I salvaged some of that kind of stuff, but everything else that was wood or metal was just rotten and corroded. Just really fucked up.

Everything I ever owned was gone. It was devastating. I was just crying and crying.

I went out on the front porch and I sat there for the longest time just crying, and all of the sudden I felt this presence staring at me or something. And I turned and looked like halfway down the block, and there was my cat, Perry, just sitting there staring at me like, "Where the fuck have you been?" Now I'm really crying.

So I walked down and he ran off. He'd become feral, almost, by that point. So he didn't trust me. Finally, he came to me and I grabbed him, and he started scratching. I was like, "I'm not letting go of you now, dude." So I brought him back to the house, and by that point I'm bleeding all over my arms.

Disco came out with one of those storage bins with the folding tops, and put him in there and zip tied it shut. I brought him to a vet and they basically said, "Well, he's malnourished, but other than that he's fairly well." They gave him some shots, and I brought him home. The kids were all freaking out and everyone cried when they saw him.

I have no idea how he survived.

[Hootie & the Blowfish] came down and wanted to volunteer. Peter was on tour with them, and they said they wanted to come down and help. A friend of ours, Craig Klein from Bonerama, was putting together this service called Arabi Wrecking Krewe to try and help out musicians from the flood, and they were going to gut all of these houses.

I put my name in the hat for Craig's team to do that. I did not know that Hootie had volunteered—next thing I know I'm getting all of these pictures from Peter. There were a good fifteen of them. Susan and Russ also joined them, and all of those people involved with Craig's team. All of the Hootie guys and all their roadies, too.

They tore out all the sheet rock—everything out of the house except for the two-by-fours and the brick siding. And it was gone, that was it. I let it sit there for two or three years afterwards, paying somebody to cut the grass just to make sure it didn't look horrible.

While we were waiting for our van to be repaired, I called Vicki. But the problem was that all the phone lines were all fucked up. Cell phones wouldn't dial out. I did reach out to Vicki and made sure she knew [we were okay], and then told her to tell everybody.

Vicki

My memory is being glued to the television, and I was just staying up all night watching. At one point I was talking to Susan and she goes, "Are you seeing this thing coming at us?" I said, "Yes I am."

I was at home watching the Weather Channel or whoever was keeping it on [constantly], and was feeling horrible and so frightened, and feeling completely helpless. And then in the morning, thinking like many people did—that we dodged this bullet. We thought, "Okay, we're alright. We're okay." But we were worried because Barry hadn't left town. He had chosen to stay. And we knew where he was; there was a place in the Warehouse District where he was supposedly staying with people he knew. It was unnerving because the friends had left and Barry was there alone.

And then the flooding started. I'm two-thousand miles away and feeling completely, just, helpless. Susan and Russ were homeless and were in their van. They had wanted to go on tour, so it was decided that it wasn't right for Miranda to be living this nomadic lifestyle. The irony was that when Miranda was younger, Susan would often say to me, "When she's thirteen, I'm sending her to you!"

Ironically enough, she was almost thirteen and they put her on a flight. She had nothing—she had, like, a backpack or a bag and that was it. They put her on a Southwest flight and I came and picked her up. One of the crew members walked her off the plane to me. The crew of this flight had taken up a donation for Miranda. They handed me, I think it was, something like seventy-five dollars. And they said, "This is for her, to help her get started and get some school clothes, whatever." They insisted. I was so touched by that. I wrote an email to Southwest commending the crew for their thoughtfulness.

Miranda was just a brave little soldier. Obviously she knows my house, she'd visited many times. But she was starting sixth grade at a brand-new school, and middle school is a very vulnerable time for anybody. The school was also very accommodating, because I told them the story. They said, "Do you have any of her vaccination records or anything?" And I said, "Nothing exists. It's all gone. All gone."

They said, "Okay, well, we'll just waive that, then."

She was very 'stiff upper lip,' like she kind of can be sometimes. I'd ask her how the day went and she'd say, "It was good! I already made friends." But of course, it wasn't great. She was traumatized. The happy side to that, though, is that she did end up making friends at this school—people who are lifers. Two of her lifelong friends are people that she met at this school in California.

I remember when I was living [in New Orleans] in the nineties, the *Times-Picayune* did a whole in-depth cover story basically saying, "It's not if. It's when. It will happen." I remember that really well. It was quite an in-depth piece about New Orleans being a bowl, and below sea level and surrounded by water. And the Corp of Engineers constructing things that they say are going to hold but they probably won't. And they didn't.

And of course, there was also wind damage. The trees were gone. But what was more deadly was the flooding.

Susan and Russ came back to look for Barry. He would call Susan's cell phone, thinking that it was a landline and that it had an answering machine and she could hear him. He was like, "Pick up! Pick up!" But there was no way to call him back, so it was horrifying. They didn't find him until December.

Russ and Susan

As told by Russ

Usually we would have the kids on the weekends, right? But that weekend, Mary asked if she could take Nick to Birmingham because it was her mom's birthday or something like that. And Sarah asked if she could take Miranda and Julie, Miranda's friend, on a semi-camping trip to go pick up a VW van that they were buying in Alabama. And Susan was going to Oklahoma to do a show with Dwight Twilley, and it was maybe going to be a live recording or something.

We had done a little tour, and before Susan left and before the kids left we had done a rehearsal with Rob and Chris to do another Covered in Vinyl. We'd done Fleetwood Mac's *Rumours* and I think [Joni Mitchell's] *Court and Spark*. And then we were going to do Cat Stevens or something like that, and we had our initial rehearsal earlier in the week. And then everyone goes out of town on Wednesday or Thursday.

So I think, "Well, I have the whole weekend; empty house. I'm going to get the downstairs pulled together." Because it was a giant storage room, basically. I was going to create a music room for us. It kind of had a partial wall—it had the studs, but it didn't have any sheetrock or anything like that. So I went to Home Depot and I bought a bunch of materials. I bought a window unit—installed an air conditioner. So I was just working sort of on my own timeframe, mostly late at night. It was cooler at night, so I could float sheetrock and that kind of thing at night. I turned up some music and would go until I was exhausted, go to sleep and wake up, and then do the same thing. I didn't put on the news; I had a mission.

And so, I was clueless until the 28th. My phone was ringing off the hook, and then once I just let the machine pick it up. And it was my mom.

"Russ! Are you home? You need to pick up the phone. And wake up." So I grabbed the phone, and I'm like, "What's up?" She says, "What are you doing home?!" And I'm like, "I'm sleeping, mom."

She goes, "You need to get up and go turn on the TV." I go, "What channel?" And she goes, "It doesn't matter."

I get up and turn on the TV and boom, it's every station. They're showing this image of this hurricane that's the size of the fucking gulf and the track is coming right at us. And I was like, "Oh my god, when did this happen?! Where'd this fucking come from?"

All of the sudden I was just in that tone of, like, panic. I've got to get the fuck out of here.

[Susan] didn't have a cell phone back then, so when she called me during the day she goes, "How's it going with the project?" And I said, "Well, that's been going well. But honey, do you know what's happening?" And she goes, "What do you mean?"

I said, "Turn on the TV and then call me back."

She calls me and she's freaking out, and she goes, "Well I only have clothes for this weekend. Can you grab a few things for me?" And I was just in a panic. I had the pets—one dog and a cat. And I couldn't find the cat carrier, and I'm glued to the TV while trying to get my head around what the hell I'm doing and where I'm going.

Do I go to Lafayette? Is that going to be far enough away? And then they were showing the traffic and they're saying everyone seems to be going west because of the track of the hurricane. None of the diagrams are showing it going west of New Orleans. So the interstate, all lanes go out of the city. There's nothing coming in. And we're surrounded by water—the only three ways to get out of the area are I-10 West, I-10 East, or the Causeway going due north. And that's it. Those are the possibilities of getting out of town.

So I had the radio on, and they're now saying "Okay, now it's a category 5." And there's winds being detected of over 170 miles an hour, which is the size of a tornado. And I'm, like, hauling gear upstairs at this time. I'm carrying some drums upstairs from the basement, and I'm thinking about floods, levees—and then they say *that,* and I'm going, "Well, the roof isn't going to hold."

Our street was okay, but mid-city in general was like marshland, you know? The highest areas of the city are close to the river. Pre-levees, everytime the river would rise and fall it'd leave soot. And that's over eons, and the ground became higher. The farther away from the river you get, the lower the ground. And there was one little ridge—Esplanade Ridge—which was a natural levee at some point. But other than that, we were in a low area of town. So with just a heavy rain, Bank Street would flood. My old house had water up to the porch and we were three-and-a-half feet off the ground and five feet above the road. And we had water up to that porch on three occasions.

So, it's like, that's what I'm thinking—this is going to dump a shit ton of water. And then I'm like, "Oh shit, well, no. The roof is going to get blown right off this thing." So I start carrying shit back downstairs and at a certain point, I've got WWL Radio on and they said, "If you're still in town, you need to get in your vehicle now and leave. Head east, because west is jammed."

The scenarios that they were painting was like, you don't want to be sitting in your car when this thing hits. And right now, the traffic is not moving. So I was like, "Well, fuck that." Whatever I had in my hands went into the car. Some things I just dropped right there at the bottom of the steps or on top of the washer and dryer.

Sean Kelly

We had a Kia Sedona minivan with a shit ton of room, and what I had in there was a bass drum, a little duffle bag with a pair of shorts and two t-shirts, some fishnet stockings for Susan and a mini skirt. That's what I grabbed for her. Not even a toiletry bag—nothing else. I didn't even have fucking socks. My brain stopped working.

My mom told me where they were; they evacuated to Lafayette. I called them and said, "Supposedly I won't be able to get there." So I'm going to head to Birmingham and go to Sonny [Pritchett, friend of the band].

And I emptied a bag of food into two big bowls for the cat, because I gave up on looking for the cat carrier and was just like, "I've got to go." I filled up the bathtub with water and I said, "Tandy, I'll be back in a couple days." We've done this a million times, right? You get out of harm's way if you need to, or you ride it out. If you get out of harm's way then you'd come back a day or two later and assess the damage, you know? And it was almost two weeks later.

I was going close to 100 miles an hour in that van. Before getting to Slidell, I-10 has these two bridges that cross over that part of Lake Pontchartrain, and the gulf is just right over there. It's right beyond that lake; it's like a bay. Right when I got on that bridge, traffic stopped. It was like I all of a sudden came up on a wall.

We're just stopped. And there's waves already hitting the bridge and splashing up and over. I was like, "Ah, fuck. Death by drowning. That's not how I want to die."

The energy in the air, it was just palpable. And I just turned off the radio and was trying to just quiet myself. And then it started to dawn on me—I'm looking in this van, and it's fucking empty. There are three empty seats, no gear to speak of, and I think I grabbed Susan's guitar. And a dog. And that was it. No cat, no neighbor, no Barry.

Had I called where he was staying, he wasn't there that day anyway. From the phone messages, he was at his friend's house downtown. So I wouldn't have known that.

Over and over, [the media was] just repeating, "If you are home listening to this, you need to get in your car, or get to public transportation, get to the Superdome to ride this thing out. You need to go. If you can go, you need to go. Now." And so, I think it was around 4:30 in the after-noon when I was in the van cruising 100 miles an hour. And it wasn't until I was stopped that I started to assess the situation.

I didn't grab our birth certificates—just the essential shit. I didn't grab any of our clothes. None of us got clothes. I didn't grab our gear, I didn't grab my drums from when I was 9 years old. I didn't grab my neighbor. I had room for some of their shit—three people and a bag, plus my full drum kit, plus Susan's favorite two guitars. And bags for all three of us. But I didn't do any of that, and it wasn't until I was sitting on that bridge not moving that it was dawning on me. That I just got in the van and left.

I got to Sonny's close to eleven, I think. It was already getting close, but the eye hit just east of New Orleans at one or two a.m., something like that. It was a stressful fucking drive up because I was going to run out of gas. I remember needing gas and I wasn't even to McComb, which is just barely into Mississippi. That van got shit gas mileage. If you're making that commitment, you get in the exit lane and that sits and moves about eight feet every five minutes. So you're in the line of traffic waiting to get to the stop sign. And there are cars in every direction on that road. It's just deadlocked every which way.

Susan was scheduled to fly home on the 30th, I think. We were trying to figure out where she's flying to, and I'm looking on Southwest's website and from Oklahoma they did have a direct to Nashville. We had a gig lined up, so initially she was flying in on the 30th and we were driving up the next day to play our show in Nashville. So it was like, "You need to fly straight to Nashville and I'll just head there."

When I got up in the morning at Sonny's, I turn on the TV and the weathermen are downtown and they're showing, you know, glass on the road and some windows blown out of the highrises and stuff. And they said, "Boy, New Orleans really dodged a bullet. This looks okay." So I thought I'd meet up with Susan that night and we'd do our gig, and then come home the next day.

So Sonny and I finish our breakfast and we're watching the news, and we're both breathing in relief. The worst scenarios didn't happen, so we'll see the destruction later. So I drive to Nashville. I was in a hotel room, and then went and got Susan. It wasn't until I got to Nashville and picked up Susan that we learned that the levees broke.

It was the next day in Nashville, and we're glued to the TV, and we're on slow-moving Internet looking at satellite images of our house. At a certain point I looked up from the computer to see on the TV that the army was there, and they had those giant trucks with the wheels that are five feet tall. And they were cruising down Bank Street. They were in five-and-a-half, six feet of water and stopped because it was getting too deep for the vehicles. And it was right before our street. And I'm like, "Okay, that's it."

Robert

Candace and I had just gotten back from New York, and our bags were literally still packed. And our friend called and said, "Hey, have you looked at the weather?" We looked at it and it was just that buzzsaw coming. And it was really organized. We were like, "Oh shit, this does not look good."

And then we turned on the TV and watched the news and there was just this parking lot on the highway going west, because the thing was coming from the east. So we're like, "Well, it's completely jammed going west and there's nobody going east, so let's go east." Candace's mom lived right around Tupelo, Mississippi, and so we went up that route, up [interstate] 59 instead of the 55 and went through Hattiesburg.

It was a really easy drive. We just packed the kid in the car—we had our bags packed. We spent an entire day getting as much as possible off the floor. Like any guitars would go to the top of closets and stuff like that. We just got out of there.

It jammed up around Hattiesburg, but if we were delayed by 45 minutes that was a lot. We made it to Candace's mom; it was Sunday, it was a dry county. And Candace's mom has absolutely no filter whatsoever, and says. 'Candy, your butt is fat, and you need a haircut!' So right about that time, our friend in Memphis called and said "I've got red wine." And I'm like, "I'm packing the car."

We got a room in Memphis, and we ended up staying on that lady's floor for, like, six weeks. We had no idea what the condition of our house was, so we had no idea if we had lost everything or if our house was okay. But it actually turned out to be on maybe the highest ground in New Orleans, and so nothing happened to our house. It was in perfect condition.

In the meantime, people were giving us furniture—they were just absolutely beautiful to us in Memphis. But we just ended up with so much shit!

And the lady whose house we were staying at, her brother was a crack addict and she was like, "If you can rehab his house, you can live there. He's in rehab right now, he'll be there for months."

Our house being one of the few houses that was completely intact, the head of Children's Hospital needed a house. Our friend, Mark's sister-in-law, in fact, [said], "Would you consider selling your house?" We're like, "Hmm, yeah."

When Mark had cleaned out his place with Disco and they were wearing hazmat suits and stuff, I was not there for that. And the only time I really witnessed Mark's place was after they had discarded things out on the street and leaning up against their house. It was like, "This is it. We're gone." And so, Candace and I drove by and just witnessed the fan blades drooping down at 90 degrees. Just straight down. Where they'd been waterlogged. He had water up to his ceiling.

And there were a couple of things still there, and I still need to send them to him. I don't think he even knows I have it—just little chatchkes. A little wooden elephant or a little wooden bust. They've been sitting in my shed for, like, seventeen years now.

I just saw his [Fender Precision] bass in pieces. Just sitting there. It was totally full of black mold, and it was just the gnarliest thing I'd ever seen, and also one of the most beautiful things I'd ever seen. And I'm like, "I'm putting it in a garbage bag and sealing up the garbage bag, I'm taking it."

And so, I hung up the pieces in my back room for like two years, because it'd been under-water for three weeks or something. All of the finish had bubbled up over the Fender logo, and everything was discolored. The headstock was—you could not possibly recreate that. And the fretboard had come delaminated from the neck itself.

The fretboard is hardwood, so it wasn't as porous—it didn't expand as much. But the neck itself sponged up. And when I got it, the neck was probably at least an eighth of an inch wider than the fretboard. After a couple of years they were back to being pretty close to the same size, so I just got a bunch of wood glue and clamps, zip ties, whatever I could do to get the fretboard back on the neck. I just glued the shit out of it, and then glued the body back together, put new electronics and a pickup in it. I used as much of the old stuff as I could—all I had to do with the tuning pegs was put some WD40 in there.

And for some weird reason, it actually played really well after that.

It was his second bass, but he was really good at breaking low E strings. That motherfucker—how many bass players do you know that break low E strings? I've seen him do it on multiple occasions. So he kind of needed a second bass to pick up.

Peter

After Susan and I got divorced—and it took a while to remember to do that; I don't know what our problem was. I think it was right around Christmas and we went to a bar, then went Christmas shopping together, which was kind of fun!

But nonetheless, Sarah and I got married and we were going to have a baby. And so we had a baby, and we moved into a house that we bought from the proceeds of the house on Filmore Avenue, where Susan and I had lived and where Susan lived. We bought a house in Arabi, St. Bernard Parish, that had belonged to Mike Mayeux and his family.

We had our family there; Miranda had a room, you know? She had a place to be when she was with us. A great memory of that is playing frisbee with Miranda on early Sunday morning. This was also when I was delivering flowers for Thibodeaux Florists on Carrollton Avenue—I was the delivery driver there for several years. And it was kind of fun; I learned all about how to drive around New Orleans. Miranda and I would deliver funeral sprays to open casket funerals, and she'd come in with me. And we'd listen to *so* much music. We listened to "Bumpin' Me Against the Wall" by Mystikal and "A Lo Cubano" by Orishas.

So anyway, we're living in this house in Arabi, and I get the call to go on tour with the Hooties. And I've got to, you know? Because that's money coming in. And I don't really love the idea of having to abandon my wife, this new baby, and my daughter while I'm out playing rock and roll every night. But that's what I do, so that was what I did.

I'm on tour, and Sarah kept up with the house and took Miranda. And there's this disturbance coming up, and it's looking bad and it's looking worse. Sarah, with some of that showbiz money, had bought a Volkswagen Westy—a camper van. She bought it on eBay, and she'd made plans to go pick it up. It was in Birmingham.

She was a little spooked from the weather, so she put the guitar collection up on our bed in the master bedroom. And she put the CPU for the computer up on the kitchen table, and parked our Volvo wagon in the driveway. She got a cab with Miranda, Julie—her best friend—and Webb. And they got to the train station and hopped on a train to Birmingham, and got the hell out of dodge. And then, boom. Shit hit the fan.

I don't remember [everything] exactly, except just watching it on the news and talking with Sarah and making sure that we had contact information. And then we couldn't get in contact, and everything was just like—it was like a blackout, almost. I was riding on a bus going to a gig.

The scope of it was breathtaking from afar. I felt so removed from my life in New Orleans all of the sudden. And so, I had to sort of take over the controls of one of the TVs on the bus to be able to watch the news and the weather, as the one guy on that tour who had a house in New Orleans and a family there.

And I realized that was all I could do, and so I did. Everything's kind of a blur, I'll be honest. One thing that we discovered, that we had never used before, was text messaging. Once we figured out that we could get texts through to people's phones—and these were flip phones still, at this point—then we were able to communicate. I heard from the impassioned, at that point newly-ex Mrs. Barry Cowsill, asking where Barry was. I was like, "I don't know. I have no idea."

[Sarah] started driving after she picked up the Westy. Had the kids in the car, car seat, everything packed in there. And she knew she wasn't going to be able to go back to New Orleans, so she thought, "Well, my grandmother lives in Little Rock [Arkansas]. So we'll go to Little Rock." And the fucking van broke down about an hour outside of Birmingham. Just bought this thing. So they had to spend a night in a church shelter.

They couldn't get anybody to repair the VW in time, so the minister of the church where they stayed the night said, "Well, I've got this van I can sell you." And since I was making showbiz bucks, she was like, "Let's go to the bank."

To their credit, the girls and Sarah tried to make it as much of an adventure as they possibly could, just to keep it on an even keel. Because that's what you do with kids. So she drove, and she drove and she drove. And she got caught in the storm path, also, at one point. She was going ahead of it, but it was really pretty brutal what she drove through.

She finally got to Little Rock, and her grandmother welcomed them to stay for a couple of days while she sort of figured out what she was going to do. Meanwhile, Susan and Russ ended up in Franklin, Tennessee, at the home of Pat McLaughlin and his wife.

So she heads to Nashville and drops Miranda off with Russ and Susan, and then the next stop is Baltimore, Maryland, where Hootie and the Blowfish are playing. And man, she hauled ass. She got there 30 minutes before we were going on, and everybody was so comforting and loving to them. I was obviously in a state of heightened reality from that—just to hold her and hold him, and know that they were okay.

So we did our show and we drove to a hotel in the van. And I sat with her in the hotel until it was time for the bus to roll, because we were rolling that night to the next show. We didn't talk much—we just sat quietly. That's one of those times where there wasn't really anything that anybody could say. The reality had fuckin' shapeshifted. In an instant. So she and Webb spent the night in the hotel. I get on the bus and roll out to wherever. The tour went on, and I had to go on the tour because I was making the showbiz bucks. And it made sense, you know?

Her dad came down from where he lived in Pennsylvania and drove them back in her van, and they stayed with him in his upstairs bedroom on, like, air mattresses for a while, until I could get there to them. And then we found an apartment, and that was where we were going to stay.

And then we took a trip down to New Orleans. It was a month and a half [later], maybe. We dropped Webb off with Susan and Russ, actually, at Sonny Pritchett's house in Birmingham. So we started driving down, and the closer we got to New Orleans, the weirder it started getting. We followed a bunch of FEMA trailers for a while. And I mean, like, 20 in a caravan.

The trees were all bent over in half by the freeway. There were just swaths of trees that were just neatly doubled. We couldn't get in the way we normally would, so we had to go through Slidell, and that was where we got off the main highway and we're driving on the surface roads which were just barren.

So we get to St. Bernard Parish, and the National Guard are there. And we explain that we want to see our house if we can get to it. We drove through that once we got cleared.

We drove down to our house and the silence was deafening. I don't know any other way to put it. We'd also just paid to have a huge tree taken down in front of our house because we were afraid it was rotten and was going to fall on our house. What could possibly be worse, right?

The house had the [spray-painted] cross on the side that says nobody was in it, and nobody's dead. The Volvo had been shoved back into the backyard down the driveway. All of my musical stuff that was in storage in the garage was all—you could see the two lines of water where Katrina and Rita had gone up to.

When we got into the house, we had to walk in through the broken front window where we had watched many petroleum sunsets, courtesy of the industry in St. Bernard.

We'd gotten this huge La-Z-Boy recliner sofa—when we got it, Susan actually was there to take delivery of it and the guys had said, "Are you sure it's going to fit in here?" And she said, "Believe me, I know my ex-husband. If he says it's going to fit, it's going to fit." And it did. I used the sofa to walk into the middle of the house.

Suffice to say, everything got inundated. We were able to walk further into the house, into the hallway. And we could look into the kitchen and could see that the fridge was leaning against the door. It was just gross; it smelled awful. The ceiling was coming down in the hallway. My complete recording outfit that I'd had on the road with Hootie and had just brought home, including a hard drive with 25 new demos; inundated.

Peter's home in St. Bernard Parish damaged by Hurricane Katrina. Photo by Robert Maché

And there were the guitars, still on the bed. The cases floated open and stuff. We couldn't get into Miranda's room because something was up against the door. And walking into the house—there was, like, this goo on the ground. We were able to get into Miranda's bedroom through the window, and we were actually able to get to the bed. And inside the bed were her three lovies—her two bears and her blanket. We were able to get those out. And so in that sense that day was a total victory.

We decided to get out of there, and then Sarah and I were like, "Maybe there's a bar open, and maybe there are some people." So we went to this bar called Cooter Brown's, at the foot of Carrollton Avenue at the river bend. We just wanted to see if we saw anybody.

And then we hit the road, and it was really weird because there were no lights in the rear-view mirror.

Coming back a year later to do work for Habitat for Humanity—the demo at Mark's place—there's a certain element of finality to it there. That was where the Drifters practiced, and that was where we had our meetings, and we hung out and had coffee, and went to birthday parties. It's like everything got gutted, on so many different levels.

The aftermath of Katrina on Peter's street in St. Bernard Parish. Photo by Robert Maché

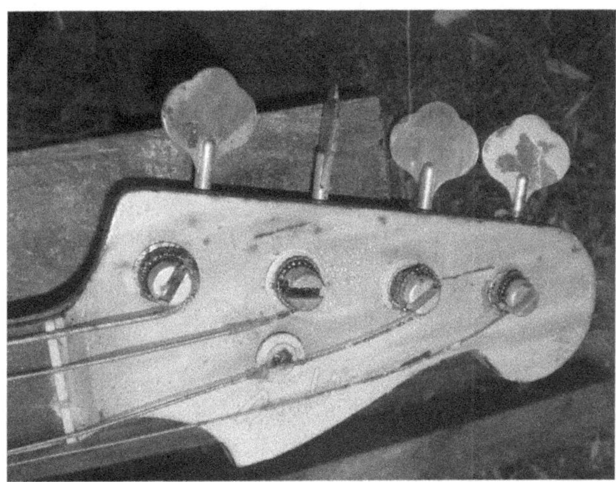

Mark's bass that Robert salvaged and eventually restored following Katrina. Photos by Robert Maché

Mark Walton's bass, damaged by Katrina, restored by Robert Maché. Photo by Mark Walton.

Sean Kelly

Chapter Twelve:
In The Family Again

"What's real about all of this is that we all loved each other so fuckin' much, and we still do. That love came out in the music we made, and I think you can hear that."

—Carlo Nuccio, 2015

May 10, 2008.

That's the day Carlo finally got sober. He'd been close to death multiple times, many of those close to him emphasize, and as Alex McMurray says, he finally "saw the light."

"He finally went in front of this judge he'd seen a few times. And [the judge] was just like, 'Mr. Nuccio, this is it. If you come into my courtroom one more time, you're going to do hard time. In Angola,'" McMurray said. "One day the light went on."

With that light came a stronger relationship with his baby sister, Lena, which she says really started when he moved into an apartment on the bottom floor of her house. He'd been attending Alcoholic Anonymous meetings and making sobriety a central focus in his life, so much so that he'd begun helping others stay off of drugs—something he rarely talked about.

"He ended up renting this apartment underneath me, and we got closer and closer," she said. "We would talk, and he would tell me—he'd say, 'Those rooms,' and he was referring to AA. He wouldn't say names to me; he was very good about not mentioning people. I just knew that he helped a lot of people."

His career got back on track, too, and one of his most notable gigs post-sobriety was playing drums on Marianne Faithfull's 2011 *Horses and High Heels* album.

Let's rewind to December of 2007. The Drifters were just over two years removed from Hurricane Katrina, and a majority had relocated to other cities—Mark in Las Vegas, Peter in Durham, North Carolina, and Robert to Memphis, Tennessee. Vicki was already back in Los Angeles, and Susan and Russ stayed in New Orleans after the storm.

On New Year's Eve, The Bangles were playing at the Fremont Experience in downtown Las Vegas, while Hootie and the Blowfish happened to be in Vegas, too, for a gig at the Silverton Casino. The Cowsills, with Russ on drums, were also in Vegas, playing at The Flamingo. Robert was in Memphis at the time, but the rest of the band decided to get together to mark this unlikely convergence.

"It was fairly quick, but it was the first time we'd been in the same room together in a long, long time," Mark said. "That was the first time that we were all happy to see each other. Nothing was negative, it was all positive. And I'd just had major surgery on my mouth, so I was really stoned on one of the medications they gave me. It was a weird thing, but it was sort of magical at the same time. Just happenstance that they were all here on the same day and then gone the next day."

The years that followed the end of the band would find Peter, Susan, and Russ' relationship healing. Because of Miranda, they didn't have the option of moving on with their lives and not communicating, especially with Peter relocating to Durham after Katrina.

"The three of us had Miranda, so we had to," Russ said. "With the rest of the band it was like, everyone could go to their quarters and do it on their own time. Or not and just sweep it under the rug, roll the rug up and throw it in the closet. The band is done, but we're not done. We can't be done.

"There's common ground amongst all three of us with our love for this child, and the fact that this child is relying on all three of us on a daily basis. She was more important than all of our challenges amongst our personal lives and those personal changes. And certainly more important than the band."

Because of that period of healing, Susan and Peter became good friends, where once there was acrimony and division. Peter and Russ' friendship got stronger, too, and remains so today.

"It just means so much," Russ said of the relationship he has today with Peter. "We can just be talking about the weather and laughing or whatever, but there's depth to it. After Katrina, every Father's Day he was the first one to wish me a happy Father's Day. Usually waking me up in the morning with a phone call."

Peter reflects on his friendship with Russ with a similar feeling of contentment.

"I think about my relationship with Russ Broussard sometimes and I'm like, 'Wow. That's a really good friendship right there,'" he said. "Because, it could very easily be a not very nice friendship or a professional relationship. But it's ended up being very sweet and very loving."

Sobriety has been a key part of Peter's own healing and growth over the past 20 years—he says that being sober "does not allow you to shrink back from your problems, or cover it up, or add that little *joie de vivre* that only 30 drinks can give."

It also, he adds, puts a new perspective on "the, sort of, garrulous nature of life with the Continental Drifters and Peter Holsapple." Overall, much of the regret he has about his alcoholism revolves around what he feels like he lost from being so consumed by drinking.

He laments: "What a bunch of bullshit. What a waste. I could've been doing a lot better things with my time, but I didn't.

"And the sad thing for me now is that, you know, I kind of missed the shot with that. I could've done a lot more than I did if I hadn't been drinking the whole time."

While getting sober was central to Peter's post-band healing, time really was the main ingredient for healing the wounds created in the final few years of the band, especially between Russ, Susan, Mark, and Robert.

"You can look at going through a catastrophe like [Katrina], and a communal one, that happened to the community of New Orleans," Vicki said. "That's a very powerful thing, and it was a very, very slow comeback on every level. And so I think even for the Drifters it's like, you get some freaking perspective. We're still here."

Indeed, Katrina was the catalyst for some reconciliation among the Drifters, namely Robert and Susan. When Barry Cowsill's body was found under a wharf three months after the hurricane, a wake was planned at an Irish pub on Decatur Street.

"I was like, 'I love Barry, I'm going,'" Robert said. "And I remember walking in and [New Orleans singer] Kim Carson had just finished playing 'Heart, Home' because she covered it. And then I just heard this voice and it was Susan going, 'Oh my god, it's Robert Maché.'

"She was kind of, like, wonderstruck and terrified at the same time that I would be there. I'm like, 'It's Barry, man. I love my Barry.' That was kind of a small icebreaker, but it was a big moment."

After that, they'd run into each other sometimes but really it was just time and space that allowed for them to be civil with each other, and ultimately close friends, again.

"It's too much energy to hold a fucking grudge, man," he said. "Now we're like besties. I trust her with my life."

And so, in 2009, the Drifters were invited to play the Threadhead Cultural Foundation's inaugural Patry, a festival held between Jazz Fest weekends that supports that organization's mission of providing grants and assistance to New Orleans artists.

"Those guys kept saying to Russ and Susan, 'We need to do a Drifters show.' And they were like, 'I don't think that'll happen.' But everybody said yes," Mark said.

Vicki says she was eager for an offer to come around for the band to reunite. After all, she's the one who's continually believed that the band would always exist in some capacity.

"It felt like I was just waiting for the call," she said.

Everyone was on board with no hesitation—as Robert says, "there was a lot of water under the bridge." So the *Vermilion* lineup made plans to reform and booked a Carrollton Station headlining gig that same weekend. They gathered beforehand to rehearse at Susan and Russ' house, opting to start their first runthrough in seven years with "A Song for You."

"We played that first song, and we're all fucking sobbing," Russ said. "And then I think we did 'Rain Song,' and again, we had to take a sobbing break. But then it just became a catharsis where we were just cracking up laughing a lot."

That rehearsal marked the first time since 2002 that the entire *Vermilion* lineup was in the same place. They didn't play it safe, either. They went full Drifters and rehearsed hours worth of songs.

"We're always suckers for punishment," Mark recalled. "We didn't say, 'Let's just learn a certain amount of songs and that's it, and let's play a nice, compact Drifters show. We just did what we always did, so it was a learning curve. Just trying to get your memory muscle back. As soon as I started going through [the songs], all of that time started flooding back, and all the memories. It was very emotional to revisit that material and know that I was going to be playing with my family again."

For some it was complete muscle memory going through Drifters songs again, with very little re-learning to do.

"It's always been muscle memory. I can play pretty much any Drifters song in my sleep," Robert said. "And Mark, he'll either remember or forget any song on any day!"

Ultimately it was the music that pulled them back together; that was why none of the personal baggage really mattered very much when it came to booking the shows.

"Everybody had families, everybody was doing different things, people had moved," Peter said. "And we loved each other socially. We adored being around each other; some of our favorite people in the world. But we knew that we would end up being back home. This was not a busman's holiday; it was really just a holiday. It had a lightheartedness to it, I think. The end of the band had gotten so heavy—for everybody. And it hurt to not be a band, because the reasons were not musical reasons. It was other stuff. That weighs on me, sometimes, to think of it like that. Because god knows it was a remarkable musical organization.

"It was like a co-op of ideas that were all equally great, and they meshed so well. And then all of the sudden you didn't have that. It's a little bit like divorce, you know? But I think there was a musical longing that made a reunion an easy thing to agree to do."

When the time came for the Threadhead show—the day before their headliner at Carrollton Station—they were just about to start playing when Robert stopped everything and got Mark's attention.

"We just got set up, we're all on stage. We're just about to go off and he goes, 'No, wait, wait! Mark! Don't play that bass, play *this* bass.'"

Robert proceeded to pull out the Fender Precision bass he salvaged from Mark's house after Katrina, which he repaired after keeping it in his shed for nearly four years. Mark immediately burst into tears.

"I was like, 'Fuck you, what are you doing to me?!'" Mark recalled. "It's like, 'Look, here's your dead grandmother! She looks like she's dead but she's alive!' I couldn't do it—I just melted down at that point.

"When I went to the house with Disco and my brother-in-law, all of my instruments had been destroyed, that included. It was laying on the ground with the neck off, the body was in three parts; everything was just a mess. So I brought it outside and I just left it on my patio in the backyard.

"I guess Robert came the next day or the day after somehow, and just saw it laying there. He picked it up, put it in his car, and brought it back to Memphis. He put it out in the shed for years and let it dry out."

The Carrollton Station show on May 2, 2009 was a classic Drifters night—playing until the early morning hours to a packed room, celebrating being back together. And when they played "Drifters" near the end of the first set, there was hardly a dry eye in the house.

"The energy was there, the humor was there, and everyone was just having a great time," Robert recalled.

Meanwhile, former Drifters went on with their own lives. Ray Ganucheau went to Los Angeles in 2009 and recorded a solo record with his old pal Jim Scott, featuring an all-star band that included Bob Glaub and Sebastian Steinberg sharing bass duties, Don Heffington on drums, Lisa Germano on violin, and John Ginty on keyboards.

At the same time, Gary Eaton continued making music, albeit in a much different capacity than his previous work. As he puts it, "I've done all kinds of weird, crazy shit."

In addition to doing some film scoring work, composing and playing on music for ESPN programming, in 2008 Gary began recording music for primarily right-wing political candidates and conservative media.

"If you've ever seen the Tucker Carlson Tonight, that's my guitar on Tucker Carlson," he reveals, adding that he was also hired to write a song for Herman Cain's 2008 presidential campaign, titled "The Herman Cain Train."

And, of course, he continued working with his wife Shelli, as well as one-time auxiliary Drifter Kevin Jarvis and Raji's regular/Drifters pal Robbie Rist, in Kingsizemaybe.

"I've been really blessed," he said.

Danny McGough spent much of these years as a touring member of Social Distortion, also playing on their 2011 album *Hard Times and Nursery Rhymes*.

In 2012, Dayna Kurtz, by then a brand new New Orleans resident who had spent years garnering critical praise and international success for her genre-bending, vocally stunning body of work, was prepping an album release show in her new home city. She knew some musicians in town but most of the regular folks she played with were in New York, aside from Robert Maché.

When putting a band together, the drummer she wanted couldn't do the gig, so she asked Robert if he had any suggestions.

"The thing about New York players is that the guys who are rock and roll guys don't play jazz very well, and the jazz guys are not feral enough to play rock and roll," Kurtz said. "And [Robert] was like, 'I think Carlo's your guy.' But he was hesitant. Carlo had burned a lot of bridges in town. Now, I'd never met Carlo when he was using, so I didn't know him from anybody, and he was actually not working a whole lot at the time *because* he had burned a lot of bridges."

They met and hit it off immediately, with Kurtz calling her and Carlo's initial connection "really special." She took him out in her band on a Netherlands tour, and they continued playing together through the formation of Kurtz's band Lulu and the Broadsides—which featured Carlo, Robert, Glenn Hartman, and the great New Orleans bassist James Singleton.

"I really wasn't even thinking about any other drummers. He was just kind of perfect. He covered so many bases so well," Kurtz said. "I'm a songwriter first, and I serve the song. If the song wants to be a mariachi song, it's a mariachi song. And if a song wants to be zydeco stomp then it's zydeco stomp. Or a swamp pop tune or a punk rock tune. It needs to go where the song wants to go, and I could never find just one player who played everything just so well. Carlo being just such a good producer and song leader himself, he really kind of dove deep to find the heart of the song."

Naturally, Kurtz says there was some creative tension between them, but playing with Carlo "felt dangerous" because of his unpredictability with everything from feel to tempo.

"It was sometimes irritating, but then you'd settle into it and it would be this whole new fucking thing," Kurtz said. "That's the thing about guys like him—they sort of de facto become a kind of bandleader in their own right. And as a result, as the bandleader of this particular band, we occasionally butted heads. But I'd say at least half the time I think he was right. His ideas were really good. He was so perfect for the Broadsides."

Dayna Kurtz's band, and ultimately Lulu and the Broadsides, became one of Carlo's main gigs in recent years. There was, as Kurtz says, a "heavy sibling energy" between the two of them—not unlike his relationships in the Drifters.

"He definitely felt like my big brother in all of the good ways and bad ways. He was so bossy, holy shit," she said with a laugh. "But he was also wildly protective. I'm a New York Jew, and he's New Orleans Italian. And the cultures are not dissimilar."

As life moved for everyone, there was more and more water under the bridge with each passing day. The band's resentment towards Razor & Tie never quite subsided, but as Russ recalls, a chance run-in with one of the owners over a decade after *Better Day* did bring a bit of closure to that situation.

By this point, Susan and Russ had been doing a regular series of shows called Covered in

Vinyl, where they played a classic album front to back with a band full of New Orleans musicians and some special guests. They were hugely successful shows that were, for a while, a staple at Carrollton Station before they ultimately moved the series to Chickie Wah Wah.

In 2013, one of the label's owners happened to be in New Orleans for Jazz Fest and got word that Susan Cowsill was doing one of her Covered in Vinyl gigs at Chickie Wah Wah.

"He and his family and some friends all came to the show," Russ said. "We were playing Bruce Springsteen and it was a packed house, and he came over. I'd already seen him once before at a show that Susan and I did in New York. He sort of gave a brief apology back then and just said 'You know, I never gave the record a full listen. I listened to four songs and said "I don't get it." I should've gone to the fifth song,'" Russ said.

The owner said he felt that if the fifth song, "Cousin," had been the opener as the band intended, he would've felt differently about the album. He even acknowledged that the A&R rep was responsible for the change in sequence that caused him to lose interest.

"That was kind of it. I was like, 'Yeah, take you and your apology and ram it up your ass,'" Russ said.

Several years later at the Jazz Fest show, the two had the chance to talk more about what happened, and Russ struck up the nerve to ask him straight out why the label seemingly dropped the ball—pressing him to explain the circumstances that led him to push the band and *Better Day* aside.

"I go, 'So, what the fuck? We were doing the work. We were working our asses off, going through this emotional toil to stay together and to keep this band going, and be supportive of one another creatively. We were doing it. We were managing the fuck out of it. And you guys just left us high and dry,'" he recalled.

"And he says, 'It was just bad timing, Russ. We were bringing in a third partner and he was going to be running it. And we're in meetings every day for over a week, doing paperwork with our attorneys and getting all of this straight to where we can sort of take a back seat and go play golf.'"

Essentially, the owner said, the album came across his desk and he just simply didn't understand what they were doing. He acknowledged that *Vermilion* had "sucked him in and wouldn't let go," but the follow up just didn't resonate.

Years later, the owner was playing golf and *Better Day* came up on his iPod. He decided to give it a listen, and when he landed on "Cousin," he was blown away.

"He said, 'I was just stunned. My knees almost buckled,'" Russ said. "He was like, 'You know, if put in an order that boosted other songs, you probably would've kept the listener all the way through the record.'

"And I was like, 'Well, shit.'"

Russ came away from that with at least a deeper understanding of what had happened, despite lingering frustrations about the label's unwillingness to give *Better Day* a shot regardless of the song sequence. And so, life carried on with yet another 'could've been/should've been' feather in the Drifters' collective cap.

There weren't any Drifters reunions after 2009, until six years later when Omnivore Recordings approached the band about doing a re-release of *Nineteen Ninety-Three*. Mark initially agreed, and to compile the album, he rescued and digitized DAT tapes from the sessions.

"Every day I'd transfer, like, ten tapes and I'd just be crying listening to it," he said. "I was so emotional about it, and then I finally went back and said, 'No, I don't want to release *Nineteen Ninety-Three*. I want to pay tribute to the band as it is, and as it was from the beginning to the end.'"

Mark ultimately combed through the archives to put together *Drifted: In the Beginning and Beyond*, a two-disc set that included early versions of "The Rain Song," and "Who We Are," demos of songs like "Karen A," a version of "Tighter, Tighter" with Rob Ladd on drums from the Kevin Salem session, and plenty of live recordings from over the years and across all lineups of the band.

Mark worked alongside Pat Thomas—musician, Drifters friend and fan, author, and noted compiler of reissues and rarities—to compile and prep the compilation for release.

In true Drifters fashion, some of the band was more involved in overseeing the project than others, but ultimately it was Mark's brainchild that he saw through. And in *truest* Drifters fashion, Mark found out about the release date just a few weeks before it was slated to come out—before anyone else in the band had a chance to listen to the entire set. There was even an advance review in the Los Angeles *Times*.

"I had to send an email to everybody trying to explain to them why I hadn't given them anything. 'Oh, by the way, it's coming out in three weeks. And oh, here's a review in the L.A. *Times*!'" he laughed. "But everybody really enjoyed it. They thought it was fantastic. And I did put my love and soul into it."

To celebrate the release, the band put together three shows—one at Tipitina's in New Orleans and two at the Morgan-Wixson Theatre in Los Angeles. The lineup for these gigs? Mark, Carlo, Ray, Gary, Danny, Peter, Susan, Vicki, Robert, and Russ. All ten Continental Drifters.

"I think there was a little bit of apprehension—it's ten people. That's a lot of people. How do we do this? Two drummers, two keyboards, more guitar players than we could ever possibly need, singers that rival The Four Freshmen," Peter said. "The Six Freshmen…The Seven Freshmen. You know? Fuck."

Getting all those Drifters together ended up being easier than some might have anticipated.

"Everybody was cool," Robert said. "It was like The Band reunion or something like that."

In a relatively rare occurrence, the band actually spent a few days rehearsing together— working through a mountain of material and conceiving the run-of-show for this behemoth of a Drifters gig.

"Everybody flew into New Orleans, we rented a rehearsal space for two or three days, maybe, and ran down the songs," Ray recalled. "It was pretty well charted out as far as sets go. It was fun. There were a few trainwrecks, but for the most part it was pretty good. I remember the crowd really responding well to the show. It was such an army of guitars on stage, so you were kind of in your own zone and hoping that it was coming across."

"I'm sure I needed [rehearsal] the most, because of course the later records I'm not on, but I did play on a lot of those tunes at the live shows," Danny adds.

Before the show, Gary remembers, everyone who drank participated in emptying a bottle of bourbon to loosen up.

"I think there was a lot of angst among certain people, so everybody just chug-a-lugged," he said.

There was also reconciliation between Gary and Vicki, who said that the two had an opportunity to talk and that Gary apologized for the way he treated her all those years earlier.

Symbolic of the evolution of the Drifters, the show started with the original Walton, Ganucheau, Nuccio, McGough, and Eaton lineup playing "The Mississippi," before the Psycho Sisters, Peter, Robert, and Russ joined them for the outro.

The stage was, as you can imagine, jam-packed at Tipitina's, but the Drifters made great use of the ten musicians by combining the various lineups. In fact, all ten Drifters were on stage all at once for songs like "Who We Are, Where We Live," though most of the set was split up according to what era a song belonged to.

The next weekend they did it again, though this time they played two nights in Los Angeles—recreating a portion of the Morgan-Wixson stage to look similar to Raji's.

"It was just the whole thing of rejoining a gang you were in a long time ago. 'Okay, let's have fun and take no prisoners,'" Danny said. "There was beautiful musical moments where I was like, 'Oh my god, this is great.'"

There was a lot of fun off-stage as well, as Robert remembers.

"Danny was just giving us great stories about touring with Tom Waits," he said. "He'd be like, 'Tom would be asking us to learn a song, and he wouldn't really give us any musical direction. But he'd look at me and go: Okay Danny, what I want from you is pomegranates and oranges.' He was just cracking us up. And of course, we all wanted his wardrobe. [Danny] is just a stellar, stellar person."

The shows at the Morgan-Wixson were both sold out, and the crowd included many of the L.A. folks that the band had played with over the years. Robert Lloyd sat in, Keith Morris was in the audience on the first night, Steve Wynn and Linda Pitmon were there for both shows, Jim Scott was there, and even John Crooke—who moved to Los Angeles after the demise of Jolene— was in attendance.

Another audience member for both nights was Nelson Bragg, a veteran L.A. songwriter and multi-instrumentalist who was then a longstanding member of Brian Wilson's solo band. Bragg was not as familiar with the Drifters prior to the show, but was friends with several Drifters (and toured with John Cowsill on the Beach Boys' 50th anniversary tour), and more notably was a massive dB's and Peter Holsapple fan.

He'd gotten into The dB's in the 1980s while in college, when *Repercussion* came out, and became a devoted fan through their breakup. He cites Peter and Chris Stamey's *Mavericks* as a hugely important album in his life at the time of its release.

"That was a life changer for me," he said. "I was deeply moved by that record."

Bragg says he knew of the Drifters when they were active but was never intimately familiar with the music before he had the chance to see them at the 2015 shows. The allure of the band's history, and the fact that they'd all lived through the debaucherous years they had together, was all the more reason for him to attend, he added.

"The band is alive! That's the greatest reason to go see them," he said. "Let's go see the band that survived. I just was so curious, feeling like an outsider. Not anymore."

The Morgan-Wixson shows made Bragg an instant fan.

"When you hear this music, you relate to it right away. Immediately. It's extremely real. It's very, very human, you know?" he said. "There's just not a lot of people that care enough about music to write songs that take work. I think this stuff is totally on a Dylan level; on a Richard Thompson level. Leonard Cohen level. We're talking about raw emotion-made music. It's the real thing."

Like so many at those shows and the Tipitina's show prior, Bragg says he "sat in awe" watching the Drifters blaze through essentially the majority of their catalog and present ten years worth of music in a four-hour show.

"I absorbed every nanosecond of both nights," Bragg recalled. "It was absolutely incredible. I was floating for two days. I floated for a month after the shows. They were so well-rehearsed. They played so well, they sang so perfectly. How does this band just get together and rehearse a few times and sound like they never stopped?"

The shows, while staged as a way to promote and sell the compilation, ended up being a chance for everyone to reconnect, to celebrate the band, and make some music together again. And it was mostly that, though as Gary recalls, he couldn't help but feel slightly removed emotionally.

"For me, I was kind of detached from it all, you know, mentally. I was glad everyone was doing well, but I was a little detached from it because my life is different now," he said. "My goals in life are different now. I feel like more of a dad now, and a working guy now. It was a little different for me."

One good thing that came from it? Gary and Peter having the chance to find common ground and have a meaningful conversation.

"It was nice talking to Pete about family," Gary said. "He and I had a really great conversation about family and life and things like that."

Peter agrees.

"I always think of Sam, his son, and how present he was in the early days of the Continental Drifters," he said. "Until I had my own child, and especially having a child in a divorce situation, I could not have begun to recognize as much of what Gary had to deal with at the time as I do now. It's another one of those things, in retrospect, that I wish I had been a little bit more attuned to."

That same detachment that Gary speaks of, Peter says he sensed it a bit from Ray as well.

"I love Ray Ganucheau very much; I care about him very much. But I think he's another guy that sort of outgrew the Drifters, or whatever the Drifters became," he said.

After that, everyone went their separate ways once more. There was some chatter about potentially recording something with all ten Drifters. Not everyone was on board with the idea, though, and it fizzled out quickly. So it goes.

Life moved on for all, and for Carlo things took a positive turn in 2016 when he met Carmen Peruyero Gomez, a teacher from Spain who was working in Wilmington, North Carolina, teaching Spanish, as part of a contract program with the Spanish government.

"One of the moms that was at my school—and we became friends—was Carlo's ex-girl-friend," Carmen said.

That year, Carmen and some colleagues visited New Orleans on Memorial Day weekend. It was the last trip that they'd have together before their contracts were up and they were set to return to work in their respective countries.

"This ex-girlfriend of Carlo told me, 'Hey, I know somebody there who can show you around," Carmen recalled. "We dated but we're still friends, so I'm going to give you his number and I'll give him your number so that you can meet. He'll show you around because he knows *everything* about New Orleans.'"

Carmen says that Carlo was actually quite apprehensive about agreeing to show her and her friends around the city. He relented, and met up with Carmen and her friends the next day to give them a tour. At the same moment that Carlo opened his car door to get out and meet Carmen, she opened the door of the hostel where they were staying to greet him.

"And he said that was the moment when he fell in love," she recalled.

The two hit it off pretty immediately, getting to know each other over the course of Carmen's trip. He asked her before she left if they could keep in touch over text, but she wasn't sure if it would work.

"I said, 'I'm leaving—I'm going back to Spain. I don't want a new relationship. Yes, we can keep texting, but just as friends. I don't want anything serious right now,'" she said.

When she got home, Carlo messaged and called Carmen "every single day."

"He was so convinced that I was the one. Since the first day," Carmen said. For her, it was a bit more complicated.

"I went to Spain, I was there in June, and then I had an offer to work in Hong Kong as a Spanish teacher," she said. "So I moved in August to Hong Kong. He said, 'Really? Spain was not far enough?'"

Carmen convinced Carlo that it was a great opportunity for her and assured him that he'd be able to visit. In February of 2017, he told Carmen that he was going to make the trip to China show her that he was serious about being with her.

"I said, 'Well, okay,' but I didn't believe that he was coming for sure. But he came," she recalled. "Our first kiss was in the Hong Kong Airport."

That, she says, was an eye-opening moment.

"It was like, 'Okay, Carmen. You can open your heart. He's serious,'" she said. Once the walls came down, Carmen fell in love, and off they went. Well, sort of.

After another year in Hong Kong, Carmen went back to Spain to finish her Master's program, where she planned to spend one more year. They were together long distance the entire time, and Carmen traveled to New Orleans to spend that summer with Carlo. It was during that summer that he began talking about wanting to marry her.

"I said, 'I'm not going to marry you. I was married before, and I don't need to get married. I love you, it's okay. We don't need to get married.' And he says, 'But I was never married, Carmen!' And I said, 'Well, that's on you!'" Carmen said with a laugh.

Carlo, she says, insisted that he'd never gotten married because he was waiting for her.

He ended up asking her parents if he could marry her when he traveled to Spain to meet them, and Carmen remembers it being an emotional conversation for everyone. It took time for her to accept Carlo's proposal, but she knew she wanted to spend her life with him and ultimately felt in her heart that it was the right move.

They got married at the New Orleans Botanical Garden on July 7, 2018.

"He was so caring. For me, my friends are the family that I picked. And for him, friends are the most important thing—well, not the *most important* thing, because music is first," she says of what attracted her to Carlo. "Having the same values, it was amazing. He was so funny, so determined; he was not worried about showing feelings. What you see is what it is. Carlo is what you see. He was honest. He was all of that. Everything that you want in a relationship, Carlo [had] it."

Carmen had what Carlo needed, too. And the people in his life took notice.

Danya Kurtz recalls meeting Carmen for the first time on a double date with the two of them and her husband, and being slightly unsure of what to expect prior to meeting her.

"We're looking at each other like, 'What kind of crazy ass fuckin' woman is going to wind up with Carlo? Is she going to be this loudmouth party girl? Is she going to be a doormat? Who winds up with Carlo?'" she said. "I met her, and I looked at him afterwards when we were alone and I was like, 'You better not fuck this up. You're never going to do better than this one!' She was all the things that he needed. She was patient and womanly in a very old fashioned way.

"Carlo was *very* old fashioned—they don't make guys like him anymore. And she, in her own way, is very old fashioned. But very kind. One of the kindest people I've ever met."

Carlo had had health problems for some time when he got together with Carmen, getting regular checkups on his liver since 2012, when he'd been receiving Interferon to treat Hepatitis C. In 2017, he started noticing that he was getting tired more easily and that his feet had become swollen. He was treated and monitored every six months, ultimately getting his energy back, before doctors found a tumor on his liver that they deemed cancerous.

"They checked it and said, 'It's cancer, but we're going to take it out and it's going to be fine,'" Carmen said.

When Hurricane Ida hit New Orleans in August 2021, Carmen and Carlo evacuated, and when they returned Carlo underwent surgery to have the tumor removed. Surgery was said to have gone well, but at his three-month check-in doctors found that the cancer was still there.

Due to prior health issues, Carlo wasn't responsive to chemotherapy and radiation, and he also had pulmonary fibrosis, meaning he wasn't a candidate for a transplant. He persisted, appealing to doctors to put him on a transplant list.

"He was rejected three times, and the last time they told him there was nothing they could do," Carmen said.

Knowing that time was not on his side, Carlo decided to throw a party.

On July 4, 2022, dozens of friends and family gathered at Carlo and Carmen's house for a celebration of what seemed like not just Carlo's life, but life in general.

"Friends from California, friends from New York, people from [New Orleans], Nashville, Asheville—everybody that could make it came," Carmen said. "We had, I think it was, more than a hundred people here that day.

"He was so thrilled. And he wanted to do it his way. He said, 'If I'm going to go, I'm going to go saying goodbye my way—surrounded by music, loving everyone that I love, while I'm still okay to do it.' He was so happy. And he was telling everyone what to do, which is so Carlo."

The beauty of that day was the fact that Carlo felt up to putting something together at all, given the state of his health at the time. As Vicki notes, it was classic Carlo.

"Some people wouldn't necessarily want to or feel up to celebrating, or don't want to be in the diminished state that they're in physically. But Carlo didn't give a shit," Vicki said. "He couldn't have been in a better frame of mind at that moment, really. It was astonishing. His stamina was astonishing."

There was a gravity to it, with everyone there understanding *why* they were there. But there was so much music, love, and joy to go around. Not only were folks like Pat McLaughlin, Glenn Hartman, Alex McMurray, and other central figures in his musical life present, but Susan, Ray, Vicki, Russ, and Danny were all there to represent the Drifter family.

Over in the Netherlands, Robert and Dayna Kurtz played "Long While" on a previously-planned European tour, in honor of Carlo and in lieu of not being able to attend the party in New Orleans.

Danny flew from L.A. to be there at Carlo's, and played alongside his old pal on multiple songs—just like the old days.

"I am so glad that I [was there]. Just to get to play with him one more time, and it was so nice to see everybody. And you know, it was difficult—definition bittersweet," he said. "I'm good at compartmentalizing stuff like that, but there were a few moments when we were playing and I got tears and stuff, and I'd be like, 'Don't crash the plane. Keep going.'

"He had a smile that would not quit that day. And I know he was probably tired as hell. But he loved being in his element; surrounded by people who loved him and who he loved."

For Lena Nuccio, one of the highlights of that beautiful day at her brother's house was getting to be among many of the people who made up the music community Carlo was part of for so many years—some of whom he quietly helped to get sober in the years since getting sober himself.

"People were coming up to me and saying, 'I just want to tell you: Your brother saved my life,'" she said. "That's the thing that I was most proud of. Carlo could be a little…proud. A little bit of an ego. But that was one thing that he didn't brag about. He really respected the confidentiality, but I know that he saved a lot, a lot, of people."

July 4 was a day full of music, friendship, family, energy, and love for Carlo. A day that certainly made an indelible mark on all who were able to be there.

When he was rejected the final time for a liver transplant, doctors insisted that he'd get the same answer no matter where else he went. He was going to die, and he ultimately decided that the best thing to do would be to stay in New Orleans and not pursue anything further.

And so, he staged his party and then continued to do gigs with Lulu and the Broadsides, Alex McMurray, and others from then on, even as his health deteriorated. He was determined to keep playing, almost intent on going out behind a drum kit.

He was also insistent that he continue doing another passion of his—cooking.

On August 20, 2022, he was scheduled for a gig with Alex McMurray at BJ's Lounge in the Bywater. Nobody was quite sure it would be happening, as his cancer had been more and more aggressive. But he wanted to do it, and so with the help of his wife, Glenn Hartman, and fellow local drummer André Bohren, Carlo prepared to play once again.

McMurray recalled: "He was getting drained the day before, so that was good. They'd drain his abdomen of all that fluid, and he always felt a lot better after that. So in the morning Carmen called me and she's like, 'Carlo had a great night's sleep. He is feeling awesome.'

"And I'm like, 'Oh, awesome.' So I call Carlo and I go, 'Carlo, how you doin', man?' And he's like, 'I'm doing good, man. We're gonna do this tonight.'"

After that call in the morning with Alex, Carlo expressed to Carmen and to Hartman that he wanted to get in the kitchen and cook.

"We told him, 'No, Carlo, you are not cooking today. We can cook tomorrow. We want you to be as good as you can for the gig. Just relax, enjoy the day,'" Carmen said.

He took a nap after that, and when he woke up he was no longer feeling as well as he had been in the morning.

"By five or six o'clock, he wasn't feeling so great, you know?" McMurray said. "We all got to BJ's early—we had the drums set up. I had Andre bring his drums; André came early in the afternoon. The idea was: Carlo would just have to come in, adjust his cymbals or whatever, and we'd just go."

Around seven, McMurray and his band got word that Carlo might not come after all. He wasn't doing well, and McMurray and his band were prepared to have Bohren substitute in the event that he couldn't make it.

Back at the Nuccio home, Carmen was getting more and more concerned, while Carlo remained hell-bent on making it to the gig.

"He said, 'I'm going to play, even if it's the last thing I'm going to do,'" she recalled.

Finally, McMurray was told that Carlo would make it to BJ's.

"We didn't know what was happening, and then finally Glenn calls me and goes, 'They're on their way,'" he said. "About 8:25 he walks in the door, and he's orange and looks like a ghost. And he had a hood on—he looked like a prize fighter. He just looked at the drums in the back of the room, and like a turtle coming out of the sea to lay its eggs, he did this slow, determined walk.

"He made it up to the bandstand, got behind the drums, and we got behind our instruments. I turned to Carlo and said, 'You ready to go?' He says, 'Yeah.' I go, 'We're going to do [a song called] "Rag Daze." Does that sound good to you?' He says, 'Yeah. Let me start it.'"

Carlo counted off the song, they played it—a little slower than normal—and the set continued as it normally would.

"He had a couple requests," McMurray said. "I'd called him earlier in the day and he wanted to do a song called 'Blurry' from the Fingerbowl days. The tempo was not decisive enough, and he got kind of lost. But the rest of the set was not too bad. And the last tune—his tempo was kind of all over the place, but we'd just sort of learned to go with him.

"He'd always be dragging, and you'd always try to fight him; the push and pull, he loved that push and pull. But on this day we were like, 'Fuck it. Let him lead.' And so we just would slow down when he slowed down. It was like, 'Whatever, Carlo's in charge.'"

The last song ended—McMurray calls it a "really high note" to end the gig on—and Carlo immediately got up from the drums. He walked out the back door with Carmen, and got into a car to go home.

"When he sat in the car, he said, 'Baby, I'm not feeling good. I'm in pain. Just drive very slow,'" she said. "I was driving fifteen miles per hour."

Carmen begged him to let her take him to the hospital, but he'd already made it clear that he didn't want to go back. His wish was to die at home.

"I said, 'I promise, Carlo. You are not going to die at the hospital. You are going to die at home.'"

Things got worse when they got home that night, and Carlo was admitted to hospice, where he spent a couple of nights before telling his wife that he wanted to go home.

And so, that's where he went. Carmen brought her husband home, singing their favorite song to him while he rested.

Carlo died on August 24, 2022.

Everybody who was with Carlo in the last months of his life praises Carmen for what she did as a caretaker and a spouse during a time of such unimaginable pain. They had a genuine love that carried them through to the day he died. And perhaps beyond.

"I swear to you, she is an angel that was just dropped down from heaven," Lena said. "She just absolutely worshiped the ground he walked on, and the feeling was mutual."

Glenn Hartman also deserves serious praise for spending every single day with Carlo and Carmen, driving them to appointments and doing whatever he could to ensure that they were taken care of.

"Glenn was with him every day. Glenn was the guy who went to the doctor with Carmen and Carlo," McMurray emphasizes.

"When he'd go to the hospital, he'd tell the hospital staff that Glenn was his rabbi so they'd let him in," Danny adds.

For Steve Caton, Carlo's collaborator on the Tori Amos records, one of his most cherished memories will forever be building Carlo an acoustic guitar—something he's been doing for several years.

Carlo would excitedly share on social media as Caton provided updates on the progress of the build, until March of 2022—just five months before Carlo died—when the guitar was finally delivered. Thrilled with the guitar, Carlo praised Caton's craftsmanship and called it his "dream guitar."

The two spoke not long after, when Carlo informed Caton that he was not in good health.

"He wasn't getting any kind of treatment, as it were. It didn't surprise me that he was weak, but I didn't leave the conversation thinking, 'Oh, he's not going to last,'" Caton said.

After Carlo died, Caton says he heard from a mutual friend about the guitar completely out of nowhere.

"In retrospect, I almost feel like that was him saying goodbye to me," he said.

Carlo's passing proved a devastating blow to the city of New Orleans as a whole, but one thing that became most apparent from his death is that he is a musical and cultural touchstone; in many ways he is New Orleans personified.

"There's no more Carlo Nuccios coming behind him to take his place. That's it," Rene Coman laments.

One of the sentiments shared by so many when Carlo died was that it didn't seem real, or even possible, given everything he fought through to get to where he finally was in life. "I Am a Tree," as the man himself said.

"He was like the giant cockroach that you can't kill. That's why I think it was so extraordinary for all of us when Carlo died," Hartman said. "That's why it didn't seem fair. After all of that, and to finally have him realizing dreams that he never thought he was even fit for. Like Carmen, and a house, and building his own home studio. If you could only imagine what was about to happen, right?"

Indeed, the unfairness of it all is that there was so much more for Carlo to do. Meeting the love of his life, buying a home, enjoying a continually fruitful career in music and writing songs again. There was so much in front of him.

"Those are all the things he wanted, and he finally got to have them. And it just really stinks that he didn't get to have them for very long," Lena Nuccio said.

One thing is certain—Carlo's imprint on New Orleans music is permanent. And with all of his accomplishments and his contributions to New Orleans music, calling him a cultural touchstone really isn't hyperbole.

To the folks who know him well, he's even bigger than that.

"It's the loss of the person that knows you and knows your value. It's like, I have one less person on the planet that thinks I'm cool," Coman said. "Plenty of times I wound up on sessions because somebody said, 'Carlo, I want you on this session. Who should I get on bass?' And he said, 'Rene Coman.' That's a very selfish way to look at it, but it's part of the weight of this.

"Not only do you lose someone that you love, but you lose someone that loved you."

"He was a bridge to a New Orleans that I never got to see, which is the New Orleans that I fell in love with: [Renowned engineer] Cosimo Matassa's studio and early rock 'n roll, Fats Domino," Dayna Kurtz said. "He was a kind of huge repository of New Orleans music history, and New Orleans history in general."

Keith Morris got to see his old pal one last time, a couple of weeks following the July 4 party, when his current band OFF! played in New Orleans. For some context, the OFF! song "Now I'm Pissed" was actually co-written by Carlo via a riff from the Bug Lamp days.

"When I introduced Carlo to the guys in OFF!, and we drove away after Carlo and I hugged and we got in the van and drove off to wherever we were going, all of the guys said, 'That's one of the nicest guys I've ever met,'" Morris said. "He was a sweetheart. I will always love the guy."

One recurring theme in the Carlo Nuccio story is how much he cared; how invested he was in those he loved, even in his darkest moments.

"He was very, very sensitive. Huge heart," Lena said. "That part of him was just trying so hard to come out, but he just had his demons that he had to fight."

He led with his heart. That's the thing that Carmen always comes back to when talking about Carlo. His big, wide-open heart.

"His heart is what I miss the most. He cares about everything. He took care of the garden, he was cutting the grass—he was so happy about the home that we made together. He used to sit outside and just contemplate," she said.

And while Carlo is no longer physically with her in the home they made, Carmen said he's never far.

"Every time I cook I go, 'Carlo, I'm cutting it wrong. How was it that you wanted me to do it?'" she said. "I talk with him a lot."

From May 10, 2008 until August 24, 2022, Carlo's biggest priority was showing love and appreciation for the people who cared for him. He gave it back.

"I can't think of a more complete about-face than what Carlo accomplished. He was the classic heart of gold guy by the end," Keith Spera said.

Danny McGough adds: "He's one person, I think, that really, really got the gratitude portion of that in a supremely profound way where he was really thankful for every day."

So maybe Steve Berlin didn't make him a "star" in the music biz sense of the word. But, you know, Carlo Nuccio *was* a star. And he burned out bright.

"I have a theory that great creativity comes from the earth," Martha Gehman, who remained in touch with Carlo until he died, said. "It just comes from the ground. [Carlo] was intuitive. I think that he was a born musician. [And] he's an incredible, incredible person."

Carlo lived a lot of life in his 61 years, but in the end he made sure that the people he loved knew and felt it. And what he found in his relationship with Carmen seems almost like a light at the end of a long tunnel that slowly got brighter as the years went by. It was that rare thing that some people spend years looking for.

Carmen says it best:

"He is the love of my life."

In 2015, all ten members of the Continental Drifters got together to play a pair of shows at the Morgan-Wixson Theatre in Santa Monica, California. Photo by Greg Allen

(right) Ray Ganucheau was back in the Drifters fold for the *Drifted* record release celebrations, 2015. Photo by Greg Allen

Carlo Nuccio rejoined the Drifters for the release of *Drifted: In the Beginning and Beyond* at the Morgan-Wixson Theatre in 2015. Photo by Greg Allen

(right) Mark, Susan, and Robert at the Morgan-Wixson Theatre in Santa Monica, California, 2015. Photo by Greg Allen

Sean Kelly

Original Drifters Carlo, Mark, and Gary Eaton back together in 2015. Photo by Greg Allen

The longest running member of the Continental Drifters, Mark holds down the bottom in 2015. Photo by Greg Allen

Peter on the keys in front of Danny McGough (with back to camera) and Carlo, Morgan-Wixson Theatre, 2015. Photo by Greg Allen

(right) Danny McGough during the 2015 Continental Drifters reunion shows for the release of *Drifted*. Photo by Greg Allen

Susan cuts loose on stage during the 2015 Drifters reunion at the Morgan-Wixson Theatre in Santa Monica, California. Photo by Julia Ewan

(below) Gary Eaton at the Morgan-Wixson Theatre, 2015. Photo by Julia Ewan

Carlo was all smiles behind the drum kit with the Continental Drifters again in 2015. Photo by Julia Ewan

(left) Flanked by Vicki (with back to camera) and Susan, Peter breaks out the accordion at the Morgan-Wixson Theatre, 2015. Photo by Julia Ewan

Vicki on stage at the Morgan-Wixson Theatre, 2015. Photo by Julia Ewan

(right) Russ keeping the beat during the reunion release show for *Drifted: In the Beginning and Beyond* at the Morgan-Wixson Theatre, 2015. Photo by Julia Ewan

Ray and Russ at the Morgan-Wixson Theatre, 2015. Photo by Julia Ewan

Gary, Robert, and Mark at the Morgan-Wixson Theatre, 2015. Photo by Julia Ewan

(right) Vicki, Russ, and Susan provide percussion during the 2015 Drifters reunion in Santa Monica, California. Photo by Julia Ewan

The Drifters take a bow at the Morgan-Wixson Theatre, 2015 (L-R: Ray, Susan, Peter, Vicki, Mark, Russ, Carlo, Danny, Robert, Gary). Photo by Julia Ewan

A Drifters family portrait, Santa Monica, California, 2015 (L-R: Carlo, Gary, Danny, Peter, Russ, Mark, Susan, Robert, Vicki, Ray). Photo by Julia Ewan

214

The Drifters keyboard trust: Peter and Danny during reunion rehearsals, 2015. Photo From the collection of Peter Holsapple.

We're a happy family: Russ, Susan, Miranda, and Peter at Jazz Fest 2023. From the collection of Russ Broussard and Susan Cowsill

Susan, Russ, Vicki, and Mark, 2023. From the collection of Russ Broussard and Susan Cowsill

Susan, Mark, and Russ (on drums) at Jazz Fest, New Orleans, 2023. From the collection of Russ Broussard and Susan Cowsill

With all of the problems that plagued the Continental Drifters—bad record deals, drama, divorces, addiction, headlocks, mouthfuls of gasoline—it was almost inevitable that they'd end up back together with so much water beneath them.

After 2015, the *Vermilion* lineup reunited a few more times—once a year from 2016 to 2018. A private party here, a club gig there, but nothing too concrete. Danny, Gary, Peter, Robert, Vicki, Russ, Susan, Mark, and Carlo came together one more time, minus Ray, in 2017 as part of the Wild Honey Foundation's star-studded tribute to The Band in Los Angeles, which raised money for autism research. Among other things, they all took on a spirited version of "The Weight" with Jackson Browne on lead vocals.

Ultimately, the 2015 shows in New Orleans and L.A. would be the one and only time that all ten Drifters were on stage together. The *Vermilion* lineup became the going concern after those performances, albeit infrequently.

In the interim, though, everyone has stayed busy. Danny and Gary continue to make music in California—Danny as a session musician and Gary under his own name. Ray plays occasionally in New Orleans, more recently recording and gigging with Tommy Malone as The Batture Boys.

Russ is the drummer for The Cowsills, John "Papa" Gros, and numerous other New Orleans acts, and his post-Drifters career included a stint with Blue Mountain as well as the legendary singer/songwriter Rodriguez.

Mark returned to the Dream Syndicate in 2012—releasing a whopping four albums with that band since 2017, most recently 2022's *Ultraviolet Battle Hymns and True Confessions*.

Vicki, with John Cowsill, is recording and releasing music with the prolific Action Skulls, their band with actor/musician Bill Mumy—marking the couple's first collaboration of their two-decade marriage. Their third album, *From A Running Horse*, was released in September of 2023. They've also recently recorded an album of songs written by Barry and Bill Cowsill called *Long After the Fire*.

Susan is with The Cowsills—touring regularly on The Turtles' annual Happy Together Tour as well as on their own, and most recently releasing their long-awaited *Rhythm of the World* album on Omnivore in 2022. It's the first Cowsills release since 1998's *Global*.

Susan and Vicki, with both of their husbands swapping on drums, finally recorded a proper Psycho Sisters album—tracked at Dockside and mixed by Jim Scott—which was released in 2014. The album, *Up On the Chair Beatrice*, features songs from their early, pre-Drifters repertoire, plus one song written by Peter.

Robert plays and tours extensively with Dayna Kurtz as both a duo and with her band Lulu and the Broadsides, and also records and tours with Memphis singer-songwriter Dan Montgomery. He also regularly performs with his wife, Candace, as a duo, and generally can almost always be found playing guitar somewhere.

The self-titled Lulu and the Broadsides debut was released in April of 2023 and features stellar guitar work from Robert, plus some topnotch Carlo performances.

Carlo also turned up on the final studio album from the late New Orleans icon Dr. John, *Things Happen That Way*—released just one month after his death and delivering more of that signature Carlo feel to the masses.

Peter joined Chris Stamey, Gene Holder, and Will Rigby to reunite The dB's in 2005 with shows in Hoboken, New Jersey and Chicago, eventually releasing the album *Falling Off the Sky* in 2012. He also released his first solo album in 21 years, *Game Day*, in 2018.

Game Day features a song about the Drifters appropriately called "Continental Drifters"—a loving reminiscence of what it was like being on such a joyous, bumpy ride with "no finer bunch of friends." One of those friends, Susan Cowsill, contributed background vocals.

> *All that beer, and all those songs*
> *And all that sound, all for one most of all*
> *Close our eyes, like getting on a train to ride*
> *Hang on tight, keep your heart and hands inside*
> *We tried*
>
> *And never was a better time had*
> *And never was a finer band*
> *In a time and a place and a different space*
> *Til it fell apart in our hands*
> *Ain't that the way it always goes with plans*

What the Drifters did together certainly impacted the direction of their lives individually, and it impacted others' lives as well. Dave Catching's trip to New Orleans with the band in 1992 proved to be pivotal to the direction of his life. He became close with Jimmy Ford after meeting him at the Monkey Hill headquarters— with Ford helping him secure a restaurant that he bought and ran until launching his Rancho de la Luna studio in the mid-1990s.

"[Ford] and I became best friends, and he ended up getting me a restaurant down there. He took me to a bar one night and introduced me to the owner, and a couple days later I was back in L.A. and he told me I had to take over the restaurant there," Catching explained. "Meeting Jimmy really changed my life."

Catching credits the Drifters, and the infamous RV trip, with connecting those dots.

"I just asked if they would mind if I would go along and help them out. At the time I think I had a lot of mushrooms and marijuana," he recalled with a laugh. "That really led me to where I am today."

Annie Clements credits her Drifters connections, namely Peter's, for leading her to the most life-changing gig of her career—playing with Sugarland.

After being recommended for the gig by fellow New Orleans native and session bassist Dave LaBruyere, Clements says that Sugarland's Kristian Bush was doing his due diligence and decided to look her up.

She explains: "I'm this kid from New Orleans. On my MySpace influences, I list: Peter Holsapple, The dB's, all of this stuff. And when I had the opportunity to audition for Sugarland, I'm probably 25 at the time.

"Kristian Bush is a huge Peter Holsapple fan, so he goes to my MySpace page and sees that I've named checked Peter and The dB's and is like, 'Oh, what the fuck? I'm going to call this girl.' That was one of the pivotal reasons why I was even considered for the audition."

That would all come full circle a few years later, when Peter was tapped to fill in for the band's keyboard player on a run of tour dates. He and Bush ended up co-writing a song on that tour called "She Won't Drive in the Rain Anymore," a song about Sarah's Katrina journey that ended up on The dB's *Falling Off the Sky*.

These days, the Drifters seem to be on a path towards something more ongoing, as opposed to the irregular reunion show or weekend jaunt. A few shows at SXSW in Austin in March of 2022 was the real impetus for thinking that something more could happen.

Everyone was in great spirits, and maybe for the first time since the initial reunion, it felt like a return to the best of times. Rehearsals in Austin began in many ways like it used to—sitting around, talking, laughing, and enjoying each other's company.

"Everybody just kind of showed up at the same time accidentally, and so we were all just sitting outside together. I haven't laughed that hard in so long," Robert said. "It just felt so good and so right."

"When we get together now, all of us, it's just a nice feeling—it's like that other family that you have," Peter adds.

One of the shows at SXSW 2022 was a showcase curated by the band's longtime friend Cameron Smith, who they met over 25 years earlier in Indianapolis, Indiana.

Smith was working at a marketing company at the time, and says he was "miserable" in his job and in his marriage. He was an avid live music goer, and had started volunteering at a small festival in Indy. He was also going down to NOLA for Jazz Fest every year by that point, and had gone down the same year of the festival in Indy to get some inspiration for the event.

He happened upon Tim Cohn, who was opening for Jolene at Carrollton Station, doing a spoken word act. He befriended Cohn and asked him to come to Indy and MC the festival.

"[Tim] called me about a month before and he goes, 'I just started dating somebody that I'm going to bring to the festival.' And I was like, 'Oh, that's cool.' He says, 'Yeah, it'll be cool to have her there, because it's Vicki Peterson from The Bangles,'" Smith said.

Vicki tagged along and became friendly with Smith. He booked the Drifters for the festival the following year, in 1997, and they stayed at his house while in town.

"It was insanity. They were all partying at the time and it was fun as hell," he said. "I had a buddy who was a chef, and he was a music fanatic. He just made this incredible leg of lamb dinner. It was the Drifters in all their glory."

It was during that party with the Drifters that Smith had a life-altering realization.

He recalled: "My wife at the time was not into it. She came home late and these lunatics were taking over our house and our yard. She just wasn't having it. I had this moment of clarity that changed the course of my life, really.

"I was just like, 'There are two paths I can go. I can keep doing what I'm doing, or I can be around people like this, and this can be the kind of life I'd have. A lot more free spirited.'"

Smith's marriage ended and he was hired to help create and run the Indy Jazz Fest, which was a huge success in its inaugural year in 1999. The second year, he booked the Drifters, while the band was smack dab in the middle of the drama between Peter, Susan, and Russ.

"It was all going down at my house," he said. "It was drama, drama, drama. It was crazy."

Over the years, Smith stayed close with the band but grew closest with Russ and Susan after the band broke up and many friendships in their orbit splintered in two directions. He ended up moving to Austin after becoming a talent buyer for Clear Channel, and today maintains a long career in the live music industry.

When SXSW came around in 2022, Smith curated a showcase at Lucy's Fried Chicken for the annual Lucy's Fried Chicken Revival. He booked some of his favorite artists for the event including X's John Doe, a reunited Blue Mountain, and, of course, the Continental Drifters.

It was a full circle moment, of sorts—the Drifters arriving at a place where a fuller-scale reunion finally felt plausible, and Smith indirectly returning the favor for what the band had inadvertently given him all those years earlier.

"From that moment, on my back porch that night in 1997, I took a huge leap of faith and started working on this concert thing. It led me into the concert world," he said. "Live music is my life, it's my religion, it's my career. They are a huge part of that."

SXSW 2022 was also where the band learned of Carlo's illness, and their Lucy's Fried Chicken set was rightfully dedicated to him.

A makeshift Drifters lineup of Robert, Susan, Vicki, and Russ, joined by Glenn Hartman on keys and Mary Lasseigne on bass—filling in for Peter and Mark—played a short set at a memorial concert for Carlo at Tipitina's in October of 2022, and the next year the *Vermilion* lineup made a triumphant return to Jazz Fest 2023, playing an afternoon slot on the main stage.

The band also returned to the Threadhead Patry and played two headlining shows—one at The Willow and the other at Chickie Wah Wah.

Making a special guest appearance during the Jazz Fest set was Savannah Jenkins, Miranda Holsapple Jenkins' daughter, born in October of 2022.

As their first batch of proper gigs since Carlo's death, these shows were performed as a tribute to their brother—with Dayna Kurtz, Glenn Hartman and Alex McMurray joining the band to play a handful of Carlo songs. And, for the first time in Drifters history, Peter sang an emotional version of Carlo's "Side Steppin' the Fire" and cried through the last verse at the Jazz Fest show.

It was a milestone of sorts, being the first time in a long time that the Drifters played an entire week's worth of shows.

And yes, it took a lot to get to a place where the Continental Drifters could play a week of shows together again, but it's been a healing journey. There's nothing complicated or messy anymore. Everyone is just overjoyed to be together again.

"This is a group of people that came to each other for security, love and comfort. And now we get to turn to each other for that again," Susan said. "We're all going to have our baggage everywhere we go, it just doesn't belong to us—I don't have somebody's underwear in mine, he doesn't have my toothbrush; we're not all in each other's bags. So it's easy."

"You know, to get where we are now, we would have to change something about how it went. And so we wouldn't be here," Russ added. "Maybe we would've had two more albums, but maybe they would have been shit. And maybe we would've all been surfacey and cordial and not ourselves."

Perhaps there's something more down the road? Nobody knows for sure what's next, but there's a definite desire to do something. Of course, as Vicki says, whether they're gigging again or just playing music on someone's porch, there will never *not* be a Continental Drifters.

How could there not be? There's so much history wrapped up in it. So many songs, so many stories, so many miles logged. The Psycho Sisters became actual sisters; Peter, Russ, Susan, and Vicki became one big family; Mark, Carlo, Ray, Robert, Danny and Gary are brothers and confidants.

And sure, maybe there were times when the drugs and drinking went overboard, and perhaps there was even a bit too much drama over the years, but none of that ever superseded what the intent and mission of the Drifters was and is.

"As for most of the giant, traumatic, important events of change that occur in my life—[which] are wrapped up outwardly in an uncomfortable package of loss, confusion, misunderstanding, and grief—that can all go down and seem like the most horrible thing to ever happen to you," Susan said. "In my personal experience, they turn out to be the absolute best thing to ever happen to you."

This thing that formed at the Batch Pad, blossomed at Raji's, and evolved in New Orleans was its own kind of flash in the pan. Something countercultural to what was happening in Los Angeles. Something counterintuitive to what every Drifter had known the music business to be. Something extraordinary, at times unusual, and never boring. It was lightning in a bottle.

But in the end, it's not only about Carlo, Mark, Gary, Danny, Ray, Peter, Susan, Vicki, Robert, and Russ. It's about all of the people who make up the Continental Drifters universe—all of the paths that were forged by the formation of this band. Musicians who became musicians because of the Drifters, people who became family; lives that became intertwined.

So while there is definitely some indisputable truth to the "Drifters" line "You don't understand," maybe there are a lot more people who *do* understand than the Drifters themselves even realize. Perhaps there's another line that truly sums it all up.

We are all drifters.

"It's just a basic, undeniable fact," Robert says of that lyric. "The connectivity is mind blowing."

It's been a long haul, as the song says. A *long* haul. But the love endures, and so does the music. That's the way they started, after all.

Drifters at SXSW 2023 (L-R: Peter, Vicki, Russ, Susan, Mark, Robert). Photo by Mike Fickel

Sean Kelly

Nick Jenkins, Savannah, and Miranda. Savannah braved her first Jazz Fest in order to see her "grand-drifters" perform in 2023. Photo by Dannal Perry

Who's That Drifter?

1. **Carlo Nuccio** (1991-1996) drums, guitar, vocals

2. **Peter Holsapple** (1992-present) vocals, keyboards, guitar, mandolin, accordion, harmonica

3. **Gary Eaton** (1991-1993) vocals, guitar

4. **Danny McGough** (1991-1992) keyboards

5. **Vick Peterson** (1993-present) vocals, guitar

6. **Russ Broussard** (1996-present) drums, rubboard, vocals

7. **Ray Ganucheau** (1991-1993) vocals, guitar

8. **Robert Maché** (1994-present) guitar, mandolin, vocals

9. **Mark Walton** (1991-present) bass, guitar, vocals

10. **Susan Cowsill** (1993-present) vocals, guitar, mandolin

Acknowledgements

Thank you to Kennedy, my best friend and love of my life, for the gift of this life together. And to Autumn and Rowan, you give me purpose and joy. I love you all.

To Vicki Stein Kelly, thank you for raising me to pursue my creativity and for believing in me every step of the way for 25 years. I miss you every day.

Thanks to Jeanne Stein, Dom Kelly, Loren O'Connell-Kelly, Catie Kelly, Kaden Harris, the Harris family, Kayleigh Denner, Noreen and Ryan Towsley, Max Werkmeister, AJ and Judith Terlouw, Nick DeRiso.

To the Continental Drifters—Peter, Vicki, Susan, Russ, Mark, Robert, Carlo, Ray, Gary, and Danny—for giving me the gift of your time, hindsight, and honesty, and for sharing this story with me. What an honor.

And especially to Susan, Peter, Russ, Miranda, and Vicki: Thank you, thank you, thank you. For everything.

To my friends Tim and Susan Lee for giving me a shot with this project. I am so proud to be doing this with Cool Dog Sound, and so grateful.

To David Jenkins for your friendship and partnership on the tribute album, Marti Jones for the stunning book cover art, and Brett Milano for the amazing foreword. To Brendan Kelly for the tribute album artwork, mixing, musicianship, and letting me bug you for help all the time.

To Carmen Peruyero Gomez and Lena Nuccio for their openness, kindness, and help in my quest to honor Carlo's legacy.

To every single person who gave me the time of day for this project, in the book and for the tribute album: Candace Maché, Dave Catching, Amy Rigby, Paula Thurber, John Crooke and Jolene, Kettle of Hawks, Don Dixon, Annette Zilinskas, Rosie Flores, Andrew Hernandez, The Talismen, Jim Fouratt, Mark McKenna, Mike Mayeux, Steve and Wish Nails, Robinson Mills, Garrison Starr, Annie Clements, Neal Weiss, Peter Blackstock, Keith Spera, John Cowsill, Paul Allen, Marshall Crenshaw, Mitch Easter, Severo Jornacion, Debbi Peterson, Scott McCaughey, Peter Buck, Jenny Conlee-Drizos, Steven Drizos, Brian Oden, Mark Bryan and Hootie & the Blowfish, Deni Bonet, Paul Rock, Nelson Bragg, Cameron Smith, John Convertino, Kevin Jarvis, Jimmy Ford, Jack Groetsch, Glenn Hartman, Malcolm Burn, Robbie Rist, Bobby Houck, Caitlin Cary, Yep Roc Records, Cheryl Pawelski and Omnivore Recordings, Sean Lakeman, Kathryn Roberts and Equation, Martha Gehman, Kim Richey, The Iguanas, Tom Stern, Monica Steward, Mikey Costanzo, Clay White, Kyle Polk, Shaun Rhoades, Neal Weiss, Keith Morris, Matt Zutell and Coast Records, Keith Morris, Ivan "Funkboy" Bodley, Karen Schoemer, Tim Sommer, Mike Mills, Bob Stein, Steve Berlin, Alex McMurray, Glenn Hartman, Dayna Kurtz, J.J. Blair, Pete Thomas, Davey Faragjer, Lenny Zenith, Gabi Lima, Rob Laufer, Robbie Rist, Brian Merrill, Nick Vincent, Lyn Bertles, Tara Austin, Robert Lloyd, Kevin Salem, Janson Lohmeyer, Jeffrey Reed, Robert Mugge, Steve Wynn, Ronnie Barnett, Brian Kehew, Fernando Perdomo, Derrick Anderson, Chris Price, George Porter Jr., Tracey Freeman, and many more.

Lyrics quoted by permission

Drifters (Susan Cowsill/Peter Holsapple)
CoCo Bunny Music BMI, admin by BMG
Bumblebee BMI/Hit Shed Music BMI, admin
by Rough Trade Songs BMI

Dallas (Gary Eaton)
God Bless This Mess Music BMI, admin by
BMG Bumblebee BMI

The Rain Song (Susan Cowsill/Vicki
Peterson)
CoCo Bunny Music BMI, admin by BMG
Bumblebee BMI/Downkiddie Music BMI

Who We Are, Where We Live (Vicki Peterson)
Ultra Vixen Music BMI

Invisible Boyfriend (Peter Holsapple)
Pertaining To Music BMI/Sony ATV Music
BMI

Mezzanine (Carlo Nuccio)
Johnny Oops Music BMI, admin by BMG
Bumblebee BMI

Here I Am (Carlo Nuccio)
Johnny Oops Music BMI, admin by BMG
Bumblebee BMI

Zoo (Carlo Nuccio)
Johnny Oops Music BMI, admin by BMG
Bumblebee BMI

**Christopher Columbus Transcontinental
Highway** (Vicki Peterson)
Ultra Vixen Music BMI

Way of the World (Susan Cowsill/Vicki
Peterson)
CoCo Bunny Music BMI, admin by BMG
Bumblebee BMI/Downkiddie Music BMI

Live on Love (Peter Holsapple)
Hit Shed Music BMI, admin by Rough Trade
Songs BMI

Na Na (Vicki Peterson)
Ultra Vixen Music BMI

Someday (Susan Cowsill)
CoCo Bunny Music BMI, admin by BMG
Bumblebee BMI

Talkin' (Susan Cowsill)
CoCo Bunny Music BMI, admin by BMG
Bumblebee BMI

Continental Drifters (Peter Holsapple)
Hit Shed Music BMI, admin by Rough Trade
Songs BMI

Discography

CONTINENTAL DRIFTERS

"The Mississippi" b/w "Johnny Oops" (single)
Singles Only Label SOL-229-7 45 (US) 1992

Continental Drifters
Monkey Hill MON 6123-2 CD (US) Nov 23,1994
Hypnotic/A&M 713561034-2 CD (Canada) 1994
Blue Rose BLU 30.103-1 CD (Germany) 1994
Razor & Tie 7930182221-2 CD (US) Feb 20, 2001 (re-release)

"Christopher Columbus Transcontinental Highway" b/w "Meet on the Ledge" (single)
Black Dog Records BD-1003-7 45 (US) Nov 1997

Vermilion
Blue Rose Records BLU CD0064 CD/ BLU LP0064 LP w/ 45 (Germany) May 25, 1998
Razor & Tie RTJC82848-2 CD (US) Oct 12, 1999

"The Rain Song" (single)
Razor & Tie RTDJ762 Promo CD single (US) 1999

Better Day
Razor & Tie 7930182864-2 CD (US) June 5, 2001
Blue Rose Records BLU DP0253 CD book/ BLU LP0253 LP/BLU CD0253 CD (Germany) 2001

Excerpts from the new album Better Day
Blue Rose PC0253 Promo CD (Germany) 2001

Listen, Listen
Blue Rose Records BLU DP0265 CD/ BLU LP0265 10" mini-LP (Germany) Nov 5, 2001

Nineteen Ninety-Three
Blue Rose Records BLU CD0304 CD (Germany) May 12, 2003

Drifted: In The Beginning & Beyond
Omnivore Recordings OVCD-132 CD (US)/ July 17, 2015

Live At The 2023 Jazz & Heritage Festival
Munck Music CD (US)/ Oct 17, 2023

White Noise & Lightning: The Best of Continental Drifters
Omnivore Recordings OVCD-557 CD/ OVLP-557 LP (US) Sep 13, 2024

COMPILATIONS/TRIBUTES

"Get Over It"/"A Song For You"
Blue Rose Collection
Blue Rose Records BLU 30.112-1 CD (Germany) 1995

"Get Over It"
So Grunge-Gee! A Taste of Alternative
Valentine Sound Productions ICH 5006 Cassette (Malaysia) 1995

"I Can't Let Go"
Sing Hollies In Reverse
eggBERT Records ER80018CD CD (US) 1995

"Get Over It"
CMJ New Music Monthly Volume 30 February 1996
College Music Journal CMJ-NMN030 CD (US) February 1996

"Mixed Messages"
Blue Rose Collection Vol. 2
Blue Rose Records BLUCD 030 CD (Germany) 1996

"Christopher Columbus Transcontinental
Highway" (Black Dog version)
Revival II: Kudzu and the Hollerin' Contest
Yep Roc Records YR 2005 CD (US) Nov 1997

"Watermark"
Musikexpress 22 – Blue Rose Records
Musikepress/Blue Rose musikexpress CD
(Germany) 1998

"Who We Are, Where We Live"
New Voices Vol. 23
Rolling Stone 23 (Germany) 1998

"Christopher Columbus Transcontinental
Highway"
Blue Rose Collection Vol. 4
Blue Rose Records BLU CD0072/Rough Trade
RTD 343.0172.2 14 CD (Germany) 1998

"The Rain Song"
Tanz & Folk Fest TFF Rudolstadt '99
No label CD 1999

"When You Dance, I Can Really Love"
*This Note's For You Too!: A Tribute To Neil
Young*
Inbetween Records IRCD 004 CD (US) /
Innerstate Records INNERSTATE 5002 CD
(Netherlands) 1999

"The Rain Song"
*Progressions #47 – New Music For Progressive
Adult Radio*
Friday Morning Quarterback Album Report
Inc. PAR47 CD (US) 1999

"The Rain Song"
*Pop Culture Press CD.10 – Bailando En La
Playa*
Pop Culture Press CD (US) 2000

"Drifters"
City Folk Live III
WFUV CFL003 CD (US) 2000

"Cousin"
Schöner Hören Vol. #9
Röder Media Service Schöner Hören 9 CD
(Germany) 2001

"Don't Do What I Did"
*HO*T FM Blue Rose Broadcasts*
Blue Rose Records BLUCD0244 (Germany) 2001

"Snow"
Blue Rose Collection Vol. 8
Blue Rose Records CD BLUCD0267 CD
(Germany) 2002

"I'm A Dreamer"
Blue Rose Collection Vol. 9
Blue Rose Records CD0290 CD (Germany)
2002

"Na Na"
*Just Good Music (Audio Super Sound
Collection Vol. 2 – Rock & Blues Vom
Feinstein*
Blue Rose Records AUD1102 CD (Germany)
2002

"Long Journey Home"
Blue Rose Nuggets 2
Blue Rose Nuggets BLU NG002 CD
(Germany) 2003

"Dallas"
Blue Rose Nuggets 3
Blue Rose Nuggets BLU NG003 CD
(Germany) 2003

"The Mississippi"
Blue Rose Nuggets 4
Blue Rose Nuggets BLU NG004 CD
(Germany) 2003

"The Rain Song"
Blue Rose Nuggets 6
Blue Rose Nuggets BLU NG006 CD
(Germany) 2004

"Highway of the Saints"
Blue Rose Nuggets 9
Blue Rose Nuggets BLU NG009 CD
(Germany) 2004

"Listen, Listen"
Blue Rose Nuggets 11
Blue Rose Nuggets BLU NG0011 CD
(Germany) 2005

"Snow" (previously unreleased)
Musicians for Minneapolis: 57 Songs for the I-35W Bridge Disaster Relief Effort
Electro-Voice 796873017169 CD (US) 2007

"Na Na"
Blue Rose Nuggets 23
Blue Rose Nuggets BLU NG0023 CD (Germany) 2007

"The Mississippi" (Live)
Blue Rose Nuggets 27
Blue Rose Nuggets BLU NG0027 CD (Germany) 2007

"Fun Fun Fun"/"Farmer's Daughter" (Live)
Blue Rose Nuggets 34
Blue Rose Nuggets BLU NG0034 CD (Germany) 2008

"Who We Are, Where We Live"
Blue Rose Nuggets 41
Blue Rose Nuggets BLU NG0041 CD (Germany) 2010

"Some of Shelly's Blues"
Blue Rose Nuggets 53
Blue Rose Nuggets BLU NG0053 CD (Germany) 2012

"Tomorrow's Gonna Be"
Blue Rose Nuggets 58
Blue Rose Nuggets BLU NG0058 CD (Germany) 2012

"Watermark"
Blue Rose Nuggets 66
Blue Rose Nuggets BLU NG0066 CD (Germany) 2014

"Who We Are, Where We Live"
1995-2015/20 Years Blue Rose Records
Blue Rose Records BLU CD0655 CD (Germany) 2015

"Way of the World"
Blue Rose Nuggets 72
Blue Rose Nuggets BLU NG0072 CD (Germany) 2015

"Mixed Messages"
Blue Rose Radio Show CD Edition
Blue Rose Records (Germany) CD 2015

"New York"
Blue Rose Nuggets 87
Blue Rose Nuggets BLU NG0087 CD (Germany) 2018

"Drifters"
Blue Rose Nuggets 93
Blue Rose Nuggets BLU NG0093 CD (Germany) 2019

"That Much a Fool"
Blue Rose Nuggets 99
Blue Rose Nuggets BLU NG0099 CD (Germany) 2019

"I Want to See the Bright Lights Tonight"
Blue Rose Nuggets 100
Blue Rose Nuggets BLU NG0100 CD (Germany) 2019

"Spring Day in Ohio"
Blue Rose Collection 17
Blue Rose Records DP0749 CD (Germany) 2022

SOLO/ADJACENT RELEASES

Peter Holsapple & Susan Cowsill and the Walkin' Tacos
Conmemorativo: A Tribute To Gram Parsons
"A Song For You"
Rhino Records R2 71269 CD (US)
Cyclope/Polydor 519 858-2 CD (Italy) 1993
(Peter, Susan, Gary, Carlo, Mark)

Double Date
Gasatanka: 13 Years of Losing Money
"Farmer's Daughter" b/w "Stoned Soul Picnic"
Gasatanka Records 519 858-2 45 (US) 1994
(Susan, Vicki, Peter, Gary)

Peter Holsapple
Out Of My Way
Monkey Hill MON 8135-2 CD (US)
Blue Rose Records BLU CD0026 (Germany)
1997
(Peter, Carlo, Susan-photos)

Carlo Nuccio
Loose Strings
Monkey Hill MON 8139-2 (CD) 1998
(Carlo, Ray)

Susan Cowsill
Just Believe It
Blue Corn Music BCM 0505 CD (US)
Blue Rose Records BLU CD0338 CD/BLU
LP0338 LP (EU) October 11, 2005
(Susan, Russ, Vicki)

Susan Cowsill
Lighthouse
Blue Rose Records BLU DP0514 CD/ BLU
LP0514 LP (Germany)
Threadhead Records US-J5D-10-0001-12 CD
(US) May 18, 2010
(Susan, Russ, Vicki)

Ray Ganucheau
Ray Ganucheau and Bande Le Rois
Plyrz Studio VQA-10-01 LP (US) November 6,
2010
(Ray)

The Psycho Sisters
"Timberline"/"This Painting"
Singles Only Label – SOL-354 45 (US) 1994
(Susan, Vicki, Peter, Gary)

The Psycho Sisters
Up On The Chair, Beatrice
RockBeat Records – ROC-3242 LP/CD (US)
August 5, 2014
Blue Rose Records – BLU DP0664 LP/CD
(Germany) 2015
(Susan, Vicki, Russ)

Peter Holsapple
Game Day
Omnivore Recordings OVCD 291 (US) July
27, 2018
(Peter, Susan)

Lulu and the Broadsides
Lulu and the Broadsides
Kismet Records – KIS1012 (CD) April 14, 2023
(Robert, Carlo)

Peter Holsapple
The Face of 68
Label 51 LAB 51019 (LP)
Label 51 LAB 51019 (CD),
January 17, 2025

116, 117, 130, 131, 132, 134, 135, 136, 137, 138, 139, 140, 142, 145, 146, 147, 149, 150, 151, 152, 153, 154, 155, 156, 157, 158, 159, 160, 161, 162, 164, 165, 166, 168, 169, 170, 172, 173, 174, 175, 176, 177, 178, 179, 180, 181, 184, 185, 186, 187, 188, 189, 191, 195, 196, 197, 199, 200, 201, 205, 210, 212, 213, 214, 215, 216, 217, 218, 219, 220, 224, 225, 228, 229 | *See also The Cowsills*

Cravin Melon: 70

Crazy Horse: 8, 28, 169, 173

Cream: 8

CREEM magazine: 96

Crenshaw, Marshall: 139, 224

Crooke, John: 134, 135, 136, 145, 202, 224

Cyclope: 228

D

du Gré, Paul: 11

Daigle, Tony: 104, 155, 156, 160

Daisy: 30

Dana and the Blue Jays: 96

Dash Rip Rock: 16

Daughters of Isis: 59

Davies, Dave: 19

Davis, Tyrone: 58

Dawson's Creek: 172

DeGeneres, Vance: 6, 7

Delgadillo, Ben: 4, 5

Denner, Kayleigh: 224

Dennis Duck: 6

Denny, Sandy: 94, 133, 134, 135, 136, 140, 145, 165

Devil Squares: 3, 45, 124

Dexter, Debbie: 45

Dillon Fence: 70

Dixie Canyon: 7

Dixon, Don: 79, 132, 134, 136, 137, 224

Dixon, Marti Jones: ii, 134, 136, 224

Dockside Studio: 98, 99, 104, 105, 107, 129, 145, 147, 155, 156, 157, 160, 177, 216

Doe, John: 136, 218

Domino, Fats: 209

Donati, Bobby: 22, 23, 24, 25, 51

Donatis: 23

Dorsey Brothers: 44

Double Date: 28, 169, 228

Doug Messenger's Studio: 14

Drake, Nick: 94, 95, 133, 134, 137

Drizos, Steven: 224

Dr. John: 216

Drum Academy: 124

Duff, Bruce: 125

Dumptruck: 78

Duritz, Adam: 150, 179

Dwight Twilley Band: 12

Dylan, Bob: 21, 28, 41, 42, 161, 202

E

eggBERT Records: 65, 226

Equation: 224

Eagles: 172

Eagles of Death Metal: 18

Earshot: 64

Easter, Mitch: 79, 96, 97, 224

Eaton, Gary: ix, xii, 3, 7, 8, 9, 10, 11, 14, 15, 17, 18, 22, 25, 26, 27, 28, 29, 30, 31, 32, 34, 41, 42, 44, 45, 46, 47, 51, 52, 59, 76, 84, 85, 93, 124, 144, 149, 152, 169, 171, 172, 198, 201, 202, 203, 211, 212, 214, 216, 219, 220, 224, 225, 228, 229

Eaton, Sam: 51, 203

Eaton, Shelli: 198

Echo Park: 155

Egan, Bob: 139

Egyptian Room: 59, 65, 105

Eicher, Stephen: 127

Electro-Voice: 228

Eleventh Dream Day: 68

El Rey Theatre: 85

Elvis: 45, 101, 102

ESPN: 198

Ewan, Julia: 212, 213, 214

F

Fabulous Thunderbirds: 41

Fairport Convention: 2, 25, 92, 94, 133, 134, 135, 137, 165

Faithfull, Marianne: 195

Fantasy Island: 30

Faragjer, Davey: 224

Farrar, Jay: 140, 141

Ferrick, Melissa: 61

Festival International de Louisiane: 169

Fickel, Mike: 220

Five Stairsteps: 28

Fleetwood Mac: vii, 2, 21, 44, 58, 78, 152, 161, 185

Flores, Rosie: 14, 17, 18, 27, 224

Flying Burrito Brothers: 21, 27

Ford "Exploder": 50

Ford, Jimmy: 28, 29, 30, 31, 50, 52, 59, 76, 123, 217, 224

Forrest, Bob: 17

Fotheringay: 133, 134, 136

Fouratt, Jim: 77, 78, 81, 82, 224

Freakwater: 68

Freeman, Tracey: 224

Fremont Experience: 195

Fricke, David: 142

Friday Morning Quarterback Album Report Inc.: 227

Frolic Room: 11, 41

Froom, Mitchell: 17

G

Christgau, Robert: 143

Sean Kelly

SONGS

9 798218 491161